William J. Weinberg has been a freelance investigative journalist specializing in environmental issues and based in New York City throughout the 1980s. Educated at the Empire State College, State University of New York, he has been heavily involved in the movements against nuclear power and nuclear weapons, military conscription and US intervention in Central America. Much of the research for his book, *War on the Land*, was undertaken during two extended periods living in Central America in 1984–85 and 1986–87. He is currently environmental editor and weekly columnist for the Lower Manhattan paper, *Downtown*. His articles have appeared in a wide range of publications, particularly in the American alternative press, but also in *The Nation* and *The Ecologist*.

War on the Land

Ecology and Politics
in Central America

Bill Weinberg

Zed Books Ltd
London and New Jersey

A catalogue record for this book is
available from the British Library

ISBN 0 86232 946 9 Hb
ISBN 0 86232 947 7 Pb

Library of Congress Cataloging-in-Publication Data

Weinberg, William J.
    War on the land : ecology and politics in Central
America / William J. Weinberg.
        p.   cm.
    Includes bibliographical references and index.
    ISBN 0-86232-946-9–ISBN 0-86232-947-7 (pbk.)
    1. Environmental policy – Central America – Case
studies. 2. Land use – Central America – Case
studies. 3. Central America – Politics and government
–1979-. 4. Central America – Social conditions –
1979-. 5. Human ecology – Central America – Case
studies. I. Title.
HC141.Z9E59   1991
363.7'056'09728–dc20
                                            91-13782
                                            CIP

Contents

Acknowledgements

My thanks and acknowledgements to:
Anne Becher, Garrick Beck, Mary Belfrage and the memory of Cedric Belfrage,
Alexander Bonilla, Gertrude Duby Blom and the Nabolom Library (San
Cristobal de Las Casas, Chiapas), Eric Boyo, Charlie Brenner, Guy Burgunder,
Evan Camp, Richard Chilton, Margery R. Coffey, Marilyn Coffey,
Confederación Universitaria Centroamericana, Pat Costner, Paul DeRienzo,
Joanne L. Dittersdorf, Empire State College (State University of New York),
Environmental Project On Central America, Sylvia Federicci, Friends Peace
Center (San Jose, Costa Rica), George Gleason, *Grupo de los Estudios
Ambientales* (Mexico City), Jane Guskin (Nicaragua Solidarity Network of
Greater New York), Mitchell Halbertstadt, Bill Hall, Linda Holland, Carl
Hultberg, Mark Izeman (NRDC), Catalina Jimenez, Joshua Karliner,
Learning Alliance, Dino Pacio Lindin, Hildegaard Dina Link, Sandy
McCroskey, Cristina Mendoza, *Mesoamerica* (San Jose, Costa Rica), Margaret
Metzinger, Karen Mogenson, Pat Mooney, Allan Nairn, Grace Nichols,
Bernard Nietschmann, Michael I. Niman, Michael Oppenheimer (EDF),
Karen Pearlston, Arturo Pozo, Patricia & Federico Rebolledo Kloques, Jim
Rensinbrink and the staff of *Downtown* magazine (NYC), José Rodrigues,
Rural Advancement Fund International, Alberto Ruz Buenfil, my friends at
Solidarity Foundation (NYC), everybody in New York Sound & Hudson
Against Atomic Development (SHAD), Sean Swezey, *The Tico Times* (San
Jose, Costa Rica), Tom Ward, WBAI Radio (Pacifica, NYC), Philip & Mary
Weinberg, the memory of Sol & Rose Weinberg, Joseph Wetmore, and
everyone who ever picked me up when hitch-hiking in Central America.

Dedicated to the memory of Jacob Aftel, 1955–90, a non-violent warrior against the nuclear threat.

'Let us forget for a moment the crimes and stupidities that have been committed in the name of development from Communist Russia to India, from the Argentina of Perón to the Egypt of Nasser, and let us look at what is happening in the United States and Western Europe: the destruction of the ecological balance, the contamination of lungs and of spirits, the psychic damage to the young, the abandoning of the elderly, the erosion of the sensibilities, the corruption of the imagination, the debasement of sex, the accumulation of wastes, the explosions of hatred. Faced as we are by all this, how can we not turn away and seek another mode of development? It is an urgent task that requires both science and imagination, both honesty and sensitivity; a task without precedence, because all the modes of development that we know, whether they come from the West or the East, lead to disaster. Under the present circumstances the race toward development is mere haste to reach ruin.'

Octavio Paz, Mexico, 1968

Preface

A word or two about how this book came to be.

I came of age politically in the anti-nuclear movement of the United States in the late 1970s and early 1980s, when citizens' groups organized non-violent occupations of atomic power plants and military installations. I participated in the blockade of California's Diablo Canyon power station in 1981, the blockade of Vandenberg Air Force Base, a launch site for missile tests, in 1983, and then Diablo Canyon again in 1984. Diablo Canyon's reactor actually began operation in 1984, protests notwithstanding. The protests in 1984 were much smaller and less effective than those of three years earlier, the last time government authorities seemed near a decision to give the plant an official OK for operation. In the wake of 1984's failed protests, I went through a re-evaluation of the anti-nuclear movement's politics.

The anti-nuclear movement had been a coalition between two broad alliances. The first was the political left, including many veterans of the earlier struggle against United States' war in Indo-China in the 1960s and early 1970s. It was with the struggle against nuclear technology that the radical left re-emerged as a potent force on the political scene in the US after a hiatus of several years following the withdrawal from Vietnam and Cambodia in 1972. For the left, the anti-nuclear movement, like the earlier anti-war movement, was part of the long struggle against the corporate-dominated system that places (to reverse the anti-nuclear movement's slogan) profits before people.

The other pillar of the anti-nuclear coalition was the environmental movement, which had been born with the massive celebrations of Earth Day in 1970. With the anti-nuclear struggle, the environmental movement, for the first time, moved into widespread grass-roots organizing for direct action. For the environmentalists, the anti-nuclear movement was part of the struggle to oppose industries and technologies that degrade the ecology.

Since the anti-nuclear movement was my first involvement in activist politics, I never realized that there was any dichotomy between the leftist concerns of social empowerment and the environmentalist concerns of ecological sanity. Therefore, I was surprised when the two pillars of the coalition went their separate ways after the movement's decline.

Indeed, it was the emergence of new issues for both the leftists and the environmentalists that led to the anti-nuclear movement's decline. With scientists warning of the terrifying greenhouse effect, many environmentalists turned their attention to preserving the planet's rainforests. And many leftists felt an urgent need to launch resistance as the United States escalated its intervention in Central America. In fact, the very week that the Diablo Canyon reactor finally received its test licence, hundreds of protestors were arrested a few hundred miles to the north, in San Francisco, at a demonstration against an official dinner honouring Henry Kissinger, the chief architect of President Ronald Reagan's interventionist Central America policy.

Implicitly I recognized that if there had been common ground for both peace activists and environmentalists in the nuclear issue, there had to be common ground elsewhere as well. In the anti-nuclear struggle the connections had been obvious – nuclear energy both poisons the environment and keeps power centralized in the hands of giant multinational corporations, which control the industry. Perhaps in other struggles the connections would be more subtle – but they had to be there.

Neither the left nor the environmentalists seemed to be in any hurry to find them, however. I spent the summer of 1984 in the San Francisco Bay Area, following both movements. I attended demonstrations against intervention in Central America organized by CISPES (Committee In Solidarity with the People of El Salvador). I also attended demonstrations at Burger King 'fast food' franchises, protesting against the use of beef imported from the deforested tropical jungle regions of Central America, organized by the self-proclaimed 'radical environmental group' Earth First! (the exclamation point is part of the name). Both these groups were concerned with the US corporate exploitation of Central America. Yet I rarely saw a single face common to both groups at demonstrations involving either group. The environmentalists were, apparently, unconcerned with the war on Central America's people, while the leftists were apparently unconcerned with the war on the land.

I found this disturbing, because I was convinced of the essential underlying unity of ecological and social concerns, and that truly effective movements would have to recognize that unity. It was especially ironic and frustrating that both the anti-intervention activists and the rainforest activists were focusing on Central America and still failed to see their common ground. Although it was not emphasized by either the leftists or ecologists, I knew that there had to be a link between the destruction of the rainforests and the destruction of human lives.

When I left the United States for a six-month trek through Mexico and Central America at the end of 1984, it was with an eye to finding that link. I networked extensively both with leftist leaders – human rights activists, labour and peasant organizers – and with the leaders of the small, marginalized environmental movement in the region.

I was disappointed to find that the dichotomy was actually far deeper in Central America than in the United States. In fact, leftists and environmentalists habitually viewed each other with nothing short of hostility in Central America, even though their rhetoric frequently attacked the same enemies (the World Bank and the International Monetary Fund head the list). Central

American leftists seemed to view enviromentalists as outsiders imposing an agenda which is antithetical to the interests of the poor, even as tools of US imperialism. The region's environmentalists viewed leftists as blinded by their own ideology to the primary need for a healthy ecology for long-term survival of humanity and the planet.

But my search for the link continued, and ultimately led to years of research and another six-month trek through the region in 1986, as well as a few shorter trips in subsequent years.

I eventually concluded that the root conflict lies in access to land. With deforestation and pesticide abuse running rampant, environmentalists seek to place as much land as possible under official protection. But with hunger and poverty also running rampant, leftists organize the peasants to take over land for agriculture. There have even been instances in which peasants have been evicted from lands that ecologists had secured to protect forests and endangered species.

Environmentalists are quick to point to population pressure as the cause of such conflicts, and are slow to recognize the factor of the hoarding of the best arable land by the 'oligarchies'. Most environmentalists cut an implicit deal with the powers-that-be: they get their nature reserves and their birth control programmes in exchange for never talking about agrarian reform. In Costa Rica and Mexico, where the leftist movements are largely non-violent, the leftists also cut an implicit deal: they challenge only peripheral lands on the so-called 'agricultural frontier' – usually rainforest areas such as Costa Rica's Limón province and Mexico's Lacandon jungle – and do not challenge the fertile agricultural heartland, firmly under the control of the oligarchies, which grow rich raising coffee, cotton, sugar and beef. This strategy pits the leftists against the environmentalists because, in the end, the peasants clear the rainforest and push back the agricultural frontier.

In three countries however – Nicaragua, El Salvador and Guatemala – the situation was sufficiently desperate that the left launched guerrilla movements aimed at liberating the agricultural heartland from the oligarchies – a strategy which had the potential to relieve the pressure on the rainforests (although that certainly was not its objective). In fact, peasant migration to Nicaragua's Miskito rainforest, which had soared under the US-backed Somoza dictatorship, virtually ceased when the revolutionary Sandinista regime launched its agrarian reform programme. And it was in Sandinista Nicaragua that the beginnings of a new kind of environmentalism began to emerge, which saw ecological recovery as indivisible from social transformation. Yet the environmentalists found it politically inexpedient to close ranks with leftist guerrillas – they would certainly lose the co-operation of local authorities in the nature reserve and birth control programmes if they did so.

Central America's agricultural heartland has been producing cash crops for export ever since the Spanish conquest of the sixteenth century, and turning this entrenched system around will certainly need generations of struggle. In those three countries, where revolutionary movements sought to liberate the real prize of that immensely fertile heartland, the power structure (the oligarchy and the military, with massive aid and direction from the United States) responded by unleashing a blood-bath. In Nicaragua, where the revolutionary movement actually seized state power, a right-wing counter-revolutionary guerrilla insurgency was launched. In El Salvador and Guatemala, leftist guerrilla movements were met with counter-insurgency operations that bordered on genocide. In all three cases, the peasants bore the brunt of the suffering.

The fact that these counter-revolutionary efforts could not have been as grimly successful as they were without the support and direction of the Pentagon and the Central Intelligence Agency (CIA), brings the problem back to where this discussion began – the effectiveness (or lack) of opposition and resistance movements here in the nations of the industrialized North – the funders of the World Bank and International Monetary Fund (IMF), the builders of the massive military machines and 'intelligence' agencies.

If our protest movements are to be effective, we must forsake the vain attempt somehow to prioritize our issues and demands – the rights of peasants to eat and to grow their maize in peace, and the rights of forests to exist. Such debates become irrelevant once one grasps the underlying unity. The global economic and political order is predicated on the exploitation and domination both of humans and of land. The violence by which this system maintains itself is both genocidal, systematically destroying human communities, and *ecocidal*, systematically destroying functioning ecosystems. The war on humans and the war on the land are merely different aspects of the same problem.

Europe's Green movements may point the way toward a new brand of politics, which recognizes the underlying unity of human and ecological concerns. This would be politics in the context of which anti-intervention activists and rainforest activists could view each other with solidarity, could co-operate and forge alliances and work towards the kind of profound changes that will be necessary in the industrial and post-industrial societies of the North in order for the nations of the South to find a mode of development that will both feed people and protect wilderness.

It is my hope that this book will be a small step in that direction.

Central America's Bioregions

El Petén

The Miskito Coast

Corcovado
Rain Forest

PACIFIC COASTAL PLAIN
(DRY FOREST PRIOR TO DEFORESTATION)

CENTRAL HIGHLANDS
(MOUNTAINS;
CONIFERS AND CLOUD FOREST
PRIOR TO DEFORESTATION)

CARIBBEAN ZONE
(RAIN FOREST PRIOR TO DEFORESTATION)

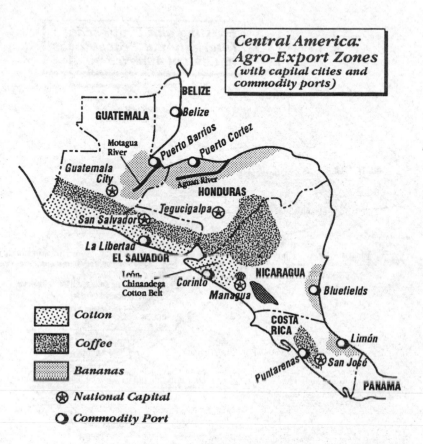

Central America:
Agro-Export Zones
(with capital cities and
commodity ports)

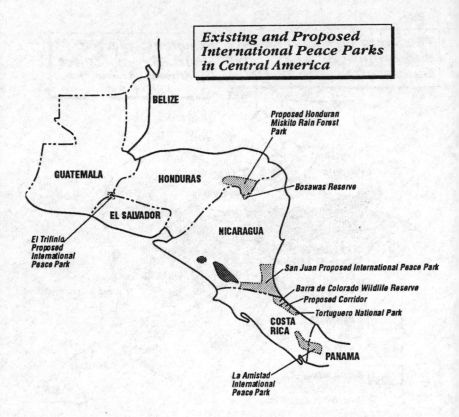

Existing and Proposed International Peace Parks in Central America

BELIZE

GUATEMALA

HONDURAS

Proposed Honduran Miskito Rain Forest Park

EL SALVADOR

Bosawas Reserve

El Triflnio Proposed International Peace Park

NICARAGUA

San Juan Proposed International Peace Park

Barra de Colorado Wildlife Reserve

Proposed Corridor

Tortuguero National Park

COSTA RICA

PANAMA

La Amistad International Peace Park

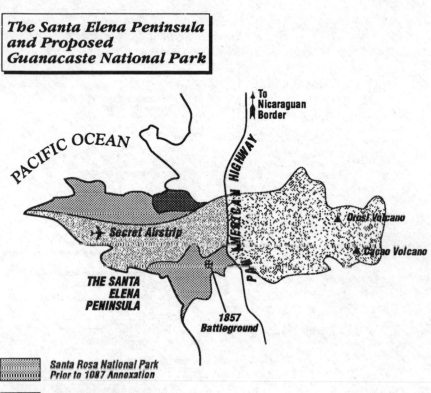

The Santa Elena Peninsula and Proposed Guanacaste National Park

To Nicaraguan Border

PACIFIC OCEAN

PAN AMERICAN HIGHWAY

Secret Airstrip

Orosí Volcano

Cacao Volcano

THE SANTA ELENA PENINSULA

1857 Battleground

Santa Rosa National Park Prior to 1987 Annexation

1987 Annexation to Santa Rosa National Park

Guanacaste Protected Zone

Murcielago Civil Guard Training Base

Part 1:
Prelude to Crisis

1. Introduction

The headlines from Central America reach us daily with reports of civil wars, revolutions, death squads and repression. The news we get almost exclusively concerns military matters – ambush attacks, assassinations, abductions, fleeing refugees, peace plans, negotiations. Clearly nations are being torn by seemingly unbridgeable ideological divisions as war and economic crisis fuel each other in a vicious cycle. But we are rarely left with a clear impression of just exactly what the fighting is all about.

Since Ronald Reagan left the White House, Central America has almost seemed to be in a time warp. The Cold War has been declared as ended, superpower tensions are at their lowest ebb since the end of World War II, the East Bloc has openly abandoned Communism, and the Soviet Union is withdrawing its commitment to support revolutionary movements in the developing world. Yet, in the final weeks of the 1980s, precisely as Romania, the last of the Soviet bloc Stalinist dictatorships, was falling to a popular uprising, President George Bush ordered the US military invasion of Panama. Three months later, the revolutionary Sandinista regime in Nicaragua was voted out as the US-orchestrated counter-revolution finally achieved its aim after nearly a decade of sustained effort. That same month, an administration more compliant with US interests than the previous one of President Oscar Arias came to power in Costa Rica, as the seeds of militarism and peasant unrest continue to emerge in this long-peaceful nation. Violence, repression and human rights abuses are escalating in El Salvador and Guatemala. A policy, ostensibly forged at the height of the Reagan Administration's anti-Soviet zeal, lives on in the post-Cold War world.

It was in 1983 that President Ronald Reagan announced the formation of the National Bipartisan Committee on Central America, a panel with a formal mandate to advise the President and Congress on US interests in Central America, the threats posed to those interests, and how Central America could be made safe for those interests. Headed by former Secretary of State Henry Kissinger, a figure notorious for having master-minded much of the Nixon White House's strategy in Indo-China, the panel became known as the Kissinger Commission. The Commission's report issued the following year became the principal justification for Reagan Administration policy in Central America. The report saw threats to US security exploiting instability in Central

America: 'hostile outside forces – Cuba, backed by the Soviet Union, and now operating through Nicaragua', which is described as 'totalitarian' and 'a crucial steppingstone for Cuban and Soviet efforts to promote armed insurgency in Central America'. The report urged that 'Marxist–Leninist' Nicaragua must be 'contained' by a permanent US military presence in the region and support for the contra insurgents. The report warned against 'power-sharing' agreements with the leftist rebels in El Salvador and recommended US military aid to the Salvadoran government ('conditional' on human-rights 'improvements' by that government – a provision Kissinger makes clear that he disagrees with in his individual commentary on the report). The report recommends resuming US military aid to Guatemala (cut off in 1977 because of gross human rights violations) and US 'public safety' assistance to Central American police forces (also cut off in the mid-1970's because of gross human rights violations). The report called for a multi-billion dollar programme of US economic aid for Central America on the scale of the Marshall Plan or the Alliance for Progress.[1]

The fact that the basic policies outlined by the Kissinger Commission remain intact, despite the thaw in US–Soviet relations, indicates that the roots of Central America's unrest and US interests in the region probably had much less to do with the 'Soviet threat' than the statements of US leaders would suggest. Indeed, the history of US political and military meddling in Central America pre-dates not only the Cuban revolution of 1959 but also the Russian revolution of 1917. The dematerializing of the 'Soviet threat', which the world seems to be witnessing in the dawn of the 1990s, may mean only that new ideological justifications will be found for maintaining Central America and the Caribbean as a US 'backyard' or 'sphere of influence'. In the *pre*-Cold War era, before the Kremlin's own expansionist tendencies conveniently provided the superb propaganda device of the 'Soviet threat' to rationalize US domination of the region, other rationalizations existed. In the era of Theodore Roosevelt, the rationalization was known as 'Manifest Destiny', and before that, in the more overt era of European colonialism, the rationalization used by the British, French, Dutch and Portuguese for the maintenance of their empires was that of the 'white man's burden'. Even as we enter the post-Cold War era, new rationalizations may be emerging – the so-called 'War on Drugs' heads the list, as interceding in the flow of cocaine, and even the comparatively harmless marijuana, north through Central America and the Caribbean is increasingly providing the new mandate for US intervention in the region. The propaganda charade continues, and efforts to arrive at and address the real roots of Central America's crisis remain consistently overlooked.

One threat the Kissinger Commission Report did *not* see in Central America is environmental degradation. The report made no mention whatsoever of pesticide abuse, tropical deforestation, erosion, flooding, drought or water contamination. Said Jeffrey Leonard, an economist with the Washington DC-based Conservation Foundation in a report he prepared for the US Agency for International Development:

Although these trends and issues were not addressed in the Kissinger

Commission's report, and generally have not received significant attention from the international community, the implications ... may be as profound (or more profound) as the current political changes occurring in the region.[2]

What is at the root of Central America's war and crisis? The answer can be summed up in a single word: land.

Central America's absurdly skewed patterns of land use provide the raw material of social unrest which has been manipulated in the East-vs.-West drama which was superimposed over the region's conflicts. Without this raw material – without the inexorable struggle over access to land – superpowers would be unable to wage their destructive geopolitical proxy wars over the isthmus.

Paradoxically, while land is at the root of the war, land is also being destroyed by the war. The same factors which have brought Central America to political crisis are also creating an ecological crisis. Until very recently, this ecological crisis rarely reached our headlines or television screens, but ultimately, it is more central to understanding what is happening in Central America than the military matters that have received widespread media attention.

The need for an understanding of what is happening in Central America is vitally important. United States tax dollars are fuelling the wars there, while money from international lending institutions, jointly funded by the United States, Western Europe and Japan, such as the World Bank and the IMF, are also propping up the status quo, which the US protects through underwriting the region's militarization and wars. As the wars grind on (often futile wars of attrition, which neither side can win) the very thing that is fought over – the land – is destroyed, rendered useless. As US policy contributes to transforming Central America's unique and incredibly diverse ecosystems into wasteland, the results will be deflected north to the US – in the form of an inexorable tide of refugees from a generation of Central Americans who have never known peace; and of the loss of a substantial part of the world's heritage of genetic diversity; and, in subtle and intricate yet real ways, loss of productive capacity and ecological health in the United States' own land. The destruction of an ecosystem *anywhere* in the world is an attack on the integrity of our planet's biosphere, with effects *everywhere*, worldwide. The biosphere recognizes no borders.

2. Ecological Destruction as the Roots of War

Central America is one of the most ecologically diverse regions of the world. While many North Americans and Europeans seem to have an image of Central America as covered with sweltering tropical jungles, in reality the isthmus contains a variety of bioregions. In addition to tropical rainforests, there are other kinds of forests, towering mountains, and fertile plains. The Spanish *conquistadores* did not find gold or silver in the region (as they did in Mexico and the Andes), but agricultural wealth to be extracted from the soil, and an Indian population to work the soil as slave labour. Eventually the Spanish crown abolished slavery, but forced labour as punishment for violating 'vagrancy laws', and the debt labour which still exists today on Central American plantations, has maintained a captive, dirt cheap labour force throughout the centuries. From the cochineal and indigo of the colonial era, the coffee and bananas that came to characterize the region by the twentieth century, to the 'non-traditional' crops such as cotton and beef of today, Central America's best land has been used to produce crops to send abroad.

This agro-export economy which has been in place for five centuries and has reduced Central America to economic dependency on foreign markets and, recently, even foreign-grown food, supplanted a vitally productive, self-contained and self-sufficient pre-Hispanic system of agriculture, which had supported sophisticated Indian cultures – complete with a written language and magnificent city-states – before the arrival of the *conquistadores*. This system of communal land holdings, without private property, produced foodstuffs (principally maize, or corn) for local consumption and sustained large populations in a society which, in many ways, was more advanced than that of contemporaneous Europe. The Spanish conquered the Indians with muskets and (more importantly) European diseases to which the Indians had no immunities – these diseases frequently wiped out whole Indian communities before the Spanish even set foot in them. The Indians, however, had a more accurate calendar than their Spanish conquerors, as well as sophisticated astronomy and architecture.

The population of Mesoamerica dropped radically in the aftermath of the Spanish conquest as Indian populations rapidly dwindled in a holocaust of massacres, disease, starvation and slavery. It would be more than a century before the region's population began to grow again, and still longer before it reached pre-Conquest levels.[1]

Geographer David Browning, in his book *El Salvador: Landscape and Society*, describes the indigenous system of land use which was eliminated along with the Indians themselves in El Salvador. Before the conquest, the dominant Indian group in El Salvador was the Pipil, who have today been almost entirely exterminated as a people with a cultural identity. The Pipil were one of the many Maya-related groups, whose territory extended to the mountains of Nicaragua, to the south and east of which, as the mountains give way to the lowland rainforest, the Maya-related groups gave way to Chibchan-related groups, such as the Miskito, Pesch, Sumo and Rama. The seat of Maya power on the eve of the conquest was in a network of city-states in the highlands of Guatemala and what is now southern Mexico, which were in turn under the cultural and political influence of the Aztec empire, based far to the north in Mexico's Anahuac Valley.

> To the Indian, private and individual ownership of the land was as meaningless as private ownership of the sky, the weather or the sea. It is probable that the *capulli*, the oldest form of Aztec territorial organization and the basic unit of settlement, was used by the Pipil Indians of El Salvador. Each family of a clan group that shared the *capulli* had a right to use part of it under conditions laid down by the local chief, the *capullec*. No one had the right to cultivate a particular piece of land in perpetuity, and indeed the migratory nature of *milpa* [seasonal maize bed] farming discouraged this. The individual family was periodically alloted a plot within the area of land that a village regarded as for its own use. To this extent, there was a sense of possession of land, but only as far as the use of land was concerned.[2]

Extermination of indigenous society was also effected through the destruction of local ecosystems upon which these societies were based. Spanish livestock-keeping claimed land that had been used by the Indians in field-to-forest rotation agriculture. In addition to depriving local Indian populations of adequate agricultural land, this development was also destructive to the ecology, since (as the Indians knew) the forest part of the cycle was essential for soil recovery. Once the Spaniards had transformed the land into permanent cattle pasture it steadily deteriorated. Eventually, more land would be needed to maintain the same quantity of cattle, prompting the Spanish ranchers to expand on to yet more Indian land. The Spanish also built aqueducts and irrigation channels, which diverted water from traditional Indian agricultural lands. Vast areas of Mesoamerica were deforested by the Spanish simply to make it look more like a 'New Spain' (the old Spain had been largely deforested centuries ago). This practice, more widespread in Mexico than Central America, led to decreased rainfall and rampant soil erosion. All of this resulted in Indian hunger and the break-up of Indian communities which, in turn, resulted in the rapid erosion of Indian language, traditions and culture. This ecocidal destruction of the land-base of Indian life facilitated the transformation of the Indians from an uncontrollable and potentially rebellious subject population to a slave labour force.[3]

That minority of Indians who survived the 'biological holocaust' unleashed by European diseases such as smallpox, yellow fever, malaria and bubonic plague, as well as the 'ecocide' that broke up indigenous communities by destroying their agriculture, was incorporated as slave labour into the new system of plantation agriculture. Due to protestations to the Spanish crown by some of the more progressive elements in the Catholic Church, the slavery became increasingly subtle – *de facto* slavery cloaked in bureaucratic obfuscation and euphemistic terminology. Outright slavery was first replaced by a system known as the *encomienda*, which meant a transfer of the Spanish crown's right to tribute to an individual, as a reward for services to the crown. Spanish captains were granted both land and Indians to work it under the *encomienda*, but the Indians were also ostensibly there to be guided, protected, educated in Spanish and converted to Christianity. The *encomienda*, in other words, was supposed to be a position of responsibility as well as privilege. Of course, it was really simply legitimized slavery. The clergy realized this and continued to protest to the crown. The *encomienda* was subsequently replaced with the *repartimiento*, which was similar to the *encomienda* except that the Indians were – ostensibly – paid for their labour. The *repartimiento*, however, rapidly became merely obligatory debt labour – the Indians were born in debt to their masters and died in debt to their masters and spent their lives working off their debt. Growing indigo or mining gold for Spanish masters, the Indians could not grow their own food. They were forced to 'buy' it from their masters – at a rate intentionally set at more than they could afford by their 'wage'. This resulted in perpetual debt. The *repartimiento* was replaced by the *latifundio* – ostensibly voluntary debt labour. The *latifundio* differed from the *repartimiento* only in that the Indians were supposedly 'free'. But they were still born and died in debt, and this kept them a captive, and virtually unpaid, labour force. The *latifundio* existed in Mexico until the Revolution of the early twentieth century, and still persists today in Guatemala and, to a somewhat lesser extent, El Salvador,[4] where distinct Indian populations have been almost completely wiped out and the exploited population is *mestizo* (mixed blood) and Ladino (Spanish-speaking), like the oligarchical class. But throughout Central America, even today, the 'oligarchs' who control the land tend to have more Spanish blood, while the peasants and captive labourers who work the land tend to have more Indian blood.

Central America can roughly be broken up into three bioregions: the central highlands, which form the spine of the isthmus; the Pacific lowlands to the south and west; and the Caribbean lowlands to the north and east. Today these bioregions have been largely converted into agro-export zones, producing, respectively, coffee, cotton and bananas.

Central America's population is largely centralized in the cool and fertile highlands – land elevated by the volcanic mountain chain that snakes along the southern and western side of the isthmus, becoming the centre of the isthmus as the land bridge narrows at Costa Rica. Along the Pacific coast, to the south and west of the mountains, the land is richly fertile, nourished with volcanic ash. Originally, much of this land was forested, but now it is used to grow coffee and, more recently, cotton.

While to the North American mind all tropical forest is simply 'jungle', in Central America there are three distinct types of tropical forest. In the intensely fertile, lowland Pacific region, the forest is known as Dry Forest, because it receives rain only during the rainy season. Five hundred years ago the entire Pacific coast of Mesoamerica, from northern Mexico to Panama, was covered by Dry Forest. Today most of this land is covered with plantations and only two per cent of the original Dry Forest cover remains. Dry Forests are home to armadillos, iguanas, coatimundis and white-face monkeys.

This Pacific lowland bioregion is the smallest of the three – comprising only a narrow strip between the Pacific shoreline and the central mountain chain – but it contains some of the richest soils anywhere on Earth. The volcanic ash that nourishes the soil is washed down by rains from the mountains above. Today the Pacific-facing slopes of these mountains are Central America's coffee production zone, while the hot, lowland plains, closer to the Pacific coast, are the cotton zone.

To the north and east of this region, in the highlands, the climate is cooler due to higher altitude and it is there that most of Central America's cities lie and the bulk of its population lives. In the more mountainous and marginal areas of the highlands, steep slopes frequently make agriculture highly problematic. Much of the highland forests are fairly similar to North America's conifer forests. On the peaks of the mountains, however, is an extremely rare – and now threatened – type of tropical forest: Cloud Forest. So called because it draws much of its water from constant low cloud cover that envelops the forests, Cloud Forest is cool, moist, mossy and home to an amazing profusion of species, many of which exist nowhere else in the world, including multicoloured frogs and brilliantly plumed birds, such as the quetzal.

On the northern and eastern side of the highlands, the land slopes down towards the broad, tropical rainforests which reach to the Caribbean coast. These lush lowlands of towering trees receive some rainfall all year round. It seems ironic that the rainforests soils, so profuse with life, are actually thin and basically incapable of supporting most types of long-term agriculture. But these forests play an important role in regulating both regional and global climate. Central America contains the two largest stretches of Tropical rainforest in the Western Hemisphere north of the Amazon Basin. The first of these is the Miskito Coast, which stretches along the Caribbean from the eastern corner of Honduras, down the eastern half of Nicaragua to the Costa Rican border; the other is El Peten in northern Guatemala. El Peten was once contiguous with rainforests across the Usumacinta River in Mexico and stretched in an unbroken expanse from the Gulf of Mexico, across northern Guatemala to the Caribbean coast in Belize – but today the Mexican rainforest has been almost entirely destroyed. The Miskito Coast and El Peten are remote and sparsely populated – on the map they are represented as large blank areas.

The animals which live there, rapidly disappearing due to deforestation, include jaguars, tapirs and howler monkeys.

Many of the people on Central America's Caribbean coast are neither *mestizo*, Ladino, nor Indian, but English-speaking blacks, descendants of rebellious slaves sent there from British-held Caribbean islands, such as Jamaica, in the seventeenth century, when the British Empire was vying with Spain to establish dominance over the region.

The best agricultural land on the northern and eastern side (the Caribbean side) of the highlands is in fertile river valleys such as the Motagua in Guatemala and the Aguan in Honduras. For the past century, this land has been used almost exclusively for banana plantations.

While coffee production in the Pacific zone and the highlands has generally been in the hands of a domestic oligarchy – such as El Salvador's so-called 'fourteen families' – banana production in the Caribbean zone is under the control of US-based multinational corporations known in Central America as *los pulpos* – the octopuses. These companies have been a powerhouse in Central American politics, crushing strikes, sponsoring revolts against unfriendly governments and, in one notorious case, pulling strings with the US Central Intelligence Agency (CIA) to arrange a *coup d'etat*. In this incident, the first Central American government to attempt a serious redistribution of land – the Jacobo Arbenz regime in Guatemala – was overthrown in 1954. The democratically elected and moderately leftist Arbenz government was deposed in a right-wing coup with the aid of the CIA after Arbenz had dared to expropriate (with full compensation) idle land belonging to the United Fruit Company (UFCo). UFCo controlled Guatemala's railroads, ports and much of the country's shipping and land. The coup resulted in a minor scandal in the US. After an anti-trust suit, a hostile corporate merger, revelations of bribes to the Honduran government not to impose an export tax (this fiasco was labelled by the media 'Bananagate') and other embarrassments, in 1975 the company's then president plunged to his death from a New York City skyscraper. But the coup in Guatemala had ushered in a decades-long reign of military government-by-terror.[5]

In 1974, in an attempt to wrest some power over *los pulpos*, the six Central American nations (not counting Belize) along with Colombia, Venezuela and the Dominican Republic formed the Union of Banana Exporting Countries (UPEB), a cartel inspired by the success of the Organization of Petroleum Exporting Countries (OPEC). But UPEB turned out to be largely a bunch of empty dreams. Unlike the OPEC nations, which can sit on their product while they wait for prices to rise or negotiations to complete, UPEB does not have this option: bananas rot; nor does industrial civilization run on bananas. US multinationals still overwhelmingly control the world banana market. Nicaragua's revolutionary Sandinista government nationalized banana operations in that country, but the state corporation, Bananic, accounts for only two per cent of the global market. Ecuador, the world's biggest supplier, also has a national company, but has declined to join UPEB.[6]

After a century of intrigues, rivalries and corporate mergers, today there are three *pulpos* in Central America. These corporations are now multi-product as well as multinational and their empires extend far beyond bananas to beef, tobacco and other commodities, but together they account for 56 per cent of the world banana market. Significantly, the names of the parent corporations of these three agricultural giants are unfamiliar to most North Americans, yet their product names and subsidiaries are household words. The three modern *pulpos* are: Castle & Cooke (also known as Standard Fruit or Dole); R. J. Reynolds (also known as Del Monte and Nabisco); and United Brands (formerly UFCo, also known as Chiquita Bananas and John Morrell Beef).[7]

The three *pulpos* are currently in a state of flux. In 1989, R. J. Reynolds (RJR) was bought out in a multi-billion dollar, hostile take-over funded by high-yield 'junk bonds', thereby incurring a gargantuan debt. The new owners, Kohlberg Kravis Roberts & Co., faced with plummetting prices for RJR shares on the stock market, decided to sell off Del Monte. In January 1990, after deals with Castle & Cooke and Citicorp Venture Capital fell through, Del Monte wound up in the hands of the Merrill Lynch Company. In April 1990, the European processed-foods division of Del Monte was bought out from Merrill Lynch by management for $375 million. RJR subsequently moved into an expansion and more aggressive marketing of its tobacco products, especially Camel cigarettes, to compensate for the loss of the giant agribusiness subsidiary. High profile advertising of RJR cigarettes, aimed at the young, and at ethnic minorities, has recently come under attack from consumers' groups in the United States.[8]

Meanwhile, Castle & Cooke is said to be considering selling off Dole to friendly investors in order to facilitate the further growth of the subsidiary, which is already believed to be the world's largest seller of fruits and vegetables.[9]

These three conglomerates each span the globe. Castle & Cooke has operations in Hawaii and California as well as the Philippines and Thailand, while Del Monte grows bananas for the Japanese market in the Philippines, asparagus for the European market in Mexico, and pineapples for the British market in Kenya, in addition to its stateside operations in Texas, Hawaii and elsewhere.[10] Malnutrition is, of course, rampant in Kenya and the Philippines, and in the early 1970s reports emerged that Del Monte was using armed agents to strong-arm local Filipino smallholders into leasing to the company.[11] However, Central America remains the mainstay of fruit production for these companies, and it has been in Central America that they have had the most influential presence in local politics.

But despite the colourful history of the *pulpos* and their destructive meddling in the region's politics, it is in the agricultural heartland of the Pacific zone and the Pacific-facing slopes of the highlands that the crisis has its deepest roots. The Caribbean zone had been sparsely inhabited before the advent of the banana plantations. In the Pacific zone, on the other hand, a thriving peasant economy existed before the introduction of agro-industry.

The first agro-industry was that of the cochineal and indigo plantations introduced by the Spanish, which ran on the slave labour (and later, debt labour) of the Indians whose land – and therefore whose self-sufficiency – had been taken by those very plantations. In 1636, a Spanish priest in El Salvador wrote:

> I have seen large Indian villages . . . practically destroyed after indigo mills have been erected near them. For most Indians that enter the mills will soon sicken as a result of the forced work . . . I speak from experience as at various times I have confessed great numbers of fever-stricken Indians and have been there when they carry them from the mills for burial . . . [A]s most of these wretches have been forced to abandon their homes and plots of maize, many of their wives and children die also. In particular this is true of the province of San Salvador where there are so many indigo mills, and all of them built close to Indian villages.[13]

This process only accelerated after Central American independence from Spain, as new export crops such as coffee were introduced.

Each wave of agricultural development resulted in displacement of peasants who had used the land for subsistence cultivation of staples such as maize and beans. Writes Walter LaFeber in *Inevitable Revolutions*:

> The effect of the coffee economy on the peasants was especially devastating: before 1820 a large majority had small farm plots, but by the 1860's about half were merely wage laborers . . . Peasants and Indians became little more than a hungry, wandering labor force to be used at will by the oligarchy.[13]

On 20 October, 1928, the following appeared in the Salvadoran newspaper *Patria*:

> Now there is nothing but coffee. In the great hacienda named California that covers the flanks of the volcano Alegria, where I visited last year, I did not find a single fruit tree. On that *finca* [farm] that extends for many *caballerias* [one *caballeria* = 45 hectares] there were formerly two hundred or more properties planted in maize, rice, beans and fruit. Now there is nothing but coffee in the highlands and pasture in the lowlands, which go on displacing the forests and the *milpas* [cornfields].

On 22 December of that year it was stated in the same paper that:

> The conquest of territory by the coffee industry is alarming. It has already occupied all the high ground and is now descending into the valleys, displacing maize, rice and beans. It goes in the manner of the conquistador, spreading hunger and misery, reducing the former proprietors to the worst conditions – woe to those who sell out.[14]

Woe indeed. Four years after those words were written the most violent episode in El Salvador's violent history took place. The military dictatorship of General Maximiliano Hernandez Martinez slaughtered nearly 30,000 people while crushing a popular uprising.[15] This act, known as the *Matanza*, or massacre, was a turning point in El Salvador's history. It is not coincidental that the uprising had centred around areas that had been communal Indian lands before the advent of the coffee plantations.[16] The *Matanza* of 1932 finished the work that began in 1881 with the Law of Extinction of Communal Lands. This law had banned the traditional system of subsistence agriculture practised by El Salvador's indigenous peoples.[17] 'The existence of lands under the ownership of communities', the law read, 'impedes agricultural development, obstructs the circulation of wealth, and . . . is contrary to the economic and social principles that the Republic has accepted.'[18] In the repression following the *Matanza*, even Indian language and dress were banned – the culture associated with traditional subsistence agriculture was effectively exterminated in El Salvador.[19] But this was not to be the end of political rebellion in El Salvador. Farabundo Marti, the martyred Communist leader of the 1932 uprising, is a name that lives on in El Salvador's leftist guerrilla insurgent group – the Farabundo Marti National Liberation Front (FMLN).

It was also in this era that the Nicaraguan revolutionary martyr Augusto Cesar Sandino, from whom the modern-day Sandinistas take their name, struggled against US military domination of his country and the disenfranchisement of the *campesinos*. Ever since the US-backed regime of Adolfo Diaz had been threatened with rebellion in 1912, 100 US Marines had been stationed in Nicaragua. Sandino was the one rebel general who refused to lay down his arms until the last Marine left Nicaraguan soil. Although his sole demand for peace was national sovereignty for a Nicaragua free of foreign troops, Sandino had a reverence for the *campesino* and the self-sufficient maize economy of the Indian past which was almost mystical in its intensity.[20] He looked forward to settling down, after the departure of the Marines, on an experimental self-sufficient co-operative farm, which he had established on the banks of the Coco River. This farm he envisioned as a model for a decentralized and locally autonomous but federated Central America, drawing from the then-popular political philosophy of revolutionary anarchism, to which he had been exposed in the labour movement when he had worked in the oilfields of Mexico.[21]

When the Marines finally departed in 1932, they left in their place the National Guard which they had trained to police the country, headed by General Anastasio Somoza. Sandino nonetheless signed a peace pact, as he had promised he would after the Marines left Nicaraguan soil, but shortly thereafter he was gunned down by National Guardsmen in civilian clothes, probably acting on the orders of General Somoza. The next day, Sandino's co-operative on the Coco River was attacked and destroyed by the National Guard, the inhabitants massacred.[22] In a 1936 *coup d'etat*, Somoza subsequently consolidated his brutal US-backed dynasty, which would run Nicaragua as a personal fiefdom until 1979.[23]

The coffee boom meant that more of Central America's land was centralized into fewer hands, less land was used to grow staples such as maize and beans for local consumption, and more hungry peasants were uprooted from their land-base and traditional lifestyle. This destructive pattern was repeated and intensified with the post-World War II cotton boom. In 1953 regional cotton production was less than 100 bales; by 1964 it exceeded one million bales. Cotton became Nicaragua's top export, second only to coffee in El Salvador and Guatemala.[24]

Those who reaped the benefits of the cotton boom were large hacienda owners who were already rich before the boom – several dozen families throughout Central America. Often, coffee plantations on the volcanic slopes expanded down into the prime cotton-growing land of the Pacific coast. Rather than cultivating this land themselves, the coffee oligarchs frequently rented it to cotton growers at a fixed rate. They thereby avoided the risks associated with occasional low cotton prices on the world market, or occasional high prices for pesticides, fertilizers, tractors and other technological inputs imported from abroad, and upon which cotton turned out to be far more dependent that coffee. Throughout the 1960s organizations such as the World Bank, the Inter-American Development Bank (IDB) and the US Agency for International Development (USAID) funded road-building to facilitate cotton cultivation in the Pacific zone, as US corporations stepped in with the technological inputs. Eventually, Central American cotton yields came to surpass those of the US Mississippi Delta. Credit for cotton poured in and a new agro-export zone was created in the Pacific coast.[25]

This resulted, of course, in a new and accelerated wave of peasant dislocation. While a great deal of Dry Forest was cleared to make way for the cotton industry, the bulk of the new cotton land had previously been producing maize by and for local *campesinos*, or peasants, who were forced out by the cotton producers. Nicaragua's Leon–Chinandega cotton belt had previously been known as *el granero* (the granary) and was legendary throughout the country as a highly productive maize area. Cotton also displaced maize in El Salvador and Guatemala.[26]

Prior to the cotton boom, Pacific zone *campesinos* had lived as sharecroppers on large haciendas, growing maize and providing labour for the owner (caring for livestock, tending crops); or they obtained access to land via the *ejidal* system, in which *campesinos* paid a small fee to use land belonging to a township or municipality, or simply used land which was untitled.[27]

With the cotton boom, previously untitled land became titled by large landowners, land belonging to townships or municipalities was transferred to large landowners, and on haciendas rents shot up way beyond what *campesinos* could afford. Haciendas which had previously allowed *campesinos* to sharecrop started demanding money rents. The cotton boom meant eviction for *campesinos*. Shantytowns proliferated along roads in the Pacific zone and slums sprang up in the villages. Slum dwellers became seasonal cotton pickers, their cheap labour allowing the cotton growers to avoid the expense of mechanical pickers. Many *campesinos*, however, saw no option other than to migrate from the Pacific zone. Some went to the big capital cities, and huge dismal shantytowns, without potable water, electricity or sewage disposal systems, spread on the outskirts of Managua, San Salvador and Guatemala City. Some migrated – often as part of government-sponsored programmes – to the rainforest of the Caribbean zone.[28]

One indirect ecological effect of the cotton boom has been the pressure placed on the rainforests by this massive influx of displaced peasants. But before turning our attention to this problem – and the spiral of resultant problems it sparked off – let us look at the direct ecological consequences of the cotton boom in the Pacific zone itself.

3. Cotton Cultivation as Ecocide

In many ways, Central America is not the ideal place to grow cotton. The humidity and heat of the Pacific zone provides fertile breeding conditions for insects and there is no winter frost to keep insect populations in check. After four or five consecutive years of cotton cultivation with excellent yields, the lowland soils began to leach and yields began to dramatically decline. In response, US companies stepped in with pesticides, chemical fertilizers and other technological fixes. In the short run, techno-fixes imported from the north seemed capable of solving any agricultural problem in the cotton zone. In the long run, however, the cotton economy was overstretching the bounds of the coastal ecology, depleting the rich soils, leading to growth of insect populations and contaminating the air, land and water of the coastal plain. Clearing cotton fields of stalks after harvest to starve insects led to wind erosion and dust storms. In the rainy season rivers became thick with silt from the fields. But the other method for combatting insects – a total-eradication pesticide strategy – proved to be even more disastrous. In fact, the era of pesticides, which was ushered in by the cotton boom, has proved to be one of Central America's worst ecological disasters.

The short-term success of the total-eradication strategy ultimately backfired with devastating consequences. In the mid-1950s crop-dusters proliferated in Central America's cotton zones and the use of DDT (discovered only in 1939) became widespread. DDT was even widely spread on coastal marshes to eliminate malaria. But with each spraying, mutant pests with a natural immunity to the pesticide survived, and bred a whole new generation of immune mutant pests. In addition, the pesticide killed off the pests' natural predators. Malaria returned with a vengeance and the number of pests attacking the cotton fields multiplied.[1] Before 1950 there were only two insect pests in the Central American cotton zones. Today there are 14. By the 1960s, scientists had found the Nicaraguan cotton bullworm to be 45 times more resistant to the pesticide methyl parathion than any previously known pest population in the world.[2]

With the number of pests increasing every season, the cotton growers, at the urging of the US chemical companies, responded by increasing the number of sprayings every season – and using increasingly toxic mixes.

The nature of this vicious cycle is described by Frances Moore Lappé and

Joseph Collins in their book *Food First*, with Nicaragua as the example:

> In Nicaragua cotton acreage was increased tenfold between 1950 and 1964.
> By the late 1950's the large growers acting on the advice of U.S. Agency for
> International Development (AID) technicians scheduled insecticide applica-
> tions an average of eight times per season as well as liberal fertilizer
> treatments. Yields increased. But by 1966 the growers found it necessary to
> apply insecticides thirty times per season. Even then cotton yields began to
> drop: from 821 pounds per acre in 1965 to 621 pounds per acre in 1968.
> Along the fertile Pacific coastal plain of Central America large cotton
> estates by the late 1960's had to schedule so many (45 to 50 a season) aerial
> sprays of a 'cocktail' of pesticides (including DDT) that cotton production
> ceased to be profitable. By 1968 Nicaragua had the dubious distinction of
> holding the world's record for the number of applications of insecticides on
> a single crop.[3]

Nicaragua became a textbook case of 'pesticide treadmill'. The average
number of pesticide applications rose from between five and ten per season in
the mid-1950s to once every four days by the late 1960s.[4]
Neither is the havoc wreaked by the pesticides limited to the cotton fields. In
fact, of the chemicals sprayed by crop-dusters, 50 to 75 per cent never reach
the target crop, but instead drift widely, contaminating local ecosystems –
including watersheds, wildlife, adjacent food crops, cattle herds and human
beings.[5] Birds are poisoned, including migratory songbirds from North
America.[6] In Costa Rica, pesticides have almost completely exterminated the
fish, crocodile and armadillo population of the Guanacaste River.[7] In
Guatemala, in recent years, pesticides have blown from the lowland cotton
zone up into the highlands, killing the natural predators of the bark beetle,
thereby causing the worst beetle attack on record in Guatemala. Meanwhile,
beneficial insects like honeybees have nearly disappeared from many areas.[8]
By the 1970s Central America was the world's highest per capita user of
pesticides and the market for 40 per cent of US global pesticide exports. And of
this 40 per cent, 75 per cent of US pesticide exports to Central America were
either banned, restricted or unregistered in the United States.[9] This results in an
ironic 'circle of poison', as the US public consumes Central American exports
such as bananas, coffee and beef, which are tainted with pesticides so deadly
that they cannot even be legally used within the United States! (The banana
plantations also use pesticides widely, and pesticides from both the cotton and
banana zones find their way into the fat tissues of livestock. For instance, in
1967 a shipment of over 300,000 pounds of beef from Nicaragua was rejected
for entry by US Food and Drug Administration officials due to excessive levels
of DDT. Many more shipments with 'acceptable' levels of various pesticides
get through entry inspections and reach US markets.) But of course the risk is
far greater for Central Americans.[10]
Employees of the cotton and banana plantations, as well as *campesino*
families who live adjacent to these lands, come into contact with huge doses of

pesticides such as DDT, Phosvel, endrin, dieldrin and DBCP, all banned in the United States, and herbicides like 2,4-D, a component of Agent Orange, on a daily basis. Since 1976, the US Environmental Protection Agency has been required by law to notify recipient governments of restricted pesticides exported by US companies. But the Agency typically sends such notice only well after the shipment has already arrived in the recipient country. More importantly, the notification says only that a particular chemical has been restricted – it does not explain why it has been restricted, what the associated risks are, or even the brand name the chemical is being peddled under.[11]

As a spokesperson from the US embassy in Costa Rica recently told a local reporter:

> It is not U.S. policy to make public names of companies that import or export these products. For, as you know, the companies would be very upset if this were to happen.[12]

If controls are abysmal at the governmental level, they are virtually non-existent on the plantation. Protective gloves, masks and other gear are seldom made available to employees by plantation managers. Few farm workers have running water in their homes to wash off the day's accumulation of pesticides – and if they live adjacent to the plantation, the homes they return to at night are also apt to be contaminated. Many bathe in streams or irrigation canals, which are contaminated with still more agro-chemicals. Instructions and warnings printed on the labels of pesticide cans are frequently only in English, while many farm labourers cannot even read Spanish – migrant Indian labourers in Guatemala often cannot even *speak* fluent Spanish. Little wonder that there is such frequent misuse of pesticides and little appreciation of their dangers.[13]

In El Salvador and Guatemala, right-wing death squads have issued death threats against people organizing against pesticide misuse, apparently viewing the charges only as a strategy to incite farm workers to rebellion. In Guatemala, a doctor who was reporting on the dangers of agro-chemicals to the country's agricultural workforce was kidnapped by one such death squad.[14]

The results of this state of affairs on human health are obvious. Here are a few facts. Today, Nicaraguans and Guatemalans have more DDT in their body fat than any other people on Earth.[15] A 1972 World Health Organization (WHO) study in Nicaragua's Leon cotton zone found samples of human breast milk to be contaminated with DDT by up to 45 times more than the 'safe' tolerance level set by the WHO.[16] The average DDT level in Guatemalan cow's milk is 90 times higher than that allowed by US standards.[17] Between 1971 and 1976, some 19,000 pesticide poisonings were reported in Central America.[18] During the 1960s and 1970s Honduras and Nicaragua were the world leaders in per capita illness and death from pesticide poisonings.[19] Every year, more than 1,000 Guatemalans receive medical treatment for exposure to pesticides – and undoubtedly thousands more suffer without treatment (and therefore without record) because they have no access to medical care.[20] Pesticides sprayed on cotton also fall on adjacent pastures where cattle graze.

Milk and meat from the cattle are brought to urban markets and consumed by the middle class. The 1972 WHO study also found that breast milk taken from women in the city of Leon had only slightly lower levels of DDT than that taken from women in Leon's agricultural areas.[21]

While other Central American crops (bananas being the classic example) were primarily or even exclusively exported north to the United States, by the 1980s nearly all Central American cotton was being exported to mills in Japan, Hong Kong and Europe.[22] Cotton is seen by US elites as a means for Central America to earn export dollars to pay off the countries' foreign debts to the US, the World Bank, the IMF and other entities in the multinational lending bureaucracy created in the post-World War II era. With an impossibly huge debt to pay off – increasing with interest every year – external pressure was added to domestic greed as an impetus to maintain an export-oriented economy.

In the 1950s and 1960s other 'non-traditional' (meaning, not coffee or bananas) crops – such as sugar and tobacco – also expanded. This expansion also took place on large land holdings, displacing tenant farmers. By the 1980s the number of landless and land-poor in El Salvador was growing faster than El Salvador's total population. As landless peasants came to support revolutionary movements in El Salvador, Guatemala and Nicaragua – movements that sought to liberate the agricultural heartland – the entire region became intensely militarized; this militarization has been overwhelmingly funded by US tax dollars. Yet, no longer is it a question of protecting the profits of a particular corporation – as it was in the CIA-sponsored Guatemalan coup of 1954 on behalf of UFCo. US intervention and its goals today are more generalized – it has to do with maintaining the entirety of Central America as an agro-export sector, doing what the 'Third World' and the debtor nations are 'supposed' to do in the modern global order: generating foreign exchange to service their foreign debt – even if the exports are no longer exclusively to the United States. For instance, since 1980, with the advent of corn syrup and artificial sweeteners, the United States has dropped to second place as an importer of Central American sugar. The top importer of Central American sugar today is the Soviet Union.[23]

In addition to agro-chemical abuse, the cotton boom has also meant the destruction of much of the Pacific zone's remaining tropical Dry Forest. A 1963 US Department of Agriculture report contained the following photo caption: 'Scene near Tiquisate, Guatemala illustrates conquest of jungle for cotton culture. Fields of cotton recently cleared reach jungle in background up to gins.'[24]

More important was the decline in basic staples and grains for local consumption – maize, beans, rice – as more and more land was turned over to cotton. Maize (what North Americans call corn) had sustained Central America's population for millennia before the arrival of the Spanish. The Maya civilization had thrived on it. Its cultivation has profound religious significance for the Indians of Guatemala, and spiritual overtones for *campesinos* throughout Central America.

In 1986, Guatemala, facing a severe maize shortage, had to import $1 million worth of corn, or 14,000 tons, from the US.[25] In 1955, Nicaragua imported 21,000 tons of grains – by 1978 this nation of rich farmlands was importing over ten times that amount.[26] El Salvador has to import nearly all of its staples.[27]

Self-sufficiency – Central America's ability to feed itself independently – declined as the cotton export sector grew, and as the minority that controlled it grew wealthy.

4. Tropical Rainforests as a Political Safety Valve

As more and more of Central America's best agricultural land was turned over to cotton cultivation and centralized in fewer and fewer hands, an inevitable question arose: what to do with the new class of landless peasants that had been created?

This is the question which is at the root of Central America's current crisis. By the 1980s, landless peasants were organizing guerrilla armies and squatter movements, and the established power structures (perhaps best termed the Oligarchy–Military–US Aid & Investment Complex) responded by militarizing – and, in the cases of El Salvador and Guatemala, precipitating a blood-bath. Landless peasants in the cities meant unsightly shantytowns and urban unrest. It was precisely to avoid such a crisis that the ruling elites decided to relocate the landless peasants into the land which was viewed as being most expendable – the vast tropical rainforests of the Caribbean zone. Like many such solutions implemented only in order to avoid recognizing and tackling the real root of the problem, it worked well in the short run, but ultimately recoiled appallingly.

American Indian historian John Mohawk has written that in the colonization of North America, as Indians were pushed further and further west to make room for white settlers, 'The military was the hammer, the frontier was the anvil.'[1] This metaphor is equally appropriate to modern Central America – or Brazil, or Indonesia, or a number of other countries where uprooted peasants are laying waste to tropical rainforest.

Beginning in the mid-1950s, Nicaragua's Leon–Chinandega 'Granary' was transformed into a cotton zone, as families with ties to the corrupt dictatorship of the Somoza dynasty registered ownership of land which had been farmed by *campesinos* (without official 'ownership') for generations. *Campesinos* who resisted relocation were forcibly evicted by Somoza's National Guard (which, as already noted, was created, trained and supervised under the direction of the US Marines who occupied Nicaragua in the 1920s and early 1930s).[2]

The National Guard was 'the hammer'; the western edge of Nicaragua's vast Miskito rainforest was 'the anvil'. In Guatemala, the army was 'the hammer', while the rainforest region of El Peten was 'the anvil'. As peasants were forcibly removed from fertile land to make way for the cotton industry, they emigrated to the agricultural frontier on the edge of the rainforests, cleared new land, and thereby pushed back the frontier. Sometimes this colonization of the rainforests by landless peasants happened 'spontaneously', sometimes under government supervision as part of official programmes – sometimes even sponsored by organizations such as USAID.[3]

But the rainforests are not as 'expendable' as the ruling elites had assumed. To start with, rainforest soils are not appropriate for growing crops such as maize and beans. In fact, they are really not appropriate for much of anything other than supporting rainforest. The soils are thin and poor; 90 per cent of the nutrients in the rainforest are in the vegetation itself – especially in the lush, verdant forest canopy – rather than in the soils. While other forests absorb nutrients from the soil, the intensely hot and humid tropical rainforests live off their own debris, rapidly recycling nutrients before they reach the forest floor.

The soils of the comparatively small Pacific zone (from which the peasants were uprooted) are among the most fertile on Earth, but the soils of the much larger Caribbean rainforest zone are shallow, rocky and acidic.

The introduction of peasant slash-and-burn agriculture into this region has been a disaster. For the first season or two, the cleared land is intensely productive. Then with the nutrients depleted, yields decline rapidly and dramatically. The relocated *campesinos* have no choice other than to abandon their spent *milpas* and burn down yet more forest to clear more land, resulting in yet another vicious cycle. With thousands of relocated peasants condemned to repeat this process year after year, the rainforest is rapidly disappearing. Nor does the forest reclaim the spent *milpas*; once the trees are felled, the protective canopy is gone, and the thin layer of soil exhausted; the land is left virtually sterile.

The resultant rampant deforestation has not only meant disaster for the rainforests and their multifarious inhabitants – including many endangered species, such as jaguars, tapirs and various kinds of monkey – the ecological effects are felt throughout Central America. In fact, destruction of the rainforests in Central America, together with those of other regions where similar dynamics are at work (such as the Amazon Basin and South-East Asia) is having an ecological impact throughout the planet Earth.

Ecologists James D. Nations and H. Jeffrey Leonard explain the results of rainforest destruction in their essay 'Grounds of Conflict in Central America':

> Undisturbed, a tropical forest acts like a giant sponge, breaking the force of torrential rains and allowing water to percolate slowly into the thin tropical soils. Gradually, the forest releases the captured water to the benefit of downstream agriculture. When tropical forests are cleared, however, precipitation rushes off sloped land and causes downstream flooding and soil erosion.

Deforestation currently results in flood damage of $3.5 million per year in the Sula Valley of Honduras, and $4.5 million per year in Honduras' Aguan River valley.[4]

> Deforestation . . . robs the soil of nutrients and makes it easy for topsoil to

wash away. Then, when millions of tons of . . . silt accumulate in river beds, downstream flooding increases, the reservoirs behind hydroelectric dams clog, and coastal harbors, mangroves and coral reefs are swamped.

But even flooding is less dangerous than the opposite, more long-term problem: decreased rainfall, even drought.

Tropical forest destruction can also induce local and regional climatic changes that take a toll on agricultural productivity . . . [F]orest clearing can . . . reduce regional precipitation . . . [A]lmost half the rain that falls on a lowland tropical forest is water recycled by the forest itself through evapo-transpiration. Forest vegetation breathes out water vapour equivalent to thousands of gallons per hectare per day. When forest is cleared, this vast recycling system is destroyed and regional rainfall may decline by as much as one third of an inch every year, markedly altering regional climate.[5]

To sum up, in addition to having their own inherent right to exist and sustain their own species, forests serve particular functions, which are essential for all living things, including human society. Ecologists have termed the most important of these functions: soil protection; the hydrological cycle; and the carbon cycle. Forests maintain soil protection by reducing rainfall run-off and controlling erosion, as tree roots absorb water. Deforestation therefore results in flooding, siltation and erosion. In the hydrological cycle, trees take in water and release it as vapour through transpiration; clouds then form from the vapour and return the moisture to the earth as rain. Deforestation therefore results in decreased rainfall. In the carbon cycle, trees absorb carbon dioxide from the air; it is returned to the air to be absorbed by other trees as old trees die and decay. As forests burn, carbon dioxide – the most significant gas contributing to the 'Greenhouse Effect' – is released into the air *en masse.*[6]

So the rainforests, the largest forests in Central America, far from being 'expendable', play a key role in regulating regional climate. The effects of their destruction will ultimately take a toll throughout the isthmus – even in the agricultural heartland of the Pacific zone across the mountains. The irony is that the peasant rainforest colonization programmes will (via deforestation) ultimately damage the very industries that uprooted the peasants from the agricultural heartland in the first place: coffee and cotton.

Furthermore, the rainforests also play a major role in regulating *global* climate. The burning of the jungles increases atmospheric levels of carbon dioxide, thereby contributing to the Greenhouse Effect and the resultant global warming. If the Greenhouse Effect continues unchecked, coastal flooding will result worldwide as the polar ice-caps melt, and coastal cities such as New York and San Francisco will be submerged. Another expected result of the Greenhouse Effect is widespread drought and severe agricultural decline in the vast North American bread-basket of the Great Plains – a bioregion geographically bigger than all of Central America. It is increasingly accepted in the scientific community that we are already witnessing the beginning of this agricultural decline due to the Greenhouse Effect.[7]

Deforestation in Central America is also contributing to the North American 'Silent Spring'. Many North American songbirds have been killed off by local psticide use, but many are now also dying because the Central American rainforests where they migrate for the winter have gone. With their winter habitat destroyed, every spring fewer songbirds return from Central America. Some ecologists speculate that North American insect populations, normally kept in check by songbirds, may soon create another serious problem for US farmers as the songbird population continues to decline. (This, in turn, is likely to result in increased pesticide use in North America.) So the integrity of ecosystems in the United States depends on the integrity of rainforest ecosystems to the south.[8]

And herein lies more irony. United States' military intervention in Central America exists to prop up a status quo which includes the rainforest colonization programmes and resultant deforestation. In fact, as previously noted, some of these programmes are even directly funded by US tax dollars.[9]

Three phases have been identified in the process of rainforest destruction in Central America. In the first, roads into the forest are cut by logging companies, which extract valuable hardwoods such as mahogany and tropical cedar, and begin the deforestation. In the second phase, relocated peasants penetrate the rainforest along the logging roads and initiate the vicious cycle of jungle slash-and-burn agriculture. In the final phase, land 'improved' (that is, deforested) by the peasants is taken over by large landowners. The peasants retreat deeper into the forest and the agricultural frontier is pushed further still. Sometimes the peasants are paid a paltry sum for the cleared land, sometimes they are evicted from it yet again by the military or private paramilitary goon squads in the employ of the large landowners, or sometimes the large landowners merely claim title to the land after it has been abandoned by the peasant families. Almost invariably, however, the land is planted with grass for pasture and turned over to cattle ranching – because after only a few seasons of cropping it is good for little else.[10]

As this process continues, vast areas of the ancient, complex, incredibly diverse rainforest are, in the space of a season or two, converted into pasture for cattle-grazing. This has been the most important factor in the frighteningly rapid decline in Central America's forest cover – from more than 60 per cent of the region's total area in 1960 to less than 40 per cent today. The rate of deforestation has increased each decade since 1950 and currently stands at 4,000 square kilometres per year and shows no sign of decreasing.[11]

Rainforests cover 12 per cent of the Earth's land surface, yet may contain up to 50 per cent of all the Earth's species. The rainforests of Central America are among the most species-diverse on the planet, and their destruction is resulting in mass extinctions – essentially it amounts to the extermination of a natural genetic storehouse which has existed for eons and has played a key role in planetary evolution.[12]

The so-called 'Hamburger Connection' to Central American deforestation has been an issue at the top of the agenda for many US environmentalists. As always, however, there is an essential unity between ecological and political crises. The advent of the beef industry is not only a key to Central America's deforestation crisis, but has also been the final spark to set off Central America's political crisis, and the subsequent US intervention in the region. It did this by causing a third wave of peasant dislocation after the first two following the coffee and cotton booms, respectively. With yet a third wave caused by the cattle boom, and the failure of the rainforest colonization programmes to serve as an adequate safety valve, Central America's social tensions were stretched to breaking point.

5. Beef Production as the Spark for Regional War

What made beef such a convenient (and dangerous) industry is that almost any land in Central America can be used to graze cattle. Other crops can be grown only in specific bioregions – bananas in the Caribbean river valleys, coffee on the Pacific side of the mountains, cotton along the Pacific plain – but beef can be produced almost anywhere in the region. Therefore, as beef credit poured into Central America in the 1960s and 1970s, the cattle interests not only gobbled up the land which had been cleared by the relocated peasants in the rainforests, but also expanded into much of what remained of subsistence maize cultivation outside the rainforest – mostly in the highland region, which the elites had considered too mountainous for agriculture – thereby aggravating the very problem that had driven the peasants to the rainforests in the first place. This expansion by agribusiness into the last stronghold of the traditional *campesino* subsistence economy pushed Central America over the edge into the abyss of crisis.

In some cases, the rural unrest produced by the cattle industry was actually used to justify the industry's expansion, as the military responded to peasant rebellion by forcibly relocating the peasant populations to the rainforest, leaving their former lands in the hands of cattle ranchers. Once in the rainforests, of course, the peasants continued the pattern whereby rainforest is converted to cornfields and then the cornfields are converted to cattle pasture. Cattle production excluded the disenfranchised peasants from the economy to an even greater extent than did the production of other crops. Cotton cultivation provides six times more employment per acre than cattle-raising, sugar seven times more, and coffee thirteen times more.[1]

Squatters' movements and rural unrest inevitably followed the cattle industry. In the late 1970s and 1980s, as Central America was plunged into crisis, *campesino* support for leftist guerrilla groups almost invariably emerged in those areas most affected by the cattle industry.

In Nicaragua pasture increased from 17,000 square kilometres in 1951 to 28,200 square kilometres in 1978, mostly at the expense of the Caribbean zone Miskito rainforest.[2] New roads, port facilities and credit for cattle production followed the uprooted *campesinos* into the forest. A post-revolutionary study on the process described it like this:

Cattlemen from the more developed regions of the country acquire the 'improvements' effected by the pioneer colonists and introduce a system of extensive cattle production . . . On selling their improved lands, the pioneer colonists move deeper into the forest, continuing the process of spontaneous expansion of the agricultural frontier.[3]

By 1973 cattle outnumbered people in Nicaragua.

Dictator Anastasio Somoza owned (in addition to much Nicaraguan ranchland), interest in six Miami beef-trading firms, which netted him $30 million per year. Nicaraguan beef exports increased 400 per cent between 1961 and 1974.[4]

Meanwhile, to the west of the Miskito rainforest, in the mountainous department of Matagalpa, thousands of peasants were displaced as their *milpas* were converted into cattle pasture. Eventually, Matagalpa became a hotbed of *campesino* support for the Sandinista guerrillas. This gave Somoza the rationale for designating the entire department a 'counter-insurgency zone'. The landless peasants were rounded up by the National Guard, and 'colonization projects' funded by USAID and the IDB resettled the displaced peasants on the agricultural frontier: the western edge of the Miskito rainforest, which was being pushed further and further east.[5]

In Guatemala in the 1960s, cattle ranching expanded from the Pacific zone into the north eastern departments of Izabal, Zacapa and Chiquimula. Virtually simultaneously, a guerrilla movement, known as MR-13, took root in these departments. Guatemala's military regime responded with its first display of brutal overkill – the terrorization of an entire peasant population in the name of 'counter-insurgency'. In 1966, a unit of US Army Special Forces ('Green Berets'), US-supplied helicopter gunships, fighter jets, bombers and napalm were introduced to assist Colonel Carlos Arana, the operation commander. Arana's troops, trained by the Green Berets, committed so many atrocities that Arana won such nicknames as 'The Jackal' and 'The Butcher of Zacapa'. Whole villages were bulldozed, crops burned in the fields as 'scorched earth' warfare, today all too common in Central America, was used for the first time. Between 1966 and 1968, 8,000 peasants had been killed in an effort to wipe out a guerrilla force of approximately 500![6]

In a tactic also pioneered by the Green Berets' 'Operation Phoenix' in Vietnam, suspected guerrilla sympathizers were hunted out and terrorized, murdered or 'disappeared'. In Guatemala, such operations were carried out by military 'death squads' in civilian clothes. Amnesty International cited one method of torture used by the death squads as consisting of enclosing a victim's head in a hood filled with insecticide.[7]

After the MR-13 guerrillas had been crushed, many of the area's landless peasants who had survived the butchery were relocated north into Guatemala's vast rainforest zone, El Peten. So the beef industry profited from the military's bloodthirsty campaign in two ways. First, the departments of Izabal, Zacapa and Chiquimula were cleared of peasants (as well as guerrillas), thereby freeing up land for cattle. Second, the relocated peasants opened up new land for cattle by clearing rainforest in the remote department of El Peten. Many of the colonization programmes in El Peten were financed by USAID. Colonel Carlos 'The Jackal' Arana was granted a large cattle ranch by the military regime in return for his services. In 1970, he would become president of Guatemala.[8]

All this, however, proved to be only a taste of things to come, as we shall see when we examine the current situation in Guatemala.

In Honduras, the expansion of the cattle industry led, not to guerrilla warfare, but to non-violent squatter movements. This is because in the mid-1970s a nationalist regime created a government bureaucracy to mediate land disputes, as well as a land reform law designed to turn idle land over to peasants. Since the nationalist dictatorship fell (in the wake of the 'Bananagate' scandal of 1975), the land reform has been bogged down by inefficiency, corruption and red tape.[9]

Nonetheless, Honduras' peasants have not supported armed guerrilla groups attempting to overthrow the government, but have instead organized non-violent land occupations in order to force the government to uphold its own laws.[10]

In these struggles, which pitted cattle ranchers against peasant families, it was the task of the land reform bureaucracy to determine who had legal title to the land. On occasion, the National Agrarian Institute (INA) has called in the army to remove squatters, and had peasant leaders thrown in jail. On other occasions, however, squatters have been granted the right to cultivate land which was found to be national or municipal. In some instances, legally-titled ranchland was even turned over to peasant families, with INA compensating the owners.[11]

But this system was set up in response to escalating violence in the Honduran countryside. Since the early 1960s there had been three massacres of peasants at the hands of cattle ranchers. Six were killed in 1965, six more in 1972, but the worst was the last, in June 1975. During a peasant occupation of a ranch called Los Horcones, peasant leaders were burned alive, two women were thrown alive, down a well, before the well was dynamited, and two foreign priests were castrated and mutilated. Prior to the massacre, the local INA office had been stormed by hundreds of goons armed with rifles. Subsequent investigation by the authorities revealed that these acts had been orchestrated by local ranchers with the financial and political support of the National Federation of Farmers and Cattlemen (FENAGH). FENAGH continues to support vigilante activity against *campesinos* by ranchers and their private security forces, and has paid military officials and bounty hunters to assassinate peasant leaders.[12]

Costa Rica has managed to avoid the bloodshed which has erupted elsewhere in Central America through, on one hand, a 'welfare state' that includes subsidies for small farmers to grow staples such as maize, beans and rice, and, on the other, a strong tradition of democracy, constitutional government and tolerance of dissent. But the one element that is indispensable for stability is missing from this prescription: land reform. As elsewhere in Central America, the beef industry has precipitated a wave of peasant dislocation which, in turn, has resulted in both deforestation and social tensions threatening to Costa

Rica's democratic institutions.[13] Displaced peasants have formed squatter movements and, in some cases, land occupations have been met with armed resistance by right-wing paramilitary groups.[14]

There is far greater awareness of ecological issues in Costa Rica than elsewhere in Central America. Ironically, however, this nation, with the highest proportion of protected wilderness areas in the western hemisphere – nearly 20 per cent of the national territory – also has the western hemisphere's fastest rate of deforestation. Costa Rica's national parks, forest reserves and wildlife refuges are in danger of becoming isolated islands of forest in vast seas of deforestation – which is somewhat futile. Furthermore, some forest reserves have been invaded by squatters, and this has led some environmentalists in Costa Rica to see militant *campesino* organizations as their enemies.[15]

This short-sighted view was also evident in the 'Plan of Action for Renewable Natural Resources' unveiled by then-President Rodrigo Carazo in the late 1970s. Although the Plan primarily addressed deforestation, it scarcely mentioned cattle ranching (the primary cause of deforestation in Costa Rica). Despite Costa Rica's lauded conservation efforts, its ambassador to the US habitually lobbies in Washington for higher beef import quotas.[16]

Geographer John P. Augelli sums up the basis of Costa Rica's dilemma:

> Settlement has spread to both oceans and to Costa Rica's borders with Nicaragua and Panama. At present, all land is either privately owned or has been set aside for national parks, forest reserves, and other public uses. As a result, for the first time in more than four centuries of post-Columbian history, Costa Ricans have no easy access to new land, and the resultant 'land hunger' is cause for concern . . . The end of the frontier coincided with an intensification of *latifundismo* [plantation agriculture], with greater importation of foreign capital and technology, and with the expansion of foreign markets – all of which tended to hasten the displacement of small-holders. The chief culprit was the growth and modernization of the country's cattle economy, coupled with some expansion in sugar and rice production.[17]

Of the Central American nations, El Salvador experienced the smallest beef boom – basically because there was little land left in the small nation for the industry to expand on to. With a large population and small area, the cotton boom provided sufficient pressure to spark off El Salvador's crisis. El Salvador also has no Caribbean rainforest zone, to which landless peasants can be relocated, unlike the other Central American nations. In the 1960s, landless Salvadoran peasants started emigrating across the border into Honduras to cultivate land there. But precisely at this time land was becoming more scarce in Honduras, due to the beef industry. The two nations briefly went to war over this issue in 1969 after the Honduran military started forcibly expelling Salvadorans. Smart-aleck *gringo* journalists dubbed the conflict the 'Soccer War' because its outbreak came on the heels of stadium riots during El Salvador-*vs*-Honduras World Cup play-offs. The media got a laugh at the exploits of hot-blooded Latins while ignoring the deeper issue that would come back to haunt Central America in the future. Today the number of landless and land-poor in El Salvador is growing faster than El Salvador's total population.[18]

Perhaps the ultimate insult is that few Central Americans can afford to eat beef. In this prime coffee-producing area often the only coffee available to drink is instant *Nescafé*. In this prime banana-producing area, the only bananas available to eat are the rejects that don't look good enough for the US market. Central America is now also a major beef producer and, thanks to what one observer terms 'United States gastro-imperialism', beef has never been more popular in Central America – Central Americans emulate the eating habits of North Americans; McDonalds has a franchise in every Central American capital. Yet only the elites of Central America can afford to patronize them. The absurd fact is that although beef-eating has never been more fashionable in Central America, never have fewer Central Americans been able to afford to eat it. The situation is described by ecologists James D. Nations and Daniel I. Komer in their essay 'Rainforests and the Hamburger Society':

The U.S. Department of Agriculture (USDA) has pointed out that as beef production increases in Central American countries, per capita beef consumption actually declines in the individual countries. Thus, in Costa Rica, where 71 per cent of all new farm land is planted in beef cattle pasture, beef production doubled between 1959 and 1972, but per capita beef consumption fell from 30 pounds to less than 19. In Honduras, between 1965 and 1975, beef production jumped by almost 300 per cent, but national per capita consumption dropped from 12 pounds to 10. By most estimates, at least two-thirds of Central America's arable land is now dedicated to cattle production, yet the region's per capita beef consumption continues to decline.

By contrast, this is the situation in the United States:

Despite slight declines in recent years, annual per capita beef consumption in the United States in 1983 surpassed 105 pounds, and an American house cat eats more beef in a year than the average Central American.[19]

Clearly, Central America's beef is going to the United States.

US per capita beef consumption has been the highest in the world ever since the post-World War II era beef boom. Hamburger chains like McDonalds and Burger King proliferated and started to scour the global market for cheaper beef. Once again, the World Bank, the IDB and other multinational lending agencies financed road-building in Central America to facilitate a new agro-export industry. Techno-inputs arrived from the North: new bloodlines from Texas and Florida ranches, artificial insemination equipment, tubes of refrigerated semen, worm medicines, fly sprays, vaccines and vitamin/mineral supplements. Since 1963, the World Bank had provided funds for cattle ranching to every Central American nation except El Salvador. Beef packing plants were opened in Central America. These proved more profitable than the ranches, because many ranches are serviced by only a few packaging plants. Some packing plants are owned by wealthy Central Americans, but others are owned by multinational corporations, such as the Costa Rican plant owned by Borden, or the Honduras plant owned by the Tela Railroad Company, a subsidiary of the banana *pulpo* United Brands. Multinationals also frequently have a hand in production. The *pulpo* Del Monte (an R. J. Reynolds subsidiary) owns ranchland in Costa Rica, and the *pulpo* Castle & Cooke has ranchland in both Costa Rica and Honduras. Goodyear's former rubber plantation in Costa Rica has been converted to a cattle ranch. The Panama-incorporated Latin American Agribusiness Development Corporation (LAAD) owns ranchland in Guatemala, Honduras, Nicaragua and Costa Rica. The list of LAAD's stockholders reads like a who's-who of *North* American agribusiness: Borden, Bank of America, Cargill, Caterpillar, Chase Manhattan Bank, John Deer, Monsanto, Ralston-Purina . . .[20]

Multinational corporations also profit from the sale of techno-inputs. Ralston-Purina began producing veterinary goods and feeds in Guatemala and El Salvador, Cargill's subsidiary Centrocom started producing feeds in Guatemala and W. R. Grace set up a frozen semen distributor in Nicaragua.[21]

Multinational development banks provided $7 billion in loans and technical assistance to Latin America for beef production between 1971 and 1977. Ninety per cent of the beef exported from Central America today goes to the United States. The expansion of the industry is justified on the grounds of improving the region's foreign exchange earnings. But the region's trade balance has deteriorated steadily over the past decade and its foreign debt has risen dramatically.[22]

According to the US Department of Agriculture, without the technical assistance of organizations such as USAID, cattle production in the American tropics would be unprofitable, if not impossible. Even with such assistance, much of the region's beef production is almost intentionally inefficient and wasteful. This applies especially in the pastures created out of former rainforest land, where a single head of cattle needs more and more land to graze with each passing year as nutrient-leaching and erosion impoverish the soil.[23]

Many large landowners in Central America leave much of their acreage fallow, or even limit investments in their productive acreage, as a hedge against inflation. They can afford to do this because they frequently have other sources of income – usually in the cities. Their land-use strategies obviously have little to do with maximizing agricultural production on the best lands. If the fallow acreage was left forested, the decision not to cultivate it might be wise. In nearly all cases, however, the owners clear and burn the vegetation simply to deter squatters or to satisfy government authorities by showing that the land is being 'used'. The burnt tracts then become unimproved pasture for beef.[24]

Where does the beef go? To again quote from 'Rainforests and the Hamburger Society':

Central America's beef exports enter the United States in 60-pound boxes of frozen, de-boned cuts packed in USDA-inspected abattoirs in the Central American countries. Transported by refrigerated container ships to port cities in Florida and California, the meat is purchased by customhouse brokers and meat packers, then sold to fast-food chains and convenience food processors throughout the country.[25]

A consumer boycott in the US recently led to Burger King abandoning Central American beef. But several other chains, including Roy Rogers and Jack-in-the-Box, admit to using imported beef, which almost certainly includes Central American beef. Others do not admit it. As one industry spokesperson is quoted as saying; 'Any chain saying they don't use imported beef is handing you a crock.'[26] Why this reliance on imported beef? Another industry spokesperson offered this explanation: 'Here's what it boils down to – $95 per cow per year in Montana, $25 in Costa Rica.'[27]

6. International Banks as Pillagers of the Land

As we have seen, the international banking community has funded and encouraged Central American cotton and beef production as a means of generating foreign exchange in order to enable the Central American nations to pay off their debts to these same institutions. But not only do the Central American nations end up even deeper in debt, because they must pay off the new loans for the development of the cattle industry, but the ecological effects of this industry have actually threatened or even destroyed some of the very projects financed by the original loans! The classic example of this is hydroelectric power.

According to a 1985 USAID report on Central America: 'The region's financial crisis, and its constraints on future development, is significantly the result of huge public power investments in nearly all of the countries.' Eighteen per cent of Costa Rica's foreign debt is attributed to the power sector. For Honduras, the figure is 33 per cent.[1]

The cattle industry, encouraged in Central America as a strategy for paying off these debts, has resulted in massive deforestation. Between 1961 and 1978, as forests declined by 39 per cent, pasture expanded by 53 per cent. This deforestation resulted in erosion, which resulted in siltation of rivers, which resulted in declining efficiency at hydroelectric dams, which resulted in electricity rationing in some Central American countries.[2]

One example is the 23-year-old Cashi hydro-dam in Costa Rica, where siltation run-off from erosion has clogged the reservoir, resulting in revenue losses of up to $274 million. Similar problems are plagueing three mega-scale hydro-dams that were built with funds from the IDB – Arenal in Costa Rica; El Cajon in Honduras; and Chixoy in Guatemala. When funding for these three projects (totalling nearly $2 billion) began in the late 1970s, the IDB failed to include outlays for maintenance or draw up plans for management of the river basins. As a result, deforestation within the watersheds doomed these projects to failure from the very beginning. In a 1986 cable to the Treasury Department (which oversees US participation in the IDB), AID warned that at Arenal 'watershed management is badly needed. An alarming amount of spontaneous colonization has occured in the area and the reservoir is silting up at a rapid rate because of erosion.' At El Cajon, *campesinos* who lost their land to the dam reservoir have remained in the watershed area (supposedly a protected zone) and are clearing land for cattle grazing right down to the edge of the reservoir.[3]

But perhaps the Chixoy has been the worst disaster of the three. Accounting for nearly one-quarter of Guatemala's national debt, by the time the dam went on line in 1987, after numerous cost over-runs, it was widely reported that much of the loan money for the project had found its way into the pockets of Guatemalan officials.[4] The government's attempt to raise electricity costs by 70 per cent to help pay the debt were dropped after it sparked off rioting in Guatemala's capital.[5]

Under pressure from the US government, Central American governments and environmentalists, the IDB recently agreed to watershed management programmes for all three of the projects, beginning in 1987. But in January 1988, the IDB announced that it had put off financing of the programmes for another year.[6] Meanwhile, other problems are in the making. For instance, erosion also threatens Honduras' IDB-funded El Nispero hydro-dam and El Salvador's Cinco de Noviembre project.[7]

Despite this litany of failure, bureaucrats still like to think big then it comes to hydroelectric power. Some of their plans have been put on hold by organized resistance. In Costa Rica, the IDB and the World Bank were recently considering construction of the Boruca Dam – with 85 per cent of its power to supply an aluminium processing plant owned by the US multinational Alcoa. The dam's reservoir would, however, have flooded a large area of the Boruca Indian Reservation, and organized resistance from the Boruca Indians has delayed start-up of the project.[8]

Costa Rican officials are currently considering building a giant hydro-dam on the Pacuare River, optimistically asserting that this single dam could meet 30 per cent of Costa Rica's total electricity needs, even though the proposed dam site is in an alleged 'protected zone' already seriously disrupted by deforestation. AID has granted $10,000 to the Costa Rican Electricity Institute to study the feasibility of the Pacuare project. This time the organized resistance has come from the international kayaker set, for whom the jungle rapids of the Pacuare are a favourite playground.[9]

Environmentalists worldwide are currently protesting against plans to develop a hydroelectric project at a spectacular hidden canyon in Costa Rica's Toro Amarillo River basin, where multiple waterfalls plummet hundreds of feet down verdant slopes of virgin forest. The Costa Rican Electricity Institute's preliminary studies in the canyon are already threatening the delicate ecology, and the IDB has already provided an $80 million loan to finance the project.[10]

A project which was conceived with almost incredible insensitivity to the problem of deforestation is the *Celulosas de Guatemala* (CELGUSA) paper pulp plant. Initiated under the corrupt military regime of General Romero Lucas García (1978–82), the plant was built by a Spanish firm in partnership with Guatemala's military-controlled state finance corporation CORFINA and funded by Spain's lending agency, Banco Exterior de España (BEE). As with the Chixoy Dam, much of the foreign money seems to have found its way into the pockets of Guatemalan bureaucrats, and kickbacks from sub-contractors have raised the total bill to more than double the original estimate.

To abandon the project at this point would be costly and embarrassing. But some Guatemalan officials have realized that in the long-run, *not* to abandon it might prove to be even more costly.[11]

The purpose of the CELGUSA plant is projected as the production of paper pulp from the pinewood that grows in Guatemala's highland region. A 1987 survey by the UN Food and Agriculture Organization (FAO) concluded that CELGUSA's projected annual consumption of 900,000 cubic metres of pinewood would soon deplete adjacent forest reserves, even if coupled with a mandatory reforestation programme. The only alternative would be to import the wood supply – which would raise questions about the plant's profitability. In light of this reality, Guatemala's new civilian government considered cancelling the project – and was immediately faced with the problem of hundreds of CELGUSA employees outraged at losing their pay-packets in the middle of a severe economic crisis. The workers held demonstrations and hunger strikes to pressure the government to continue the project. The ultimate fate of the CELGUSA fiasco is still uncertain.[12]

In the last months of military rule in Guatemala, in 1986, CELGUSA had worked around the clock to fell as many trees as possible before the civilian government took over. The out-going military regime had tipped CELGUSA a wink, even though the firm was failing to follow through on its promise to replant cleared areas.[13] Among the species found in the forests threatened by CELGUSA is the quetzal – a small bird, resplendent with long, flowing green tail feathers and red crown – which was sacred to the Maya Indians and is the national symbol of Guatemala. Guatemala's unit of currency is even named for this bird, which is rapidly disappearing from Central America due to the destruction of its highland forest habitat. Some take it as symbolic that as the exquisite quetzal declines in Central America, the huge, black, ominous *zopilote* – or vulture, which feeds on carrion – is proliferating.

Through the multilateral development banks, US tax dollars are funding environmentally destructive projects in underdeveloped countries. The United States is the largest contributor to the World Bank and the IDB and is also a major contributor to the Western Europe-dominated IMF. Reviled by leftists and nationalists throughout the developing world as a bureaucratic and economic means of imperialist domination by the wealthy northern nations, these institutions have also come under fire by environmentalists on many occasions. Highly concerned with their public relations image, the multilateral banks have frequently made policy statements professing sensitivity towards ecological concerns in response to criticism from the environmental movement. The disparity between statements made for public consumption and statements made in internal documents is, however, revealing. In response to a round of criticism, World Bank representative Ernesto Franco said in 1970: 'The Bank is taking steps . . . to assure that the projects financed by it do not have serious adverse ecological consequences . . .'[14] Yet, a March 1984 World Bank Internal Memorandum states:

As a matter of routine, environmental issues are not considered . . . The

Bank does not have the capacity to conduct sector work on environmental issues on a routine basis.[15]

Today, the impending Greenhouse Effect has suddenly focused world attention on the plight of the rainforests and once again a wave of criticism is mounting and, once again, the World Bank's response is the promotion of a new image of its supposed ecological consciousness. In May 1987, the World Bank's new President, Barber Conable, said publicly:

We will strengthen the Bank's long standing policy of scrutinizing development projects for their environmental impact and withholding support for those where safeguards are inadequate.[16]

Such disparities are also evident in World Bank policy on indigenous peoples. In Central America, as in the Amazon and elsewhere, indigenous tribal cultures are threatened by the development of such World Bank-funded projects as dams and mines on their traditional lands. Speaking at the UN International Labour Organization's Convention on Tribal and Indigenous Populations, at Geneva, Switzerland, in September 1986, World Bank senior legal expert Carlos Escudero admitted that, in fact, the World Bank's published policy guidelines for development in tribal areas are not those that it actually observes. Escudero announced that the World Bank's real policy for development of tribal areas is described in a confidential document, not publicly available. Escudero maintained that these confidential internal policy guidelines do attempt to ensure respect for tribal identity, but must be taken in conjunction with World Bank policy on 'resettlement' and 'rehabilitation' (also kept secret) which is applied after compulsory relocations to make way for development. Escudero rejected the notion that the consent of tribal peoples should be sought before implementation of projects on their lands.[17]

The recent steps taken by the World Bank in response to international criticism include augmenting their staff of in-house ecologists. But these ecologists are hired to do research, not to make policy. It remains to be seen whether the policy-makers will take the ecological research into consideration – and whether the changes at the World Bank will amount to anything more than slicker public relations.

7. Central America as North America's Garbage Dump

Perhaps the most cynical and unscrupulous 'development projects' fall under the category of 'Garbage Imperialism'. In this chilling new phenomenon, industrialized nations are exporting their toxic and human waste to the 'Third World'. Seeking a way to avoid the expense of conforming to the more stringent environmental regulations in their own countries, industries are looking to underdeveloped countries to serve as waste dumps. If the waste can be packaged as something useful – fertilizer or roadfill – the underdeveloped countries can be induced to *buy* the stuff!

In June 1988, nearly 4,000 tons of highly toxic PCB-contaminated chemical waste from Italy was discovered in over 2,000 drums, sacks and other containers in Nigeria; local residents are falling sick. Wastes from industrialized nations have also wound up in Zimbabwe, Guinea and Haiti.[1]

In February 1987, two ships contracted by a Norwegian shipping firm sailed from the United States with a cargo of toxic industrial ash from Philadelphia. The first ship landed in Haiti, where several thousand tons of the ash were unloaded, ostensibly as agricultural fertilizer. The second ship was also bound for Haiti, but changed course after receiving word that protest had erupted on the island when word got out about the nature of the first shipment. The ship altered course for the African country of Guinea, where 15 tons of the ash were dumped on a coastal island. Nearly all of the island's trees were soon dead. Before turning to Haiti and Guinea, however, Philadelphia had attempted to dump the waste on a Central American nation.[2]

What is this waste, where did it come from, and why is Philadelphia so eager to send it out of their country?

In 1986 Philadelphia was left holding 250,000 tons of dioxin-laden ash from the city's municipal waste incineration programme after the New Jersey waste dump, where the ash used to go, was closed. Seven US states rejected Philadelphia's request to unload the ash in their waste dumps. Then, in November 1986 the city struck a $9 million deal with the Norwegian firm, Bulkhandling Incorporated, to have the ash sent to the municipal government of Bocas del Toro, Panama as part of a 'development project'! The idea was that the ash, full of dioxin and toxic heavy metals, would be used to build a road through an unspoiled coastal wetland, to facilitate tourism. Fortunately, Panamanian environmentalists got word of the plan and pressured their government to call a halt to it.[3]

As the landfills where the US cities dump their garbage are rapidly filling, city governments are looking to solid waste incinerators as an alternative. But these plans have provoked an outcry from environmentalists because these incinerators produce hazardous toxic ash. One US firm, International Asphalt and Petroleum, thinks it has found the solution to this dilemma: have the incinerators built in the 'Third World' countries where life is cheap. The firm has drawn up plans to build an incinerator that would burn up to 1.8 billion pounds per year of domestic and industrial garbage from the US while generating electricity for Honduras. It is projected that the 'cogeneration incinerator' will be built in a remote part of Honduras' Miskito rainforest department of Gracias a Dios. International Asphalt and Petroleum's proposal for the project makes no mention of environmental controls or ash disposal, even though the minimum proposed 400 million pounds of burned waste per year would result in four million pounds per year of unburned waste being released into the atmosphere, according to Pat Costner, a Greenpeace activist working to stop the plant. She says that this unburned waste, once in the atmosphere, could poison wildlife, livestock, or local people.[4]

Central America may also become a dump for US domestic sewage. A lawsuit recently prohibited the city of Los Angeles from continuing to dump its sewage into Santa Monica Bay after 1 January 1988. Los Angeles cannot sell its sludge as fertilizer in the United States because it does not meet the US Environmental Protection Agency's minimum standards, due to its high levels of toxic household and industrial pollutants. In 1987, the Los Angeles-based Applied Recovery Technologies attempted to strike a deal with the Honduran government to dump raw sewage sludge in 90 square kilometres of Honduran coastal wetlands, claiming that the wetlands would then generate organic fertilizers. Honduras rejected the plan as a result of public protest after local environmentalists got wind of it and began to organize.[5]

Applied Recovery Technologies also tried to strike a similar deal with Guatemala, proposing a sale of thousands of tons of Los Angeles' sewage to a Guatemala fertilizer firm. The Guatemalan Congress responded with a resolution prohibiting the importation of human faeces. Said the resolution: 'For reasons of national dignity we must not permit our territory to become the repository of the human waste from super-developed cities.'[6]

The idea of exporting human faeces to Central America is rather like sending coal to Newcastle, as the saying goes. Central America does not even have adequate systems to deal with its own human waste, and diseases related to contamination of drinking water by faeces – such as diarrhoea, dysentery and hepatitis – are grave health problems in the region. Diarrhoea is the number one killer of children in most Central American nations.[7]

While so far most 'Garbage Imperialism' schemes for Central America have been nipped in the bud, the International Asphalt and Petroleum solid waste cogeneration incinerator in the Honduran rainforest has, at the time of writing, yet to be stopped.

Similar schemes are being proposed to the Central American governments virtually constantly, and as the debt crisis worsens Central America's ruling elites will doubtless find these proposals harder to resist. Nicaragua's new government only recently rejected a deal brokered by a Nicaraguan expatriate based in Miami to pave a road through the Miskito rainforest with toxin-laden municipal incinerator ash from north-east US cities.[8]

While, as we have seen, funding always seems to be available for ecologically destructive projects, the US frequently seems to drag its feet on projects for environmental recovery. In 1981, 25 Caribbean nations formulated a policy called the Caribbean Action Plan (CAP), as part of the Regional Seas project of the United Nations Environment Programme (UNEP). Under CAP the 25 nations have committed themselves to work on such efforts as watershed management, marine ecosystem protection and contingency programmes for dealing with oil spills (such as that which devastated mangrove forests on Panama's Caribbean coast in 1986). The 25 nations include both the Central American nations and the United States (representing Puerto Rico and the US Virgin Islands). The United States is the only participating country with adequate resources to get CAP off the ground, yet it has neither contributed nor pledged funds to the effort. Critics warn that lack of US support could threaten the project's survival, and charge that this lack of support has been due to the participation of Cuba and Sandinista Nicaragua in the project.[9]

Funding (via participation in the IDB and World Bank) mega-scale hydro-dam projects without funding (via participation in programmes such as CAP) watershed management projects is one way in which the United States government contributes to Central America's ecological crisis. In the 1980s this ecological crisis has led to a political crisis, which has prompted the US government to do something that has, paradoxically, profoundly worsened Central America's ecological crisis – fund and orchestrate proxy wars and generalized militarization of the entire region.

Part 2:
The Crisis

The militarization of Central America has only succeeded in worsening the very crisis to which it is a response – including the ecological roots of that crisis. This is a regional crisis, with common roots in all the Central American nations. Yet there is no single generalized war in Central America, but several local guerrilla struggles. Let us see how the militarization has specifically affected the ecology of each country in the region.

8. Guatemala: The Hamburger Connection to Genocide?

Social unrest as well as tropical deforestation have followed the cattle industry in Guatemala, both chronologically and geographically. The cattle industry pushed the Maya Indians from what little of their highland subsistence agriculture economy still remained by the 1980s, resulting in their support of guerrilla movements. The military responded with a programme aimed at destroying Maya culture, with its historical and spiritual links to the land and the cultivation of maize. The cattle industry has, therefore, meant massacres and relocation camps as well as the destruction of rainforest in Guatemala.

Guatemala, the most populous and economically powerful of the Central American nations, also suffers from some of the worst poverty, repression and human rights abuses in the region; and has had one of the most violent histories of any nation in the region. The now almost forgotten era of Guatemala's 'Social Revolution' between the fall of the long Jorge Ubico dictatorship in 1944 and the CIA-backed coup of 1954, has been almost erased from the national memory. The 1944 *coup d'etat*-cum-student and worker uprising, which toppled Ubico's 14-year reign, was partially incited, albeit unintentionally, by anti-Fascist propaganda from the United States then inundating Latin America due to US involvement in World War II. (Venezuela was a vital source of oil for the Allies). Indeed, Ubico had openly expressed pro-Nazi sympathies until US diplomats had a little talk with him – although his loyalty to his Washington masters was sufficient for him to have German properties in Guatemala confiscated and suspected Nazi sympathizers extradited to detention camps in Texas. The US government, while hoping to sway Latin American opinion away from support for the Axis, certainly never had any desire to remove such figures as Ubico from power. (The 14-year dictatorship of El Salvador's General Maximiliano Hernandez Martinez was also toppled by a general strike in 1944.) After World War II ended, Washington began to view the changes in Guatemala with growing unease.[1]

Shortly after Ubico was toppled, national elections were held. The first president of the Guatemalan Spring was Dr Juan José Arevalo, whose somewhat fuzzy vision of 'spiritual socialism' was quite strongly and explicitly anti-Communist. Nonetheless, it succeeded in provoking 22 attempted *coups d'etat* from conservative elements in the Guatemalan military. In 1950, Jacobo Arbenz, one of the leaders of the 1944 uprising against Ubico, was elected to the presidency, and moved Guatemala sharply to the left. Having run on a platform of agrarian reform with strong support from organized labour, he slashed the military budget, began organizing among the Maya Indians – and, with full compensation based on the company's own tax estimates, expropriated unused lands of the United Fruit Company. This proved to be fatal.[2]

This expropriation had been a long time in the making. Under pressure from labour unions, Arevalo had passed a law requiring landowners to rent to neighbouring *campesinos* those portions of their estates not under cultivation, at a rate not to exceed five per cent of the value of their harvests. By 1951, with Arbenz in power, a right-wing backlash was being organized, as large landowners, led by UFCo, initiated a policy of 'lockouts' on plantations in an effort to induce agricultural workers to take up arms against the government. Arbenz responded by enacting the more sweeping agrarian reform law. This, he hoped, would deprive conservative elements of their power altogether by setting actual limits on the amount of land which can be owned under a single holding, and empowering *campesino* organizations to expropriate lands that exceeded those limits.[3]

Despite the fact that Arbenz had the support of Guatemala's Communist Party, however, he saw the country's land problem as feudalism and sought to correct it by introducing capitalism to the Indians and *campesinos*. Read Title I of the Arbenz Reform Law:

The essential objectives of the Agrarian Reform are:
A) To develop a capitalist economy among the peasants and in agriculture generally
B) To award land to the *campesinos*, peons and agricultural workers who possess none or possess little
C) To facilitate the investment of new capital in agriculture by means of capitalist rental of nationalized lands . . .

Arbenz sought to limit expropriations to those lands that private owners could not profitably exploit anyway – therefore, many of the expropriated properties were of poor quality land. Following the coup which ousted Arbenz, one Guatemalan exile who had worked with the Arevalo and Arbenz governments, and refers to the 1944–54 decade as 'years of springtime in the land of eternal tyranny', recognized the limitations of the Arbenz land reform:

Indians remained the poorest segment of the large class of impoverished rural peasants who depend upon availability of rental lands and wage labor in order to eke out a meager living on their marginal plots.[4]

Nonetheless, following the enactment of the agrarian reform, Ladino landowners in the Maya Highlands felt threatened as the Indians gained some political power for the first time. Arbenz began to lose his few remaining friends in the military; and UFCo, once its lands had been affected, was infuriated.[5]

UFCo had close connections with the highest levels of the US government. Both the Dulles brothers – CIA Director Allen Dulles and Secretary of State John Foster Dulles – had done private legal work for UFCo as senior members of the New York law firm Sullivan and Cromwell, involving UFCo's take-over of the Guatemalan railways. (Another lucrative Sullivan and Cromwell client was Standard Oil of New Jersey, today known as Exxon, the Rockefeller titan on behalf of whose interests the nationalist Mossadeq government in Iran had been overthrown with CIA collusion two years earlier.) The *coup d'etat* which returned Guatemala to military rule was organized from Washington and Boston, where UFCo was based, as President Eisenhower warned Congress that Guatemala was 'spreading Marxist tentacles' throughout Central America. The final 'justification' for the move came when Arbenz, justifiably worried about Yankee intervention by this time, arranged for a secret purchase of arms from Czechoslovakia after US pressure had blocked attempted purchases from Western powers. (Czechoslovakia, which had also recently sold arms to South Africa, doubtless saw the deal as simple commerce.) On 17 June, 1954, CIA-trained mercenaries, led by right-wing Guatemalan military officers, entered Guatemalan territory from their base camps in Honduras, while CIA-contracted US Air Force fighters bombarded the Guatemalan capital. The 'Social Revolution' was over.[6]

The long reign of terror under successive military regimes that followed the coup was so complete that the very words 'agrarian reform' became virtually taboo, and, as we shall see, remain so today, even after civilian government was ostensibly restored in the 1980s.

Resistance and unrest began to re-emerge in the 1960s, and was met with brutal and overwhelming represssion in a cycle that would escalate until the repression finally took on genocidal elements in the 1980s. And, as will be seen, this cycle of rebellion and repression always followed the development of the cattle industry, both chronologically and geographically.

'The cult of maize is finished!'

We have already seen how the expansion of the cattle industry into the north-eastern departments of Izabal, Zacapa and Chiquimula in the 1960s resulted in a wave of peasant dislocation, which led to peasant support for the MR-13 guerrillas and subsequent bloody repression by the military regime. This proved to be not the end, but only the beginning. In the 1980s a new and even more bloody spiral of rebellion and repression was sparked off as the cattle industry expanded into new areas – the mountainous north-western departments of El Quiche, Alta Verapaz and Huehuetenango. These departments make up a region known as the Maya Highlands. While the peasants of Izabal, Zacapa and Chiquimula were Ladinos (Spanish-speaking *mestizos*, like most Central Americans) the peasants of the Maya Highlands are Maya Indians who are culturally distinct from other Guatemalans. For centuries they have kept alive their traditional dress, calendar and languages – Quiche, Ixil, Mam and Chuj. Their mythology and identity as a people still centres around the yearly cycle of communally planting and harvesting maize. Therefore, not only their livelihood, but their very sense of place in the universe was threatened by the incursion of cattle into their lands.

For decades Ladino incursions into the Indian lands of the Maya Highlands had been pushing the Indians on to smaller and more marginal plots. While the new Ladino landowners often left much of their land fallow, the Indians farmed their increasingly meagre lands as intensively as possible, even cultivating maize on near-vertical slopes where erosion is an almost insurmountable problem. With inadequate lands to survive solely by subsistence agriculture, many Indians were forced to provide seasonal migrant labour for the coffee and cotton plantations to the south, in the Pacific lowlands. This meant starvation wages, exposure to pesticides and the erosion of traditional Maya culture (wearing traditional Maya dress is often prohibited on the plantations, while speaking Spanish is obligatory).

Under the agrarian reform of the Jacobo Arbenz government, the Indians were encouraged to form *sindicatos* (unions) empowered to 'denounce' local landowners whose holdings exceeded the legal limits, and 'agrarian committees' empowered to expropriate such landholdings. After the CIA-backed coup of 1954, however, all such experiments came to an abrupt end as the newly-installed military dictatorship quickly reversed the agrarian reform. In the ensuing years conditions slowly worsened for the Indians; but when the cattle boom reached the Maya Highlands in the 1970s they began rapidly worsening.[7]

The military is big business in Guatemala. Every military man who has occupied the presidency in Guatemala since the early 1970s is said to have ended his term a millionaire several times over. The military has an even bigger hand in cattle than other industries, with large chunks of land being given to middle and high ranking officers for ranching. Together with oil exploitation, nickel mining and hydroelectric power (the Chixoy dam on the Alta Verapaz-Quiche border), the beef boom provided the justification for a massive road-building operation in the Maya Highlands in the 1970s and into the 1980s. The region became known in bureaucratese as the 'Northern Transversal Strip' – often called by Guatemalans 'The Zone of the Generals' because of the military money and presence there. The development of the Northern Transversal Strip meant yet more poverty for the Indians, as more Ladinos arrived to squeeze them off their already insufficient lands. In the words of one Guatemalan official: 'The government gave away or sold land titles to outsiders. It went to the politicians, the rich, the military. They all grabbed what they could.'[8]

As credit for the development of the Northern Transversal Strip poured in from foreign banks, among those who 'grabbed what they could' were multinational oil and mining companies, and – most significantly – private cattle ranchers. The military began using the typical underhanded strong-arm tactics to force Indian *campesinos* from their land. Increasingly, Indians were pushed north, away from their traditional highland communities and into the edge of the wilderness that slopes down towards the tropical rainforest that lies across the Mexican border. In 1976, an Indian peasant co-operative in Huehuetenango, which had been clearing the edge of the forest and fighting insect pests for a year, was finally ready to plant when an armed unit arrived and ordered the co-operative to 'plant grass seed in the cleared area and then move'. Father Bill Woods, a Maryknoll priest who had been organizing the co-operative, was in the process of making the case known when he was killed in a mysterious aeroplane crash.[9]

On 29 May 1978, over 100 Indians were massacred at the village of Panzos in Alta Verapaz as they were in the midst of petitioning local officers for the return of land seized by the military.[10]

This proved to be a major turning point in the Maya Highlands. Prior to the massacre, a guerrilla group operating in the Highlands, the Guerilla Army of the Poor (EGP), had been small and marginalized. After the massacre, it quickly grew, gaining a base of support among the Indians.[11]

In the early 1980s, as this Indian guerrilla movement began gaining ground, the Guatemalan military launched a counter-insurgency programme in the Maya Highlands, which in magnitude, sophistication and brutality dwarfed the one against the MR-13 to the east in the 1960s. This counter-insurgency programme was more than just sheer terrorization – it was a systematic attack on the Indian culture which had come to support the guerrillas. The stakes were higher this time than they had been in the 1960s, because of the ethnic overtones of the conflict. The Indians, who had always been excluded from a share of political power, are actually a majority in Guatemala. General Oscar Mejia Victores, Guatemala's last military ruler, summed up the ultimate goal of the counter-insurgency programme: 'We must get rid of the words "indigenous" and "Indian"'.[12]

The first phase of the programme was 'pacification' – a 'scorched earth' campaign in which Indian villages suspected of being strongholds of guerrilla support were simply destroyed, the crops burned in the fields, the inhabitants massacred. Between 1981 and 1983, when the 'pacification' was declared completed, over 20,000 Indians had been killed, 250 villages destroyed and nearly one million people displaced.[13]

The second phase was 'consolidation', in which the military restructured the countryside of the Maya Highlands along new lines. The 'pacification' had sent a flood of refugees north, through the expanse of trackless mountains and forest, across the border into Mexico, where today thousands still languish in refugee camps (placing population pressure on Mexico's last, threatened strip of tropical rainforest). Others fled south to the squalid shantytowns of Guatemala's capital, and became 'internal refugees'. But many of those who remained in the Maya Highlands were forcibly relocated to newly-built military-controlled 'model villages'. Displaced residents from outlying destroyed villages would be centralized in the 'model villages', usually built on the ruins of a more centrally located destroyed village. The 'model villages' are based on the 'strategic hamlets' built by the US in Vietnam to isolate the peasants from the Viet Cong guerrillas. The Guatemalan 'model villages', however, were seen both as a means of breaking the Indians' guerrilla loyalties and expanding the military business ventures of the Northern Transversal Strip. In fact, the military's administrative apparatus for running the 'model villages' is designated 'development poles'. There are four 'development poles' – two in El Quiche, one each in Alta Verapaz and Huehuetenango.[14]

Programmes within the model villages are all ultimately aimed at weakening traditional Indian culture and shifting Indian loyalty from the EGP to the military. One military base in each of the four 'development poles' co-ordinates security forces in the area and serves as a boarding school for children orphaned by the massacres. Much of their 'education' consists of being marched around with mock rifles, preparing them for participation in the 'civil patrols', participation in which is obligatory for all males over 18 years old. Each model village has a civil patrol, led by a former soldier, armed with rifles and empowered to enforce curfews and land allocations – and imprison and punish violators. In the civil patrols, young men are pressured to join the military, where they are subject to further indoctrination. Many model villagers are also subjected to seven-to-ten month 're-education programmes' to sever guerrilla loyalties. These courses include intensive instruction in Spanish for those who speak only Maya tongues – the military made an effort to discourage the speaking of traditional Indian languages in the model villages. While the Catholic Church was discouraged from taking an active role in the life of the new villages (local church workers had been influential in early organizing of the Indian communities to defend their meagre lands), fundamentalist Protestant sects from the US have had easy access to the settlements. These groups, which preach unquestioning obedience to authority, have been allowed to build their churches in prominent and central locations in the model villages, and are often responsible for distributing food and basic goods under military supervision. The result has been a mass conversion of Indians to evangelical Protestantism. (In addition to the 'Liberation Theology' tendency that existed among some Catholic church-workers in the Highlands, the 'folk Catholicism' of the Indians includes many elements which have survived from the pre-Hispanic religion of the Mayas, that invariably centre around the relationship to the land and maize. It is worth noting that the mastermind of the model villages programme, General Efrain Rios Montt, Guatemala's president when the programme was conceived in 1982, is a 'born-again' follower of a California-based fundamentalist Protestant sect.)[15]

But the most ambitious schemes in the model villages programme were aimed at both uprooting Indian culture and accelerating the transformation of the Maya Highlands into the Northern Transversal Strip – they were designed to simultaneously rupture the Indian's mystical connection to the land and make money for the military. Using funds from USAID and other aid agencies, the military would distribute food to the Indians. Relying on the military rather than the land for their food, the Indians would cultivate non-traditional export cash crops, such as broccoli and asparagus – under military auspices, of course. Significantly, the food that the Indians received in return for their labour (rather than a monetary wage) did not include maize. Military-linked companies would export the crops, and the military would save money that it would otherwise have to spend on salaries. The programmes would sever the 'maize-earth-man' relationship of the Mayas and the ancient rituals that surround it and reduce the Indians to a permanent agro-export labour force. This was to have been the final outcome of the counter-insurgency plan. The 'pacification' phase had been dubbed 'Guns and Beans' (interpreted as 'if you're with us, you eat; if not, we shoot you'); the 'consolidation' phase had been dubbed 'Roofs, Work and Tortillas'. This third and final phase, dubbed 'Food for Work', would complete the transformation of the Maya Highlands into an agro-export zone and the eradication of the Maya culture as more than a quaint, colourful backdrop of dress and ceremony to encourage tourism.[16] In this period Guatemalan military leaders frequently boasted: 'The cult of maize is finished!'[17]

This final phase has, however, been mostly a lot of empty dreams, due to insufficient funds to underwrite anything as massive as the complete elimination of the Maya maize subsistence economy. General Rios Montt was removed from power in a 1983 coup that brought the equally brutal but less visionary General Mejia Victores to the presidency. The steep hillsides around the model villages are still growing maize. But the model villages programme and the militarization of the Maya Highlands continue unchallenged, despite the return of a civilian president to the Guatemalan National Palace. The military presence in the Maya Highlands – everything from cattle ranching to mining to 'scorched earth' campaigns – has taken its toll on the region's ecology.

For the most part, the 'scorched earth' campaigns could not precisely be termed warfare, because only one side was armed. It was the Indian population which bore the brunt of the repression, rather than the leaders of the EGP. While virtually all the EGP fighters were Indians, the command was comprised almost exclusively of Ladinos – mostly leftist students and intellectuals from the cities who moved into the Maya Highlands to organize the Indians when they deemed the region ripe for rebellion. (Indeed, the EGP's logo is a stylized portrait of the Argentine-born freelance revolutionary Che Guevara, who had held a post in the agrarian reform bureaucracy under the Arbenz government and is a hero and martyr for the left throughout Latin America – but is certainly a meaningless figure for most Maya Indians.) As the counter-insurgency operation began, there were occasions when the guerrillas would come out of the mountains to an Indian village, put up their flag and declare the village 'liberated' – then retreat to the mountains, leaving the defenceless village to fend for itself. If the villagers left up the flag, they were inviting a massacre and the destruction of their village by the military; if they took it down, they were inviting reprisals in the form of a few killings of villagers by the guerrillas. It is due to such insensitive strategic blunders by the guerrillas, as well as the overwhelming repression by the military, that Indian support for the EGP has, in fact, eroded in recent years.[18]

El Peten

Since 1979, the EGP has been part of an umbrella coalition with Guatemala's other guerrilla groups, known as the Guatemalan National Revolutionary Union (URNG). It is interesting to note that Guatemala's three major guerrilla groups are active in areas corresponding to Guatemala's three major bioregions. The EGP is active in the mountainous Maya Highlands. To the south, as the highlands slope down to the coffee country, and then the cotton country of the fertile Pacific coastal plain, the Revolutionary Organization of the People in Arms (ORPA) is active, facing plantation owners with the choice of either paying their seasonal Indian migrant labour the minimum wage or getting their plantations burned down. (Ironically, the anti-government guerrillas of the ORPA are actually enforcing Guatemala's laws!)

To the north-east of the Maya Highlands, in the vast, sparsely inhabited rainforest department of El Peten, the Rebel Armed Forces (FAR), built on the remnants of the leadership of the crushed MR-13, roams the jungle and occasionally launches ambushes. As previously noted, this region has been subject to widespread deforestation by colonization programmes by landless peasants from the Highlands, and the cattle ranches that follow in their wake. Attempting widespread cultivation of maize in the jungle is folly, and El Peten is littered with massive testaments to this folly – the ruins of the pyramids and temples of the city-states of the Classic Maya era, such as Uaxactun and Tikal (today a tourist attraction). The Classic Maya civilization, which was far more sophisticated than contemporaneous Europe in such sciences as mathematics, astronomy and architecture, rapidly declined around 900 AD. The massive ceremonial centres (including the tallest buildings in the western hemisphere at that time) were abandoned centuries before the arrival of the Spanish. Today, many archaeologists hypothesize that one of the key factors leading to this mysterious, sudden demise of an advanced civilization was the inability of the rainforest ecosystem to support the slash-and-burn maize agriculture needed to maintain the city-states. In the centuries following the decline, the rainforest gradually reclaimed the fields and the cities. (The ancient Maya, it must be noted, did not have any cattle!)[19]

In contrast, to the south of the rainforest, in the Maya Highlands, where the land is fertile enough to sustain long-term maize cultivation, the Maya Indian culture was still dominant when the Spanish arrived. The Highland Maya did not build massive ceremonial city-states, but their culture has proved to be almost incredibly tenacious. It survived the genocide of the Spanish *conquistadores* and it still survives today, despite the new genocide of the modern militarists.[20]

Today, El Peten is administered by the military-controlled Peten Development Corporation (FYDEP), which, basically, has been handing over El Peten's resources to friends, favourites and/or the highest bidder. El Peten was once a major source of hardwood trees such as mahogany for export, but today the region is almost completely shorn of such trees, thanks to plunder by logging companies (usually with some military money involved). In recent years logging sites have become a favourite target for FAR ambushes. Another source of wealth in El Peten is archaeological relics from the Classic Maya era, only a fraction of which have been unearthed by scientists. While Tikal has become a tourist attraction, with daily flights into the remote site from

Guatemala City, many more ruins of ancient Maya ceremonial centres remain undeveloped, sometimes even unexcavated, deep in the rainforest. During the military regime of General Romero Lucas Garcia (1978–82), the (illegal) export of Maya artefacts became a thriving business, as squads of uniformed soldiers, using army engineering equipment and chain saws, carved up stelae and dug trenches through ruined temples in search of saleable artefacts. (The FAR has also been accused of filching from the ruins, although their efforts could not have even approached those of the military, simply due to their vastly inferior resources and manpower, if nothing else.) After 40 years of such 'administration' of El Peten, FYDEP is now destined to be abolished by the new civilian government and, ostensibly, handed over to civilian authorities for the first time. With the FAR guerrillas active in the region, however, the military is certain to maintain a heavy presence in El Peten.[21]

Another modern threat to the rainforest of El Peten comes from oil companies which are exploring the region with an eye towards drilling. Their progress has been considerably slowed by attacks and harassment by the FAR. In May 1986, the FAR occupied a seismic survey camp of Geo-Source, a Texas-based firm working under contract for Esso Central America, the regional subsidiary of the massive multinational Exxon, flagship of the Rockefeller empire. An exploratory drill was destroyed and a rented helicopter burned to a crisp by the guerrillas after its company occupants were ordered to step out. The stranded Geo-Source personnel were given a compass, a pair of machetes and directions to the nearest village. Tractors, patrol cars and other equipment were destroyed in other raids during the same period. Geo-Source subsequently suspended its operations in Guatemala, leaving in limbo the 740,000 acres of El Peten which a 1985 contract with the Guatemalan government had granted to Esso Central America for exploration rights. Fearing similar attacks, Amoco's seismic survey sub-contractor pulled out of Guatemala only a month later.

Hispanoil, the Spanish state company, is already exploiting Guatemalan oil and has even built a 135-mile pipeline from its jungle oil fields to the Caribbean port of Santo Tomas. In late 1985 the FAR burned several Hispanoil trucks and the military responded by sending 1,000 troops to the oilfields.[22]

In the short-run, these attacks have doubtless been costly to the FAR in political terms. Hundreds of El Peten workers lost their jobs when the seismic survey firms pulled out. The attacks may, however, have deprived the Guatemalan government of important economic gains and, of course, one of the primary goals of guerrilla warfare is to attack the country's economic infrastructure. The Central American nations have to import virtually all of their oil – a tremendous economic burden, especially at times when the price of oil is high and the price of the principal Central American agro-exports is low. But oil is the biggest pillar of the Mexican economy and areas of Mexico adjacent to El Peten have been successfully exploited by the Mexican state company Pemex. In fact, oil exploitation is a leading cause of deforestation in this region of Mexico.[23]

With the Guatemalan government as a 55 per cent partner in all oil deals, El

Peten is being eyed for exploitation both by domestic bureaucrats and the massive, mostly US-based multinational oil concerns (whose wealth and power dwarf those of most national governments – certainly any of the Central American national governments). Mobil and Chevron have both expressed an interest in exploring in Guatemala and are said to be waiting in the wings to see the results of the Exxon and Amoco explorations.[24]

For now, the FAR seems to have unilateral veto power over these explorations. A 1986 communique from the FAR contended that the group has interests of ecology at heart and is 'protecting the nation's resources from imperialist exploitation'. Does this mean that there would be greater ecological sensitivity in a post-revolutionary Guatemala, should the government fall and the guerrilla leaders take power (a prospect that hardly seems imminent)? One long-time observer laughed at this notion, pointing to the absurd situation in Angola, where Cuban troops protected the facilities of US oil companies from attacks by US-backed rebels![25]

The FAR have also pledged to sabotage any efforts to construct a massive hydro-complex that is being considered for the Usumacinta River, which forms the Mexican border through the rainforest. The dam is under consideration as a joint project by the Mexican and Guatemalan governments. The project has drawn fire from environmentalists who say it could flood up to 500 square miles of rainforest and submerge at least two classic Maya sites – Yaxchilan on the Mexican shore, and Piedras Negras on the Guatemalan side. The rainforest on the Mexican side has already been almost completely destroyed by oil and cattle interests and peasant colonization – all that survives is a sliver along the Usumacinta, known as the Lacandon.[26]

Chemical warfare

Military counter-insurgency measures against the FAR have, of course, taken a toll on the fragile rainforest ecology of El Peten. The dense cover of rainforest foliage provides the perfect environment for a small guerrilla band to wander at will (the FAR is estimated at far less than 500 troops). The US military's response to a similar problem in Vietnam was to simply eliminate the cover by spraying the jungle with chemical defoliants such as Agent Orange. Therefore, many viewed with suspicion the US Drug Enforcement Administration's recent programme of herbicide spraying in El Peten, ostensibly aimed at eradicating marijuana crops – especially as Guatemala is not believed to produce or export any significant amount of marijuana.[27]

The spraying took place between April and June 1987 and was briefly resumed in January 1988. The Drug Enforcement Administration (DEA) aircraft took off across the border in Belize (which, unlike Guatemala, *does* have a notorious reputation as a major source of marijuana). A vast area of El Peten was sprayed, including parts of Tikal National Park. Because the flights originated in another country, it has been difficult for Guatemalan officials to even determine exactly what herbicide was sprayed on their territory.

Glyphosate has been confirmed, but there are also unconfirmed reports of paraquat and 2,4,5-T, a component of Agent Orange. As protest at the programme mounted, the US Embassy in Guatemala City issued a self-contradictory statement asserting that the chemicals used 'are not harmful to people, livestock or the environment,' but will 'affect almost all of the vegetation'. ('Not harmful to the environment' but will 'affect almost all of the vegetation'?!) The statement also claimed that the aircraft used by the DEA are 'civilian planes that carry no weapons and are flown by civilian pilots'. Eventually the Guatemalan government admitted that the guerrillas were the target of the spraying – but this could hardly have been more obvious: the sprayed areas corresponded precisely to the areas of guerrilla activity – the FAR stronghold of El Peten and the EGP stronghold of northern Alta Verapaz, El Quiche and Huehuetenango. (After the repression in the Maya Highlands, the EGP bands fled into the trackless wilderness in the extreme north of these departments, where they remain today, tunnelling into the mountainsides and occasionally venturing down to the roads and villages to ambush military patrols.) At the same time that the DEA planes were spraying in 1987, the Guatemalan military requested (and received) US assistance in airlifting troops by military transport helicopter into the north of El Quiche in an effort to rout EGP strongholds. (The US loaned the helicopters.) Simultaneously, a massive fire of unknown origin was destroying 1,500 square kilometres of rainforest in El Peten – far exceeding the area of jungle usually put to the torch by slash-and-burn agriculture. Guatemalan news reports speculated that the fire was started by napalm, which may have been used along with the defoliants against the FAR.[28]

By June 1987, 14 people and hundreds of cattle had died after exposure to the herbicides – usually by drinking contaminated water – and hundreds more were poisoned, experiencing ulcerations, vomiting and respiratory problems. Guatemala's Congressional Committee on Environmental Protection declared the sprayings illegal, as they had not been approved by the nation's Congress, and decried the operation as a 'violation of Guatemala's national sovereignty by the US'. Guatemalan Interior Minister Juan Rodil, the man who originally made the deal with the US agency, is currently facing litigation for the effects of the spraying both on people and the environment in El Peten. The Guatemalan Human Rights Commission, an exile group based in Mexico City, charged that the sprayings are a violation of the Geneva Convention prohibition of chemical warfare. At the time of writing, more sprayings are scheduled but they may be suspended due to the outcry of protest.[29]

Is reform possible?

Guatemala is no longer the 'banana republic' it once was. UFCo's massive land holdings, railroad and port facilities were broken up as a result of an anti-trust suit in the US courts (sparked off by fallout from the CIA's 1954 coup on behalf of the company). Today the former R. J. Reynolds subsidiary Del

Monte is active in Guatemala, although it frequently contracts local farmers to grow its bananas instead of owning all of the land outright, as UFCo had. Together with its sub-contractors, Del Monte is the largest private employer in Guatemala, and many of its lands formerly belonged to UFCo.[30]

The recent crash in world cotton prices has led to a reduction of nearly 50 per cent in Guatemalan cotton cultivation.[31] It remains to be seen what will happen to this prime Pacific agricultural land. Landless peasants led by a populist priest from the Pacific zone, Father Andres Giron, are demanding that it be turned over to small farmers for cultivation of staples such as maize. The peasants have pressed their demands with massive cross-country marches on the National Palace in Guatemala City, hoes in hand. But the agro-export sector (supported by the still-powerful military, which periodically menaces the civilian government with rumblings of a *coup d'etat*) is pushing for converting the land to new 'non-traditional' export crops, such as asparagus and cucumber. Nonetheless, a tentative agrarian reform programme initiated by the civilian government has already turned over a few parcels of land to Father Giron and his followers.[32] This is Guatemala's first agrarian reform programme since the Arbenz administration of the 1950s, and the current civilian President Vinicio Cerezo hastens to emphasize that it is being done 'without fanfare, slogans or labels'. It is not even officially called 'agrarian reform' – a term that became taboo under the 30-year string of military dictatorships following the fall of the Arbenz regime. Even today, under an ostensibly civilian government, those who talk of 'agrarian reform' risk assassination, 'disappearance' and torture by military-linked death squads. The Mutual Support Group (GAM) of the families of the 'disappeared' still hold weekly vigils in front of the National Palace to demand the return of their missing loved ones. So, as President Cerezo himself recently admitted, the reality of Guatemalan politics 'rules out any [land] redistribution policy'.[33]

The 1990 presidential elections in Guatemala were marred by controversy surrounding the candidacy of General Efrain Rios Montt, the man who had masterminded the ethnocidal counter-insurgency programme in the Maya Highlands as the country's dictator in the early 1980s. He had come to power in the 1982 coup which ousted General Lucas Garcia, and proceeded to streamline the counter-insurgency plan with concepts and nomenclature far slicker and more sophisticated than such crude euphemisms as General Garcia's 'rural pacification'. It was Rios Montt who launched the drive to actually eradicate Mayan cultural identity with the 'Guns and Beans' programme, making extensive use of right-wing evangelical sects to indoctrinate the Indians in the 'model villages', as well as using terror as an instrument against those who would resist indoctrination. When accused of a 'scorched earth policy', Rios Montt stated: 'We have no scorched earth policy. We have a policy of scorched communists.'[34]

Rios Montt was ousted in the 1983 coup which brought General Mejia Victores to power, motivated by conservative Catholic fears that the Montt regime was attempting to establish a fundamentalist Protestant theocracy in Guatemala. Rios Montt is today attempting to make his political come-back.

In August 1990 the Citizens' Register of Guatemala rejected his candidacy on the basis that the constitution forbids 'the chief or leaders of a coup, armed revolution or other similar movement . . . or those who assumed power that way' from running for president. The retired general has pledged that he will use all legal means available to reverse the decision. As I write, the case is still pending.[35]

While the carnage in neighbouring El Salvador and the militarization in neighbouring Honduras has been overwhelmingly funded by US taxdollars and carried out with US weapons, Guatemala was forced to look elsewhere for such 'assistance' after the Carter Administration, in 1977, cut off military aid to the nation due to its exceptionally poor human rights record. Since then, many Guatemalan military leaders have developed a sense of pride in their ability to crush Communist insurgency without US aid, as opposed to their counterparts in El Salvador. (Although, it must be noted that the overwhelming majority of the victims of the Guatemalan counter-insurgency were not even guerrillas, much less 'Communists'!)

Yet Guatemala's military budget is maintained at a level far beyond what can be supported by the nation's own economic means. As a 1985 EGP document reads: 'The military objectives of concentration and control of the popultion require enormous costs . . . The magnitude of this military effort must be supported by outside financing.' The US is only now beginning to resume military aid to Guatemala, after President Reagan's claim that the nation had received a 'bum rap'; in the interim, Guatemala had turned for military aid to Israel, which served as a 'US proxy' in the words of one Israeli official. Israel has served as such a proxy in South Africa and elsewhere around the globe where direct US military aid would be politically inexpedient – even to the Argentine military dictatorship which had displayed openly anti-Jewish tendencies. In the 1980s, Israel dramatically stepped up its involvement in Central America.

While Israel has provided military material and training to El Salvador, Honduras, the Nicaraguan contras and even Costa Rica, it is Guatemala that has become Israel's mainstay in Central America. Israel has provided Guatemala with computers, military transport aircraft, armed personnel carriers, grenade-launchers and other equipment. The Israeli Galil automatic assault rifle became general issue in the Guatemalan army, and Israeli technicians have even set up an arms factory in Guatemala to produce replacement parts for the rifle. Israeli advisers have provided counter-insurgency training to Guatemala. In the words of General Lucas García, Ríos Montt's predecessor and architect of the pacification programme: 'Israel was the only country that gave us military support in our battle against the guerrillas.'[36] Guatemala also received police aid from West Germany following the Carter-era law banning US assistance to foreign police forces, in response to mounting reports of human rights abuses. But US Federal Bureau of Investigation training of the Guatemalan police resumed under the Reagan Administration facilitated by one of the ever-widening loopholes in the law.[37]

Conservation programmes

Guatemala today has a conservation movement that has been sufficiently influential to induce the government to declare 18 national parks (the largest of which encompasses the Mayan ruins of Tikal), but funding for the national parks programme is extremely limited and effective protection of these areas is at best uncertain. A smaller-scale programme of protected areas is run by a conservation centre at the National University of San Carlos in Guatemala City. This programme's small but carefully managed reserves, known as 'Biotopos', are generally designed to provide a sanctuary for a specific threatened species.[38] For instance, there is a Biotopo to protect the manatee on Lake Izabal, and another one to protect the quetzal in the Cloud Forest of Baja Verapaz.[39]

In February 1990, President Vinicio Cerezo signed the Protected Areas Law, which ambitiously declares 44 new 'special protection areas'. Thirty per cent of the national territory has been opened up to be studied for consideration of such designation, but the law does not actually establish borders for the new reserves. The proposal is that boundaries are to be drawn up after studies have arrived at estimates of each site's significance and a realistic approach to resolving conflicts over its natural resources. Most of the study areas are small and isolated, with the notable exception of a large area covering the northern third of El Peten. The studies are being conducted by the Nature Conservancy, an international environmental group, which will report its findings to the Guatemalan Congress.[40]

Considering that the quetzal is the national bird of Guatemala, the destruction of its habitat is akin to the plunder of the ancient Maya temples of El Peten: an attack on Guatemala's cultural identity. Wrote Guatemala's Ministry of Education in 1974:

Ornithologists and ecologists, as well as researchers of the ancient Maya civilization, are extremely concerned about the environmental dangers facing the Quetzal and its natural habitat . . . [T]he Quetzal is our national symbol; it is also our *nahual*, our inseparable protector; with all the powerful inner mystical connotations that it implies. Our historic past has lived under the protection of the Quetzal; our present does and our future shall.[41]

In December 1981, Professor Mario Dary, founder of the Biotopo programme, was murdered in Guatemala City.[42] Nobody has ever been brought to trial for the crime, but it has been speculated that lumber interests with ties to the military felt threatened by Professor Dary's efforts to preserve the highland forest habitat of the quetzal and may have had a hand in the killing.[43] In a nation where opposition leaders, peasant organizers and human rights activists frequently 'disappear', it is also dangerous to be an environmentalist.

Guatemala is only beginning, shakily and tentatively, to emerge from a generations-long nightmare of military terror in which corruption was institutionalized and dissent was met with total repression. The reign of the generals climaxed with the genocidal effort to exterminate the culture of the Maya Indians because, ultimately, the Maya people's mere existence was an obstacle to the generals' development plans. This effort, for all its sophistication and naked brutality, fell short of its ambitious aims. But Maya culture is still threatened and the military only ceded the reins of state power after the guerrilla movement had been safely crushed and the Indians terrorized into a modicum of submission. The development plans at the root of the bloodshed still remain. And the limits of freedom and dissent that will be tolerated by the military under the ostensibly civilian government are clearly, if unofficially, defined.

The under-funded and wholly inadequate national parks programme notwithstanding, it is unlikely that Guatemala will be able to meaningfully confront its ecological crisis until its 'democracy' has enough breathing space to challenge military development plans and institute a meaningful agrarian reform without fear of provoking a return to the nightmare. For this change to come about, those nations which have aided, and continue to aid, the Guatemalan security forces, including the United States, Israel and Germany, will have to come to terms with the role that this aid has played, and still plays, in perpetuating environmental destruction and injustice. And this, in turn, can happen only with an informed and active citizenry applying pressure to these governments from below.

9.   El Salvador: Civil War as Ecocide

The disenfranchisement of El Salvador's campesinos *from their traditional lands has a long history of violence and repression. In the 1980s, it finally plunged the country into civil war, as a leftist guerrilla movement gained support among the peasants. With massive US aid and direction, the Salvadoran military has responded by unleashing a programme of ecocide, the destruction of the ecology which sustains life in areas held by or sympathetic to the guerrillas – a programme modelled on similar strategies used by the US military in Indo-China 20 years earlier.*

Of all the Central American nations, El Salvador is closest to being in a state of total war. This has been the case ever since 1980, one of the most cataclysmic years in that country's history. A civilian junta had come to power the previous year, but massacres of peaceful trade union demonstrations in the capital, San Salvador, and the death-squad assassination of the country's Archbishop, Oscar Romero, who had been publicly decrying the repression, indicated that the ostensibly civilian element of rule was meaningless. The junta splintered, and some former members closed ranks with Marxist guerrilla leaders, believing that armed struggle was the only lever for change. The various guerrilla factions coalesced under a single umbrella – the Farabundo Marti National Liberation Front (FMLN). The FMLN launched a premature and overly optimistic 'final offensive', which was crushed. A gruelling and brutal war of attrition ensued.[1]

In the ten years since then, it has not been popular support that has kept the Salvadoran government from falling. It has been an immense war effort, armed, underwritten and directed by the United States, and modelled on counter-insurgency techniques developed by the Pentagon and the CIA in the laboratory of Indo-China in the 1960s.

The Vietnam analogy

Systematic destruction of the ecology – ecocide – was virtually an official policy of the US armed forces in Indo-China. Forests and agricultural land as well as villages in areas of insurgent activity were laid to waste by aerial bombardment with explosives and flammable chemical agents such as napalm and white phosphorus. Thousands of square miles of forest were cleared by bulldozers to facilitate military activity. An electronically-activated and satellite-co-ordinated network of minefields known as the 'automated battlefield' wreaked havoc on the land.

Where insurgent forces hid under jungle cover, the US military destroyed the foliage by aerial spraying of highly toxic herbicides such as Agent Orange. Rice fields were chemically destroyed to deprive guerrillas of food and to force peasants into military-controlled 'strategic hamlets'. In addition to wreaking the environmental damage for which such attacks were *intended*, the attacks also set in motion a destructive cycle, as deforestation led to erosion, and the erosion of land poisoned by chemical defoliants led to the contamination – with, for example, dioxin – of local water sources due to run-off from the herbicide. Over the course of the conflict, half of Vietnam's inland forest was destroyed, along with 41 per cent of its coastal forest. Four per cent of Vietnam's bird species and three per cent of its plant species became extinct. Forty per cent of Vietnam's rubber plantations, a pillar of the nation's economy, were destroyed. The Stockholm International Peace Research Institute estimates that most of South Vietnam will take 40 years or more to recover from the environmental effects of the war, and that some areas will never recover. Partially a result of this ecocide, even today, 20 years later, Vietnam is still plagued by food shortages.[2]

Twenty years after the cataclysm of the doomed US war effort, as Vietnam appeals for international aid to stave off an impending famine, US officials and commentators point to Vietnamese economic mismanagement. But war correspondent John Pilger, who reported from Vietnam for ten years during the war, wrote after a recent visit that:

> Much of North Vietnam is a moonscape from which visible signs of life – houses, factories, schools, hospitals, pagodas, churches – have been obliterated. In some forests there are no longer birds and animals . . .[3]

The principle of guerrilla warfare first stated by Mao Zedong and adopted by Latin American revolutionaries, beginning with the legendary Che Guevara, is that guerrillas must be 'fish swimming in the sea of the people' – they must be able to disappear indistinguishably into a rural population which supports them. The goal of counter-insurgency operations is, therefore, to 'drain the sea'. The ecocide in Indo-China was part of the attempt to 'drain the sea' by destroying Vietnamese peasant society.

Since rural guerrilla movements began to gain ground in the early 1980s, this tactic of 'draining the sea' has been implemented in areas of Central America, threatening to unleash devastating ecocide on the scale of that done in Indo-China 20 years before. Nowhere have efforts gone farther in this direction than in El Salvador.

'Land to the tiller'

The El Salvador–Vietnam analogy is not simply a creation of US liberals. Many of the very helicopters currently attacking peasant populations in El Salvador were actually used by the US military for similar purposes in Vietnam. Many of the names of US operations in Vietnam keep appearing in El Salvador in the 1980s. The first of these is 'Land to the Tiller' – the insufficient, corrupt, bureaucratized agrarian reform programme which failed in its attempt to win over the hearts and minds of Vietnamese peasants and sever their guerrilla loyalties. Funded, organized and administered by the American

Institute for Free Labor Development (the AFL-CIO's 'third world' development agency, or AIFLD), the Salvadoran 'Land to the Tiller' programme was modelled directly on its failed Vietnam predecessor. USAID originally introduced AIFLD to El Salvador, to organize the *campesinos*, as part of the Alliance for Progress in the early 1960s – the same time that it was introduced to Vietnam.[4] Philip Agee, former CIA agent and author of the best-selling exposé *CIA Diary*, describes AIFLD as a 'CIA-controlled labor center financed through AID'.[5] Companies donating finance to AIFLD have included W.R. Grace, Shell, ITT, IBM, Exxon and UFCo.[6]

Not until 1980, however, with a guerrilla insurgency quickly gaining support among the peasants (and an ostensibly civilian government in power to give the programme an aura of legitimacy), did AIFLD begin a programme in El Salvador as extensive as its earlier one in Vietnam.

The mastermind of the Salvadoran programme, AIFLD bureaucrat Roy Prosterman, had actually been one of the main architects of the Vietnamese programme. In selling it to El Salvador's newly-created civilian junta (especially to junta leader and future president José Napoleon Duarte, the 'centrist' chosen by the US government as the most expedient figure to lead El Salvador), Prosterman even boasted that guerrilla recruitment in Vietnam declined when the 'Land to the Tiller' programme was implemented – ignoring the obvious: the disastrous ultimate outcome.[7]

The Alliance for Progress, which initially brought AIFLD to El Salvador, had been the US response to the threat of armed rebellion in Latin America after the example of the 1959 Cuban revolution. The AIFLD programme in Vietnam had been one pillar of US counter-insurgency strategy for the nation. In both of these scenarios, reform and development was aimed at 'winning over' the populace, while concomitant military operations aimed at crushing revolutionary movements.[8] The 1980s 'Land to the Tiller' programme in El Salvador fits the pattern. But such a view has its inherent limitations: agrarian reform simply cannot work if it is imposed from above by distant bureaucracies and, ultimately, the reformists and the militarists work at cross-purposes.

From its inception, El Salvador's agrarian reform was a top-down operation, directed and funded by the United States. A 1980 internal AID document acknowledged that the programme:

> [C]ould prove troublesome because it was decreed without advance discussion except in very limited government circles, and we are told it is considered by key Salvadoran officials as a misguided and U.S.-imposed initiative.[9]

The land reform was divided into three phases:

Phase I called for the take-over of all properties of over 500 hectares, which accounted for about 15 per cent of El Salvador's agricultural land. This phase was carried out, but in such a way that of that 15 per cent nationalized, nearly 70 per cent had been cattle ranchland, which has extremely low productivity for other forms of agriculture without extensive inputs, such as fertilizer – and such inputs were not forthcoming.[10]

Phase II, the 'heart of the reform', would have allowed peasants to purchase title to land worked on estates between 100 and 500 hectares – around 60 per cent of El Salvador's agricultural land. Due to strong opposition by landowners, Phase II was postponed, and then cancelled.[11]

Phase III was aimed at relatively small rental lands, around 10 per cent of El Salvador's agricultural land. This included much poor land that needed to remain fallow for a year or two before replanting to allow nutrients to replenish the soil – something the peasant beneficiaries could not afford to do.[12]

A 1981 evaluation by one AID consultant concluded that if cultivated every year, most Phase III plots 'would be converted into sterile desert'.[13] An evaluation by the hunger advocacy organization Oxfam America noted that Phase III completely failed to take land-use patterns into account. 'To do so would have required a commitment to rural development instead of pacification and counter-insurgency.'[14]

But the most important area that the agrarian reform did not touch was El Salvador's agricultural heartland. This most productive land remained under coffee and cotton cultivation.[15]

Some of the redistributed land was organized by AIFLD into peasant co-operatives, but little changed – the same *campesinos* worked the same land with the same inadequate resources – only now they worked it for a technocrat instead of an oligarch. As one observer put it: 'Before, you had an absentee landlord; now you have an absentee administrator.'[16]

But with the 1982 elections, which brought the far right to power, 'Land to the Tiller' changed from an overly-bureaucratized fiasco into a nightmare of state-sponsored terror. *Campesino* leaders organizing for enforcement of the agrarian reform law were abducted, tortured, raped, mutilated and assassinated by death squads, secret military-linked units which wear civilian clothes. In some cases, land titles were even taken back by the former owners. By the time Duarte, the US favourite with the CIA-financed campaign, was elected President in 1984, the agrarian reform had degenerated beyond the point of resurrection. Said a 1985 AID report: 'Hope for El Salvador's economic and social problems rests largely on the development of light industry, agroindustry and non-farm sources of employment.'[17]

Presumably, this refers to hand-binding computer microchips for California's Silicon Valley, as in the sweatshops of South East Asia, or intermediary assembly of product parts for final assembly and sale in the US, as in the US-owned factories of northern Mexico. This kind of industry has already taken hold in the Free Trade Zone near San Salvador, where strikes are outlawed and foreign corporations can operate exempt from taxation and minimum wage laws.[18]

From a purely political standpoint, 'Land to the Tiller' could claim a measure of success. At a critical moment, it helped lend an aura of legitimacy to a government the US was attempting to prop up in El Salvador, winning crucial economic and military aid from the US Congress. The massive influx of US aid (over $1,000,000 every day) is all that keeps the Salvadoran economy even barely afloat at this point. This tiny nation receives more US aid than any other in the world after Israel, Egypt and (depending on the year) sometimes Turkey or Pakistan. Even with this aid, basic foods such as maize and beans are increasingly in short supply, especially in remote areas.[19]

The seemingly inexorable cycle persists. El Salvador needs to export coffee in order to pay off old loans. Keeping the best lands under coffee cultivation means squeezing the rural poor on to poor lands, which they have to overwork in order to survive – thereby rendering the land (and, ultimately, themselves) even poorer. This inequitable situation results in *campesino* support for the leftist guerrillas. The government (with massive US military aid and direction) launches a counter-insurgency war against the guerrillas. The economic crisis worsens as the country falls still deeper into debt and resources are diverted into the war effort (prompting yet more domestic privation and reliance on the agro-export sector). Finally, the war effort practically irreversibly damages the economy by accelerating destruction of the land.

Operation Phoenix

As the CIA was quietly funnelling money into the presidential campaign of the 'moderate' Duarte, a figure chosen primarily for public consumption in the US, it was simultaneously working with Duarte's far-right enemies in the Salvadoran military to streamline the counter-insurgency programme in the Salvadoran countryside. In 1986, a more ominous phrase from the Vietnam war resurfaced in El Salvador: 'Operation Phoenix'. By this point the FMLN guerrillas had control of a great deal of Salvadoran territory, including almost all of the northern department of Chalatenango, much of Morazan department, and Guazapa Volcano, which is just outside the capital, San Salvador.[20] In such areas the FMLN maintains virtual political autonomy, organizing the peasants, running its own field hospitals, clinics, radio station and even makeshift weapons factories.[21] 'Operation Phoenix' aimed at 'draining the sea' by simply making the FMLN-controlled zones uninhabitable. Elite Salvadoran troops, often trained by US Green Berets who were veterans of the Vietnamese 'Operation Phoenix', were helicoptered into guerrilla territory to burn cornfields, granaries and houses.[22] Once again, the targets and victims of these 'scorched earth' operations were civilian *campesinos*. The aim was simply to depopulate the targeted areas. Hundreds of peasants were assassinated or massacred, and many thousands – ultimately more than 20,000 – fled north from Chalatenango across the border into Honduras, seeking refuge.[23]

The Green Berets' CIA-directed 'Operation Phoenix' in Vietnam had been a search-and-destroy programme directed against suspected Vietcong sympathizers, which by conservative estimates claimed 20,000 lives between 1968 and 1971.[24] A search-and-destroy mission conducted under the Salvadoran Operation Phoenix in Morazan province by the Green Beret-trained Atlacatl Battalion in 1981 resulted in the massacre of hundreds of civilians.[25] In 1985, a former lieutenant of the Salvadoran military and graduate of West Point (the US military academy in New York State) named Ricardo Ernesto Castro, told a Washington DC press conference of participating in a massacre of 24 unarmed women and children during a search-and-destroy mission near the Lempa River in 1981. 'The cries of the children calling out to their mothers made me sick,' Castro told the reporters.[26]

Speculation that Green Beret 'advisors' are actually participating in search-and-destroy missions in El Salvador have gained credibility in light of recent events. On 31 March 1987, a rebel attack on a military garrison resulted in the first known death of a US advisor in combat in El Salvador – 27-year-old Green Beret Staff Sergeant Gregory A. Fronius.[27]

Former Lieutenant Ricardo Ernesto Castro also told the Washington press conference that he had commanded four assassination missions against suspected 'subversives', claiming about a dozen lives. He also revealed that he had worked as a translator in a CIA training course for the Salvadoran military on 'interrogation techniques'. He said that the US trainer suggested that suspects be kept 'completely disoriented' during interrogation.[28]

The nature of such 'disorientation' techniques is graphically illustrated in the case of Graciela Menendez, who was a 34-year-old Salvadoran employee of USAID when she was arrested at her office on 16 September 1985 by two members of the US Embassy security staff and charged with being an agent of the guerrillas. She was taken to the Embassy, where she was questioned about alleged FMLN infiltrators among Embassy personnel, before being handed over to the Salvadoran Treasury Police, notorious for their brutal 'interrogation techniques'. She was held incommunicado for two weeks, during which time she was repeatedly interrogated, tortured and raped. Blindfolded and often naked, she was kept awake with drugs and jets of cold water from a hose. She was threatened with the death of her parents and husband if she failed to co-operate. After being forced to sign a statement admitting to being a guerrilla sympathizer, she was turned over to a military court. After eight more days of captivity – this time in a women's prison – she was released by a judge on the grounds of insubstantial evidence, and allowed to leave El Salvador with a Red Cross escort.[29]

Menendez later told reporters that while in the hands of the Treasury Police she was frequently questioned by US agents who justified their participation with the line 'We pay the bills'.[30]

By 1987, the campaign had become largely an air war. The predominant tactic was aerial attack on areas of guerrilla control, with incendiary bombs and sometimes napalm and white phosphorus. (Production of napalm in the US was banned following the outcry in the wake of the Vietnam war; El Salvador is believed to purchase its napalm from France with, of course, US military aid dollars.) In 1984 SALPRESS, an independent Salvadoran press organization, reported that,

Between April 6 and 12 in the province of Cuscutlan, Air Force bombs destroyed 286 houses, killed more than 116 head of cattle, and burned the entire corn and grain crops and most of the zone's fruit trees. That is to say, the bombs destroyed the entire productive infrastructure which the *campesinos* of this area rely on for their precarious sustenance.

The bombing has accelerated since those words were written.[31]

But the effects of this military ecocide are best summed up by the *campesinos* themselves. On 24 February 1988 an advertisement was placed in the Salvadoran daily *El Mundo* by a group called 'The Communities of Northern Morazan'. It read:

We, the people who inhabit the town of Perquin and surrounding areas, are very worried by the grave damage caused by the devastating forest fires provoked by the bombardment and indiscriminate mortar attack, as well as by soldiers in their patrols and operations. The Armed Forces commonly burn the woods in this time of year [ie, the dry season]. The fires are accelerating the destruction of the heritage of this zone: forests, logging areas, crops of coffee and basic grains. By deforesting great areas of this zone, the fires and bombardments have notably affected the rain cycle. The duration of the rainy season has diminished in recent years. The levels of the creeks and rivers have dropped. The situation is becoming more acute, and we are worried because it is already affecting us directly. Our crops have diminished and this has aggravated our already agonizing economic situation.

The army has said that it is burning the mountains as part of its operations against the guerillas. But in practice the fires clearly do not hurt the guerillas, but rather hurt us, the civilian population.

We call upon the Ministry of Agriculture and Ranching, with which we are working on reforestation projects in our area, to vigorously protest before the high command of the Armed Forces these practices of burning, bombardment and indiscriminate mortar attack which are destroying our forests, our crops, and our heritage.[32]

By heritage – *patrimonio* – the *campesinos* mean, in part, their right to work the land.

Cultural extermination

Beginning with the 1881 law banning communal land holdings, accelerating with the *Matanza* of 1932 and the repression of Indian language and culture in its aftermath, and continuing today with the admitted failure of the land reform and USAID calling instead for the integration of landless peasants into an urban industrial economy, the process which has torn peasants from the land and fuelled rebellion has been one of cultural extermination. The culture under attack is that of the *campesinos*, rooted in the older Indian culture with its profound reverence for the land and maize. Perhaps it is not coincidental that the FMLN rebels have the most support in the northern province of Chalatenango – one of the last areas of El Salvador where the Maya-related Pipil Indian language, dress and culture still had been firmly maintained until being almost completely wiped out by the dictator Maximiliano Hernandez Martinez in the early 1930s.[35]

This situation, in which military terror is used as the means to enforce an absurdly inequitable system of land distribution, is a prescription for civil war. Civil war plus modern military technology equals ecocide.

In October 1987, over 4,000 Salvadoran refugees voluntarily repatriated from their Honduran refugee camp to their Salvadoran villages, as a part of the Central American peace plan.[36] Since the repatriation, there have been aerial bombardments dangerously close to some of the villages. On 11 February, 1990, six repatriates were killed in an Air Force raid on a resettlement camp in northern Chalatenango province, following ground fighting in the region.[37] It remains to be seen whether these repatriated refugees will be able to reclaim their heritage, or whether the US-funded ecocide will continue.

The March 1989 presidential elections in El Salvador only served to further polarize the country. The FMLN rebels agreed to honour the election results if the vote were to be postponed for six months in order to arrange for guarantees, which would allow leftist candidates to campaign without fear of right-wing terrorist retaliation and assure against fraud. The proposal was rejected, the left was divided as to whether to participate in the election or boycott it in protest, and the right came to power.[38] With Duarte dying of cancer and discredited on the left and right alike, the party whose candidate won the election, the Nationalist Republican Alliance (ARENA), is the only one available for US policy-makers to attempt to pass off as 'centrist' – even though ARENA is the same party that ushered in the reign of death-squad terror which destroyed the agrarian reform programme in 1982.[39] Although the new ARENA president, Alfredo Cristiani, has cultivated a moderate image (with the help of a high-powered US public relations firm), it is widely recognized that the real brains behind ARENA (and Cristiani) are those of the party's founder – former army major Roberto D'Aubuisson, who used his training at the International Police Academy in Washington DC to organize, train and lead death squads in his native land.[40] D'Aubuisson has been implicated in many killings, most notoriously that of El Salvador's Archbishop Oscar Romero, who had been speaking out against the death squad repression, in 1980. D'Aubuisson's arrest after Romero's assassination only prompted his friends in the military to oust those who gave the arrest order. He was shortly released and never brought to trial – an eloquent testimony to the real nature of political power in El Salvador.[41]

The first year of the ARENA government has seen a dramatic escalation of human rights abuses, as critics had predicted. In November 1989, hundreds of civilians were killed in the midst of military repression of a guerrilla offensive on San Salvador.[42] The offensive was driven back and the military immediately followed up with attacks on church workers who condemned the repression.

Seventeen Episcopal lay workers were arrested in one sweep,[43] while six Jesuit priests were killed along with two women in a pre-dawn raid on a university.[44] In response to US pressure, nine soldiers have been arrested on charges of participating in this massacre, and the US media make much of the fact that for the first time since the outbreak of El Salvador's civil war in 1980, members of the security forces may be imprisoned in connection with human rights violations.[45]

Rarely reported in the media, however, is that the regime of death squads is also a regime of ecocide. Widespread concern for restoration of the environment is unlikely to emerge in El Salvador until peace is achieved. This is contingent, in part, on whether activists in the world human rights, peace and environmental movements can launch a strong enough political mandate to successfully call a halt to El Salvador's blank cheque from Washington DC.

Conservation programmes

El Salvador's National Parks' System – still in its infancy – has been pushed to the back-burner of the national agenda by the war. So much of the country is deforested, densely populated and severely degraded that very little potential parkland remains. Nonetheless, 18 areas have been set aside for their unusual natural characteristics, most notably the Montecristo Cloud Forest in the north-western corner of the country, near the Guatemalan and Honduran borders. This reserve protects a great number of species, including quetzals. A Montecristo Ecologist Group, named after the Cloud Forest, works on issues that reflect El Salvador's severely degraded environment, such as deforestation and pesticide abuse.[33] Of less interest to naturalists is Cerro Verde Volcano, where, at great expense, the government recently built a convention centre and luxury hotel at the summit so that the eruptions of neighbouring Izalgo Volcano could be watched in comfort by wealthy tourists who would spend much-needed US dollars. Just as construction was completed, however, it seemed that Izalgo stopped erupting . . .[34]

10. Honduras: Militarization as Ecocide

Historically, Honduras has been relatively peaceful by Central American standards, despite extreme underdevelopment. This is due to the fact that it has had a fairly equitable distribution of land and peasants have at least been able to feed their families. The absence of a domestic oligarchy, however, has left a power vacuum which has been filled by banana companies, the CIA and the Pentagon. These institutions have played an even more central role in governing Honduras than they have in other Central American nations. In the 1980s, Honduras was intensely militarized as it became a staging ground for the Nicaraguan counter-revolution. This militarization has displaced peasants from their traditional lands just as surely as any agro-export industry – taking an overall grave ecological toll and fuelling both unrest as well as deforestation.

In Honduras, as in every Central American country, political unrest has been preceded by ecologically destructive land-use patterns, which have forced *campesinos* from their land.

But the development of these patterns in Honduras was considerably hindered by the fact that the mountainous territory was for long ignored by the Spanish crown – even by Central American standards. While Mexico and the Andes, with vast resources of silver and gold, became the centres of the Spanish empire in the New World, Central America remained an underdeveloped backwater. *Within* Central America itself, Honduras, along with Costa Rica, was the underdeveloped backwater which did not share in the comparative agricultural wealth of Guatemala, El Salvador and Nicaragua. And Honduras, unlike Costa Rica, did not become a trail-blazer into the post-colonial export crops like coffee. It remained severely underdeveloped.[1]

Ironically, the severe underdevelopment of Honduras has the same roots as its relative stability (again by Central American standards) and, in some ways, this relative stability has actually proved contrary to the country's best interests. It is partially because Honduras has no mass-supported revolutionary movement that in the 1980s the United States government chose it as the best place to install an extensive military infrastructure from which to police the more turbulent Central American nations – especially Nicaragua. The direct US military presence in Honduras today is greater than in any other Central American nation (excluding Panama); and, as we shall see, this military presence is environmentally destructive in the extreme.

Banana republic

As in the other Central American nations, the Honduran system of land use was born of genocide. The first waves of peasant dislocation began in the early days of the Spanish colonial era, as the Indian population was exterminated and exported as slave labour to the wealthier parts of the Spanish empire. Former Indian communal lands were allotted to the captains and foot-soldiers of the *conquistador* armies – the size of the allotment was in proportion to rank. The allotments for captains and knights were measured in *caballerias* (knights' units, or gentlemen's units), while those for the foot-soldiers were measured in *peonias* (peons' units), the former being hundreds of times larger than the latter. Those holdings measured in *caballerias* were most frequently turned over to cattle production. In the words of one ecologist: 'As the Indian population disappeared, livestock took its place.'[2] The 'peons', meanwhile, were left to intermarry with the remaining Indians, adopt their subsistence maize economy, and become what is today Honduras' *campesino* population. In some ways, the *campesinos* were actually aided by the fact that Honduras remained a remote and unimportant backwater of the Spanish empire. After independence, land laws (in 1836, 1870 and 1936) continued to protect *campesinos'* access to communal fields. Due to poor transportation in the mountainous region and lack of capital among the country's elite, Honduras did not share in the coffee boom that began in the 1880s and continued until the international market collapsed in the Great Depression of the 1930s. Therefore, Honduras never developed a coffee oligarchy.[3]

This had a good side and a bad side. The good side was that Honduras did not experience the wave of *campesino* displacement associated with the coffee boom elsewhere in Central America; communal lands were not taken over. While Guatemalan and Salvadoran peasants were being 'pauperized', in Honduras 'each department had sufficient agricultural land and each *campesino* was able to have the land necessary to support himself and his family.'[4] It is noteworthy that Honduras was simultaneously the poorest and (aside from Costa Rica) the most equitable nation in Central America.

The bad side was that without a strong domestic oligarchy, Honduras was even more easily subject to outside manipulation than the other Central American nations. The first manipulators were the banana companies. Gaining huge tracts of land from the Honduran government in exchange for building railways, US banana firms controlled 80 per cent of all Honduran banana lands by 1910. In 1929, UFCo bought out its competitor, the Cuyamel Fruit Company, and thereby gained a virtual monopoly over Honduran banana production. The rivalry between the two concerns nearly plunged Honduras into civil war. In 1924, US troops landed in Honduras in response to a conflict within the Honduran elite over the presidential succession. Washington justified sending the troops on the grounds that governments would not be allowed to gain power by force. However, it turned out that the usurper to the presidency was being backed by UFCo, while his rival was being backed by the Cuyamel Fruit Company! The conflict appeared to be over which company was to control the country's rail lines. Washington sent a functionary to Honduras to negotiate a presidential succession mutually agreeable to the banana companies. Cuyamel Fruit Company was subsequently taken over by UFCo, and the candidate UFCo had backed ruled the country for 17 years.[5]

The banana boom, however, affected only lands in the Caribbean coastal lowlands, a sparsely populated area, more suited to bananas than maize. It was not until in the post-World War II era that roads were built through the mountains (including the Pan-American Highway), allowing new industries – coffee, cotton and, especially, cattle – to affect areas of traditional agriculture and dense population. The results of this expansion were increased rents for tenant farmers, and illegally claimed communal lands.[6]

As this process accelerated, peasant squatter groups formed and rancher vigilante groups (often with ties to the military) formed in response. *Campesinos* were pushed on to small, marginal plots, often on steep hillsides. Today, *campesinos* are pushing their lands past ecological limits. The dictates of survival have forced them to abandon the three-to-five-year fallow cycle, necessary for the regeneration of such fragile and marginal lands, making for devastating erosion and decreased yields. Peasants also migrate to the agricultural frontier on the edge of the Miskito rainforest in the departments of Gracias a Dios, Olancho and Colon. They are followed to the rainforest by cattle ranchers who, following the usual pattern, evict the peasants from the cleared land. At the current rate, the Honduran rainforest will be completely depleted in 20 years. But the agro-export sector, which initially pushed the peasants from their land, is now experiencing the effects of deforestation: decreased rainfall, watershed depletion, erosion, sedimentation and flooding. Sedimentation is now seriously threatening the reservoir which provides water for the Honduran capital, Tegucigalpa – and at a time when peasant displacement is causing a population explosion in the city.[7]

The new power bloc

In the 1980s, however, yet another form of ecologically destructive land use resulted in a wave of peasant dislocation. This time it was not coffee, cotton, cattle, or any other agro-export. It was militarism. Just as the absence of a powerful domestic oligarchy allowed the turn-of-the-century banana companies to gain more influence over Honduras than over any other Central American country, in the 1980s, as Washington responded to Central America's crisis with a programme of militarization, this political vacuum in Honduras was filled by the Pentagon and the CIA.

But, ostensibly, Honduras is 'at peace'. There is no peasant uprising, civil war or popular guerrilla movement there. The gargantuan military build-up in this poorest of the Central American nations (Honduras is second only to Haiti as the poorest nation in the western hemisphere) has been in response to perceived threats in neighbouring nations – most importantly Nicaragua across the south-eastern border, where the leftist Sandinista regime seemed to have provoked in the Reagan Administration a state of pathological obsession. Since the Sandinistas came to power in Nicaragua in 1979, the US has established in Honduras military bases, military roads, a network of airstrips and a regional military training base. Joint US–Honduran military manoeuvres involving thousands of troops – usually along the Nicaraguan border – became a yearly ritual.[8] The contras, the CIA-created right-wing Nicaraguan guerrilla insurgency, actually set up a state-within-a-state in Honduras, with a sprawling network of base camps and airstrips along the Nicaraguan border.

Having already developed so much military infrastructure in Honduras to facilitate the 'destabilization' of Nicaragua, the Pentagon is currently seriously considering relocating the US Southern Command to this country. A 1977 treaty mandates that the Southern Command relocate from the Panama Canal Zone (where it is situated at present) by the end of the century. With the relocation of the Southern Command to Honduras, the militarization of the country would be both intensified and made permanent. In this light, the fact that the contras seem to have outlived their usefulness (following the election of the US-backed opposition to power in Nicaragua) does not mean that Honduras will necessarily be in any way demilitarized.[9]

In the 1980s, some 16,000 Hondurans were displaced by the US military and the contras. Peasants who farmed land outside the Honduran military base at Palmerola were evicted when the base was expanded to facilitate 1,200 US troops in addition to the Honduran forces.[10] The Honduran Coffee Producers' Association (AHPROCAFE) estimates that 2,000 small growers have had to flee 46 villages in El Paraiso, the department on the Nicaraguan border where the contras located their state-within-a-state. These internal refugees added to the ranks of the thousands of Salvadoran and Nicaraguan refugees already in Honduras.[11] Militarization in the form of mined roads ringing an 81-square-mile zone of base camps and air strips, along with contra terrorization of the local populace, has brought economic ruin and widespread displacement to El Paraiso. AHPROCAFE has even filed a $15 million suit against the United States government on behalf of El Paraiso farmers who have had their land damaged by or lost to the US-backed Nicaraguan rebel army.[12]

According to the president of the coffee producers' association of Danli, a town in El Paraiso, hundreds of local farmers have suffered economically from the contra presence. All local farmers are deeply in debt and cannot sell their land to move farther from the border because nobody will buy land in the contra zone. Many farmers forced from their land by the contra presence have relocated north into the Miskito rainforest, accelerating the cycle of slash-and-burn agriculture there. The displaced growers were among 50,000 Honduran families producing a $500 million-per-year coffee crop which provides Honduras' second largest source of foreign currency, after bananas. The contra war and militarization of Honduras have meant agricultural abandonment just as surely as did the cattle boom.[13]

Ending US support for the contras, the first requisite for restoring the economy, agriculture and ecology of El Paraiso, now seems both imminent and inevitable with the transfer of power from the Sandinista regime in Nicaragua. But it may not be sufficient to solve the problem alone. Many Hondurans now fear what former CIA Director Allen Dulles once called 'the disposal problem': what do you do with nearly 20,000 armed insurgents abandoned on Honduran soil? Fear abounds that with the end of Washington support, the contras will turn to banditry and looting to survive (while the leadership returns to prestigious positions in the new Nicaraguan order, or possibly snorts cocaine in Miami). The Honduran Foreign Minister has appealed to the United Nations for an international peace-keeping force to oversee the evacuation of the contra forces from Honduran territory.[14]

The frequent joint military manoeuvres have also taken a toll on Honduras' environment. The Honduran State Forestry Corporation (COHDEFOR) reported that the 'Cabanas '86' US–Honduran military manoeuvres destroyed 10 per cent of the pine forests in the savannas near the Nicaraguan border.[15] In addition to 'war games', these activities include the building of military roads through the forests. A spokesperson for the US Army reserves, which frequently participate in the Honduran manoeuvres, recently told *The Washington Post* that engineering projects in Honduras are 'less environmentally constrained' than in the United States.

> If you're building a road, you don't have to worry about the width of the culverts, about the Environmental Protection Agency or about the environmentalists. Those are not concerns down there.[16]

The Miskito coast

The new military roads also provide a pathway for landless *campesinos* to colonize previously untouched areas of the Honduran rainforest. Since the Honduran rainforest is part of the Miskito, which is divided by the Honduran–Nicaraguan border, it has been greatly (and adversely) affected by the militarization along the border.[17]

Following the Nicaraguan border north east from the coffee-producing department of El Paraiso, one reaches the departments of Gracias a Dios, Olancho, Yoro and Mosquitia, where the mountains give way to the lowland Miskito rainforest, and where contras and peasant colonists encroach on the sparsely inhabited traditional territory of the indigenous Miskito Indians. All of Honduras' rainforest is in this border zone, which is subject to political tension and militarization. Since conflict broke out between the Sandinista government and the Miskito Indians, some 20,000 Nicaraguan Miskitos have fled across the border on to the Honduran side of the rainforest. Much of the rainforest there has been cleared to make way for Miskito refugee camps. The militarization has spread into the rainforest as the contras have attempted to turn these refugee camps into military base camps for anti-Sandinista attacks, playing upon the pre-existing tensions between the Miskitos and Sandinistas.[18] (See also chapter 11.)

A 1988 COHDEFOR report on the environmental impact of the contras in Honduras concluded, 'Perhaps the most troubling news is that the contra war is destroying the Rio Platano zone,' a rainforest reserve protected under the United Nations Man and Biosphere programme. The Rio Platano reserve shelters species already extinct elsewhere in Central America. The reserve's human population has doubled due to the influx of Nicaraguan Miskito Indian refugees, placing it under serious stress. The Rio Platano reserve is also threatened by plans to build a new USAID-funded road connecting Tegucigalpa and the new US military base at Puerto Lempira on the Honduran Miskito Coast. Because this road would have cut right through the reserve, it has, for the moment, been shelved due to pressure on AID from ecologists.[19]

The Man and Biosphere reserves aim at incorporating limited human populations into the protected natural environment, and the Rio Platano reserve is designed to protect the traditional lifestyle of the Honduran Miskito Indians, as well as to protect the endangered rainforest species.[20] The Nicaraguan refugees in the reserve are also Miskito Indians (in this remote rainforest area the border along the Coco River is more or less arbitrary, and cuts through the heart of the Miskito's traditional tribal territory). With the contra/CIA attempt to organize the Miskitos into an anti-Sandinista guerrilla army, Miskito culture and territory has been greatly militarized and their traditional lifestyle has come under attack. Officials from the United Nations High Commission for Refugees, which ostensibly administrates the Miskito refugee camps, have charged that the contra-allied Miskito guerrilla group KISAN have harassed, kidnapped and conscripted the Indian refugees, and used the camps as paramilitary training grounds.[21]

The introduction of the contras and the cattle industry into the Miskito rainforest is also taking its toll on another Indian group which inhabits the region, the little-known and extremely sparsely numbered Pesch (also known as Paya) of Olancho department, distant relatives of the Miskito. Although the Pesch received legal title to their traditional lands in 1864, much of it has recently been gobbled up by Ladino cattle interests with the indifference or collusion of the Honduran government. In the early 1970s, the Pesch joined with the small group of Jicaque Indians in the neighbouring department of Yoro to press their land claims with the Honduran government's National Agrarian Institute, and in 1978 founded the National Federation of Tribes for the Liberation of the Honduran Indian, or FENATRILIH. FENATRILIH continues the struggle to reclaim usurped Indian lands and to preserve what remains of Indian culture and language. As elsewhere in Central America, usurpation of Indian land means destruction of Indian culture, because without adequate lands to feed themselves, the Pesch are forced to sell their labour to the Ladino economy in order to survive – which means speaking Spanish on the job and leads to the erosion of their indigenous culture.[22]

A March 1988 investigation by the Honduran non-profit-making organization Mopawi, which attempts to promote grass-roots-based alternative sustainable development among the indigenous groups of the Miskito rainforest, found that timber interests were actually felling mahogany and other hardwoods within the boundaries of the Rio Platano Biosphere Reserve.

A post marking the boundary of the reserve had been defaced; what just a year earlier had been primary forest around it was now chopped down . . . [E]xpedition members observed a logging truck hauling three massive mahogany logs out of the reserve; bosses of the logging company were conspicuous, with holsters and sidearms.[23]

More chemical warfare?

The banana companies (today, United Brands and Castle & Cooke's Standard Fruit, with about equal operations) are still an overwhelming economic force in Honduras. But as a power bloc in Honduran politics they have largely been superseded by the Pentagon and the CIA.[25]

When, in February 1986, a mysterious disaster struck, nobody was sure which power bloc to blame. Honduran newspapers reported that in Villanueva, a village in the north-west of the country near the banana city of San Pedro Sula, 20 people turned up in clinics with skin sores and respiratory ailments, which they said were caused by a yellowish mist. Some reported that shortly before the mist descended on them, they heard the sound of an aircraft overhead. One of the first victims has since refused to speak to reporters, claiming that his life had been threatened. He declined to say whether he had been menaced by military or civilians. As rumours spread that the mist had been sprayed by a military aircraft, the US Embassy in Tegucigalpa issued a statement denying that the US is testing any chemical weapons in Honduras; the Honduran military has remained silent on the matter.[26]

The Honduran Congress appointed a commission to investigate the reports, but it seems unlikely that we will ever know which of the two most likely possibilities is responsible: Was the mist a chemical warfare agent released by the US military? or was it an extremely toxic pesticide mix released by one of the US banana companies? The answer is in some ways irrelevant. Agro-industry and militarization both have the same two interrelated consequences: *campesino* displacement and ecocide.

Honduras is a dangerous place for those who protest against either the militarization or the concomitant *campesino* displacement. In her book *Don't Worry Gringo: A Honduran Woman Speaks from the Heart*, Elvia Alvarado, a Honduran *campesina* and grandmother to eleven who, through her work with the Catholic Church, founded the Honduran Federation of Campesina Women, which became part of Honduras' largest and most active peasant group, the National Congress of Rural Workers, tells of her imprisonment and torture.[27] Amnesty International writes that the use of 'disappearance' and torture against peasant organizers in Honduras is 'frequently reported'. Dr Ramon Custodio Lopez, leader of the Honduran Committee for the Defense of Human Rights, or CODEH, the nation's only independent human rights watchdog, has been the victim of numerous attacks, including the firebombing of his office.[28] In 1988, in the first case of human rights violations heard before the Inter-American Court of Human Rights (an Organization of American States-sponsored body based in Costa Rica) the Honduran government was found guilty of the 'disappearance' of two student activists. Honduras was ordered to pay damages to the victim's families. The testimony of government defectors at the trial revealed the existence of a semi-official secret elite death-squad, known as the 316 Battalion, which had been trained by the CIA in Texas.[29]

Overshadowed by events in neighbouring El Salvador and Nicaragua, Honduras is rarely noticed by the Western media. The non-violent land occupations of the Honduran *campesino* movement face adversaries in two interlinked forces – the cattle industry and the military – the very forces which have drawn criticism from, respectively, rainforest activists and anti-intervention activists in the US and Europe. North American and European environmentalists opposing the cattle industry's rape of the Miskito rainforest, and anti-intervention activists opposing the militarization of Central America, could both apply pressure to bring the destruction in Honduras to the world's attention.

Conservation programmes

Honduras has the most recently established National Parks' system in Central America. The first National Park was established at La Tigra Cloud Forest just north of Tegucigalpa in 1979. (Copan National Park near the Guatemalan border, which incorporates the ruins of the ancient Maya city of the same name, is administered separately from the other National Parks.) The Honduran Ecological Association, Honduras' most prominent environmental group, works against deforestation and road construction into virgin forest areas under a campaign called 'A Green Honduras by the Year 2000'. This Association is also active against the solid-waste incinerator a US firm hopes to build in the Honduran Miskito rainforest.[24] (See chapter 7.)

11. Nicaragua: Ecology and Revolution

The Sandinista revolution, which came to power in 1979, attempted to address the inequitable land distribution which has historically meant both hunger and ecological destruction in Nicaragua. Experiments with alternative development and appropriate technology, including relatively pesticide-free agriculture, were launched. The CIA-orchestrated counter-revolution, however, succeeded in diverting the Sandinistas' attentions from meaningful transformation of Nicaraguan society to militarism and mere survival. This counter-revolution partially achieved its aims when the Sandinistas were voted out in February of 1990, but it remains to be seen if the revolutionary agenda will be completely repealed.

US political domination has been far more blatant in Nicaragua than anywhere else in Central America. The country was actually taken over in 1856 by a gang of United States mercenaries led by the adventurer William Walker and funded by the industrialist Cornelius Vanderbilt, who hoped to build a canal through the country, or at least establish a monopoly on overland ocean-to-ocean transport through the isthmus. Walker's government reinstituted slavery, which had centuries since been abolished in Central America, declared English the official language – and immediately gained legal recognition by the United States. Fortunately, it was short-lived. Walker got too greedy: he double-crossed Vanderbilt and attempted to take over neighbouring Honduras and Costa Rica. He was captured by the British, who were then vying with the United States for influence in the region, and handed over to an Honduran firing squad.[1]

Later in the nineteenth century, the US began sponsoring and arming a conservative rebellion against President José Santos Zelaya, after his nationalist regime had balked at allowing the US to build a canal through Nicaragua. In 1909, Zelaya ordered the execution of two US mercenaries who had been captured mining Nicaraguan troop ships on the San Juan river. The US responded by demanding Zelaya's resignation, and sending a warship to the Nicaraguan coast to ensure that this demand be met.[2]

When Zelaya's US-supported successor, Adolfo Diaz, was threatened with rebellion in 1912, US Marines came to his aid. They remained in the country almost continuously until 1932, by which point they had trained the Nicaraguan National Guard, headed by Anastasio Somoza. Somoza would consolidate control over the presidency and establish a family dynasty in Nicaragua, amassing much of the country's land and resources in the kind of government that would one day be termed a 'kleptocracy'. After his death, power would pass to a son, Luis, and after *his* death, to another son, also named Anastasio.[3]

Despite US support, blatant corruption and the murder of opposition figures finally culminated in the 1979 uprising which toppled the dictatorship and brought the revolutionary regime of the Sandinista National Liberation Front (FSLN) to power.

The Sandinistas had learned the lessons of such experiments as Guatemala's 1944–54 'Social Revolution', which attempted to implement meaningful reforms while leaving the conservative military apparatus in place. Following the example of the Cuban revolution, the new regime created a new army under the control of the Sandinista party. In contrast to the Cuban example, however, the Sandinistas did not send former leaders of the National Guard to the firing squad; on the contrary, they abolished the death penalty.[4] Many former National Guardsmen fled to Miami, as had Somoza, taking with him the country's national treasury. The CIA began working with these exiles to topple the Sandinistas, applying a variation of the 'covert destabilization' recipe which had worked in Iran in 1952, Guatemala in 1954, Brazil in 1964, and Chile in 1973.[6] Every trick in the book was used, from right-wing guerrilla terror to economic sabotage, in an effort to make Nicaragua ungovernable and to divert the Sandinistas from revolutionary change to unpopular militarism.[5] In February 1990, this effort finally achieved its aims, at least in part, as the FSLN was voted out and a US-backed coalition was voted in.

Let us now see how the Nicaraguan revolution approached issues concerning ecology, the extent of the impact in this regard by the counter-revolutionary effort, and what are the prospects for the future under the new US-supported government.

Somocismo: an anti-ecological regime

In addition to being a brutal dictatorship, the Somoza regime had been profoundly anti-ecological. There is a direct link between the facts that by the 1970s the Somoza family owned 20 per cent of prime Nicaraguan farmland and that 30 per cent of Nicaraguan tropical rainforest had been destroyed.[6] The rainforest was destroyed by *campesinos* who had been pushed from their land to make way for the ecologically disastrous cotton industry, which relied heavily on pesticides and other inputs. While all Central American countries became a 'dumping ground' for dangerous pesticides, which are either restricted or banned in the countries where they are produced, Nicaragua also became a *testing ground* for new experimental pesticides – with the Nicaraguan citizenry serving as the guinea-pigs. In 1952, the German multinational, Bayer, tested the highly toxic methyl parathion in Nicaragua, applying over 1.2 million pounds of the deadly chemical in the Leon cotton zone. The consequent wave of deaths and illnesses among local field workers and their families prompted the Nicaraguan Ministry of Agriculture to ban methyl parathion, but within two years President Anastasio Somoza Garcia had overturned the ban. In 1967, the next ruling Somoza, Anastasio Somoza Debayle (Somoza Garcia's son) inaugurated the Cotton Experimental Center in Posoltega, where multinationals could test their new pesticides for $1,000 a shot, thereby avoiding more expensive testing in the country of origin. This experimental centre also became the vehicle for the introduction of new pesticide products into the Nicaraguan market. Under Somoza, Nicaragua consistently led the Central American nations in sheer volume of pesticides applied to crops. USAID granted Somoza's Nicaragua multimillion dollar loans for pesticide imports.[7]

When the new revolutionary government came to power, it inherited a country devastated by decades of ecological mismanagement, years of civil war and a 1972 earthquake. Much that had been destroyed by the earthquake had never been rebuilt. Financial aid for reconstruction had poured into the country from the US and elsewhere, but most of it was pocketed by the Somozas. In addition, upon fleeing the country in 1979, Somoza drained the national treasury. Already a millionaire several times over, Somoza took Nicaragua's reserves of gold and cash with him to exile in Miami – thereby assuring the new government an even greater economic crisis than it would have faced anyway.[8] Nonetheless, after the Sandinista victory there was a tremendous burst of enthusiasm in Nicaragua for rebuilding the country along new lines. Ecologists throughout Central America looked to Nicaragua with hope, as the new government pledged to set an example for the region.

Ecology and 'destabilization'

While many of these hopes have been fulfilled, progress was slowed considerably by the US-sponsored war and economic aggression against Nicaragua. As Alexander Bonilla, a Costa Rican ecologist who networks with other environmentalists throughout the region told me in 1988:

> I don't recall any ecological consciousness in Nicaragua in the era of Somoza . . . there was corruption almost everywhere. Somoza reaped the profits of intense exploitation of the land. The Somoza regime was an anti-ecological regime. I believe the Sandinistas are more clear on the importance of the ecology, more conscious of environmental conservation. However, due to economic, political and military pressures, they now have other priorities. Conservation of natural resources is not a priority for them at the moment.[9]

Inevitably, post-revolutionary Nicaragua was going to face grave economic problems. But the Reagan Administration worsened the problem formidably by applying the standard CIA 'destabilization' recipe. The contra guerrilla insurgency was created from the remnants of Somoza's hated National Guard, and sponsored to attack economic infrastructure and terrorize the populace. In 1985, the Reagan Administration ordered a US economic embargo of Nicaragua. For a nation which, for generations, had been almost completely dependent on imports from and markets in the United States, the results were devastating. Prior to the embargo, the United States had been the market for 100 per cent of Nicaragua's bananas, 76 per cent of its tobacco, 37 per cent of its beef and 35 per cent of its sugar. Nearly a quarter of a million people have been relocated from the contra war zone – which includes Nicaragua's key coffee, tobacco and maize areas. The Sandinista government placed the total economic losses due to the contra war at $1.8 billion, and total economic losses due to the embargo at $279.7 million.[10] Together, the two tactics conspired to send Nicaragua plummeting into a crisis of scarcity, dramatic currency devaluation and inflation, and resultant chaos and entropy. Cars and buses are falling apart, even the most basic items are in short supply. The capital city of Managua shuts off water for a number of days every week to every neighbourhood on a rotating basis, because the decrepit pumping system (made in the US) is falling apart and cannot accommodate the city's booming population, and because the economic embargo made it impossible to fix it or even to buy replacement parts.[11]

The ecological leanings of the FSLN were relegated to the back-burner of the national agenda while, in response to the US aggression, military defence of the revolution was promoted to the forefront. The most obvious effect has been the redirection of Nicaragua's meagre resources away from programmes of environmental restoration, and into the war effort. In the first weeks of the new government, the Nicaraguan Institute of Natural Resources and the Environment (IRENA) was founded. Four months later, IRENA created the National Parks Service, which its Sandinista director, Lorenzo Cardenal, described as 'one of the youngest park services in the world'. In 1985, IRENA's budget was cut by 40 per cent, and reduced by another 10 per cent the following year, considerably impeding programmes of reforestation, watershed management, soil erosion control and conservation of genetic diversity. Masaya Volcano, the only national park created under the Somoza regime, was founded by Jaime Incer, who became the chief of IRENA and is an energetic figure in Nicaragua's environmental movement (he had proposed to Somoza the creation of a similar agency before the revolution). In a 1983 plan, IRENA targeted an ambitious 18 per cent of Nicaragua's land to be designated as national park, which would have given the nation one of the planet's highest percentages of protected wilderness. Today, however, protected areas account for only .01 per cent of Nicaragua's territory, and Masaya Volcano remains the only national park. Plans to found a second national park in Saslaya, a large wilderness area on the edge of the Miskito rainforest, were put on hold in 1983 after the contras kidnapped the new park's administrator and two rangers.[12]

As US environmental activist Joshua Karliner wrote:

> To be an environmentalist in Nicaragua is to be a target of the contras . . . In 1984, Marvin Jose Lopez, director of IRENA in the northern city of Ocotal, was ambushed and killed on a dawn inspection of a reforestation project. Numerous nurseries, research stations, and fire-control projects have been destroyed; and in the last three years, more than seventy-five government environmental and natural resource employees have been kidnapped or killed, with over fifty of the dead from IRENA and the State Forestry Corporation.[13]

In addition to attacking personnel, the contras have also burned forest, as in a 1983 attack on the Northeast Forestry Project in which 400 square kilometres of reforested coastal pine were destroyed. In a 1983 attack on the Pacific port of Corinto, the contras blew up a tank full of methyl parathion that had just been unloaded on the docks, releasing the deadly pesticide into the atmosphere.[14]

With the Reagan Administration order for USAID to pull out of Nicaragua, AID-funded reforestation efforts were postponed.[15]

Under Somoza, Nicaragua maintained a thriving export trade in endangered species' products – jaguar pelts, crocodile hides, and live exotic birds as pets. IRENA banned the export of endangered species, but without available resources to enforce the ban, an illegal traffic in exotic wild animals flourished in Nicaragua – and is said to have been a source of funding for the contras. In 1985, in response to the economic crisis, IRENA itself lifted some of the bans on wildlife export.[16]

Among the projects that generated enthusiasm in the early days of the revolution was development of the Momotombo Volcano geothermal plant, which had been left incomplete by Somoza and was seen as a clean, ecologically sound source of energy. The plant is supposed to generate electricity from steam produced by the earth's natural heat in the volcanic area. But, the plant's shafts are now reaching magma with high levels of sulphur, arsenic and other toxins; the wastes are flowing into Lake Managua and killing fish by the thousands. The lack of available resources and the economic embargo delayed completion of the plant. It has yet to produce any electricity and its ultimate fate remains uncertain as it continues to contaminate Lake Managua.[17]

Lake Managua is under stress from other pollution as well. It receives 70,000 pounds of raw sewage every day from the city of Managua, Nicaragua's capital. The lake also contains toxic levels of mercury which, under Somoza, was dumped with impunity by the US electrochemical firm Penwalt, and mercury-contaminated water has reached into Managua's reservoir. In 1980, the new government cracked down on Penwalt, which had been dumping in Lake Managua since 1968. The United Nations Environment Programme (UNEP) earmarked $1 million to study Lake Managua and modernize IRENA's water analysis capabilities, while France contributed funds to a watershed restoration programme for the Lake Managua basin. But Sandinista plans to build sewage treatment plants were postponed indefinitely – again, because of the war and economic chaos.[18]

Agrarian reform

One of the Sandinistas' primary goals was a restructuring of Nicaragua's agriculture. The banana *pulpo* active in Nicaragua, Castle & Cooke's Standard Fruit, had been the nation's largest foreign-owned enterprise before the revolutionary victory of 1979. In 1982, Standard Fruit pulled out of Nicaragua, and its lands were taken over by the state. The Overseas Private Investment

Corporation (OPIC), the US agency which insures US corporate holdings abroad against expropriation by local governments, was called in to rule whether Standard Fruit left voluntarily (as the FSLN claims) or whether its holdings were taken over (as Standard Fruit claims). Friction between the company and the new Nicaraguan government may have begun in 1980, when the Ministry of Labor banned all uses of the pesticide DBCP – widely used on banana plantations throughout Central America – and impounded all existing stocks, after the agent was found to cause sterility in production workers in California (and cancer in laboratory rats).[20]

The Sandinistas launched the most far-reaching agrarian reform programme in Central America. Before the victory of 1979, a *campesino* organization – the Association of Rural Workers (ATC) – had been an important base of Sandinista support, especially in the cotton zone of Leon. Land reform, therefore, began in Leon days before Somoza had even given up power in Managua, as the ATC occupied Somoza-owned plantations. Once in power in Managua, the Sandinistas outlawed land seizures by peasants and workers. In some cases, they even returned land taken over by the ATC to the original owners, if it could not be proved that they were 'Somozistas' (cronies of the ousted dictator). But they made good their promise to the ATC to initiate a programme of land reform; not to do so would have been politically disastrous. The ATC was pressing its demands with public rallies and demonstrations and even after the programme had been initiated, the ATC would on occasion publicly protest that the redistribution was too slow, or was not reaching enough *campesinos*.[21]

Upon assuming power, the Sandinistas found themselves in control of more than 20 per cent of Nicaragua's farmland, as land abandoned by Somoza and his 'cronies' who fled the country with him was expropriated. When the new agrarian reform law was passed in 1981, it proved to reflect the political balancing act that characterized the first years of the revolution – it was carefully crafted to avoid losing the support of either the landless and land-poor *campesinos* who had been a base of grass-roots support for the Sandinistas in much of the countryside, or the large landowners, many of whom had made an alliance with the Sandinistas as part of an anti-Somoza coalition. Unlike all previous attempts at land reform in Central America, the Nicaraguan programme actually placed no ceiling on land ownership. At issue was not how much land was owned, but what was being done with it. Private property was protected if an owner contributed to the Nicaraguan economy by producing and using land efficiently. Land kept idle, however, was subject to expropriation.[22]

The expropriated land was either broken up and titled to individual *campesinos* or designated as co-operatives or state farms. After 1985, the Sandinistas began to give greater priority to titling individual *campesino* families, having found that smallholders almost invariably produce better than large farms – perhaps partially because the state farms and co-operatives had become favourite targets for contra attacks.[23] The land reform law also called for providing titled smallholders with fertilizers and other inputs, but once again, due to the economic crisis and the diversion of resources into the war effort, such inputs were frequently not available to smallholders, particularly those in remote areas. This situation occasionally led to tensions between *campesinos* and the Sandinista government.[24]

Escape from the 'pesticide treadmill'

Concomitant with the agrarian reform was a concerted effort to get the cotton industry off of the 'pesticide treadmill'. At the forefront of this effort was a programme of Integrated Pest Management (IPM), which called for maximizing the use of non-chemical pest controls, such as the reintroduction of natural predators. In 1982, an advisory panel of Nicaraguan IPM specialists, the National Committee on Integrated Control, was formed and began to recommend to local growers area-wide cotton-pest management programmes. By 1984, Nicaragua had the largest IPM programme in Central America, and possibly the largest in all of Latin America. Rather than relying on the 'scheduled spraying' promoted by the multinational chemical companies (in which, as we have noted, crops are routinely sprayed every few days), the IPM programme called for the planting of a small, pre- and post-harvest 'trap crops' of cotton which serve intentionally to attract the boll weevils and other pests. An early build-up of the boll weevil population can then be prevented with a relatively small amount of pesticide spraying. In addition, nationwide laws were passed imposing fines for growers who failed to comply with fixed dates for cutting and ploughing-under old cotton stalks as a non-pesticide means of controlling between-season carry-over of the boll weevil population.[25]

The pesticides used in the IPM programme were chosen carefully. They may be extremely toxic, but they will not leave lasting residues in the environment, as does DDT. Methyl parathion is one such pesticide which was planned for use in the IPM programme. When the contra attack on Corinto in 1983 destroyed the shipment of methyl parathion, the government was forced to fall back on more environmentally dangerous pesticides which had been impounded and warehoused. The attack came at a key moment in the boll weevil cycle and dealt a serious blow to the IPM programme.[26]

Nonetheless, the IPM programme produced very impressive results. By 1982, the shift away from the most environmentally dangerous pesticides had resulted in a complete halt in the importation of DDT, endrin and dieldrin. In 1982, the government created the National Pesticide Commission to develop new pesticide regulations aimed at worker safety – such as colour-coded labels for workers unable to read.[27] The University of Leon developed a three-year masters' programme in IPM, mainly for technicians on state cotton farms. The University of Leon also has an IPM research laboratory, funded by CARE, where experiments currently underway include attempts to breed a virus that will attack only cotton pests.[28]

The IPM programme reached its peak of success in 1983. Pesticide imports decreased, despite a significant increase in the area planted in cotton. IPM workers projected cutting pesticide use in Leon by 50 per cent within a few years. Sadly, these hopes have not been realized – the IPM programme has virtually collapsed in recent years. In the words of Dr Sean Sweezey, a University of California IPM specialist who has worked extensively with the Leon programme: 'The kind of progress that we witnessed between 1981 and 1983 has slowed to a snail's pace since then because of the war and aggression.'[29] According to Bill Hall, a US environmental activist who closely monitors the situation in Nicaragua, with scarce resources diverted to the war effort, the Sandinista government ultimately stopped even attempting to crack down on a thriving illicit traffic in black market pesticides brought in from Costa Rica to the south. Pesticides that have ostensibly been banned are nonetheless used openly on the cotton fields. Said Hall in 1988: 'The pesticide crisis reflects the economic crisis. The commitment is there, but it's on hold.'[30]

Agricultural destabilization: the Sandinista revolution v. the 'Green revolution'

The Reagan Administration aggression against Nicaragua not only instrumented an economic crisis, but an agricultural crisis as well. The most obvious means of instrumenting this crisis was the contra war. Farms were favourite targets for the mercenary army. Even small *campesino* plots were singled out for attack if they received fertilizers or other inputs from the Sandinistas under the land reform programme.[31] In some cases, the Sandinistas forcibly relocated peasant populations away from areas of contra activity to create 'free-fire zones'.[32] In short, the contra war created yet another wave of rural displacement.

The crisis has taken its toll. Beans and maize tortillas became increasingly scarce and expensive.[33] But there are more subtle factors than military attacks involved in this crisis.

Since the so-called 'Green Revolution' transformed world agriculture in the post-World War II era, Nicaragua – like virtually every other nation on the planet – has been dependent on hybrid 'high-yield variety' seeds which are developed and sold by a handful of multinational corporations. Two factors contribute to this dependency. The first is that once the hybrid seeds become widely used, the native strains become extinct. Unless a special effort is made to preserve the indigenous varieties, the entire genetic heritage of an agricultural region can disappear in a single season. With all the cornfields planted in a newly-introduced hybrid, the last surviving samples of the local native variety of maize are simply ground up into tortillas and eaten.

Once the native strains are gone, a nation has no choice other than to purchase hybrids from the multinationals. Which brings us to the second factor: while unaltered native strains will produce new seeds with each new crop, the hybrids do not remain genetically pure season after season. When second-generation hybrids are planted, yields decline dramatically. Seeds from the previous year's hybrid crop are often sterile or highly vulnerable.

Therefore, to maintain high yields (or, in some cases, any yields at all), new hybrid seeds must be purchased each season. Growers are forced back to the market with every planting.[34]

Furthermore, it has been pointed out that the term 'high-yield variety' is deceiving. The hybrids *only* produce high yields as part of a package with other 'Green Revolution' inputs such as pesticides and chemical fertilizers – also available only from the multinationals. This dependency increases with each season. In addition to the 'pesticide treadmill', which demands increased sprayings as more and more pests develop resistance to the sprays, there is also a 'fertilizer treadmill'. With each season of reliance on inorganic chemical fertilizer (instead of manure, compost, crop rotation and other traditional methods), the quantity of organic matter in the soil declines. The result is that more and more chemical fertilizer is needed to produce the same amount of the crop.[35]

Only large farmers can afford to purchase seeds, pesticides and fertilizers every season. In Central America the Green Revolution has, therefore, played an integral part in the *campesino* displacement which has given rise to the region's political turmoil.

This process promises to continue and even accelerate as 'high-yield varieties' become more technologically 'sophisticated' (always in the name of combating world hunger, of course!). The next step appears to be to achieve new genetically-engineered seed varieties through chromosome-splicing. Says a senior science administrator at AID:

> In the long run, techniques such as recombinant DNA, protoplast fusion, and the . . . development of truly pest-resistant plants, drought-and-salt-tolerant varieties, and energy-efficient nitrogen-fixing bacteria may be achieved.

And although such developments will be of 'revolutionary value' to US farmers, they 'will be even more helpful to the resource-poor farmers of the developing countries', and will become 'the nucleus of technological packages that the Third World farmers will accept.'[36] The first recombinant DNA corn seed was projected as ready to be marketed in 1989.[37]

One of the primary goals in the bio-engineering of seed stock is to produce crop strains which are resistant to pesticides, thereby allowing still greater levels of spraying. Not surprisingly, this type of research is being undertaken by some of the same corporations which also produce pesticides, including Monsanto, DuPont and Ciba-Geigy.[38]

The inherent vulnerability of an agricultural system that relies on a handful of 'high-yield varieties' was demonstrated in no uncertain terms in 1970, when the genetically uniform US corn crop was decimated by the Southern Corn Leaf Blight. New hybrids resistant to the blight were developed. But the blight drove home the importance of maintaining a reservoir of genetic material from which new hybrids can be developed to insure against future disasters. In the words of Pat Mooney, a seed expert with Rural Advancement Fund

International; 'The hybrids are bred more towards the needs of the food processors than the farmers. Therefore new genes are needed constantly to fight vulnerability.'[39]

It is for such purposes that the US Department of Agriculture (USDA) maintains a vast seed bank in Fort Collins, Colorado. This facility contains samples of native varieties from every region of the planet – including many varieties which are now extinct in their country of origin. A great many strains originating in Central America are warehoused at Fort Collins, because Central America is one of the most genetically prolific regions of the world. Write the authors of *Food First*:

The heritage of genetic diversity has not been evenly spread over the earth. In the 1920's, the Russian plant geneticist N.I. Vavilov discovered eight major and three minor centers of extreme plant gene diversity, all located in underdeveloped countries (along the Tropic of Cancer and the Tropic of Capricorn), in mountainous regions isolated by steep terrain or other natural barriers. These centers represent only one fortieth of the world's land area but have been the source of almost all our food plants. From these reservoirs have come many of the most valuable strains and genes used by plant geneticists in the last fifty years.

Central America is one of the so-called 'Vavilov Centers'. For instance, all of our corn and tomatoes are dependent on seed varieties with Central American origins.[40] Which is why Central America's current situation is so ironic. Central America is in the position of having to purchase from the multinationals hybrid seeds, which were created with Central American native stock. This position is more ironic, but no less vulnerable, than that of any other underdeveloped country: if the multinationals were to withhold sale of seeds and inputs from a given nation, that nation would be plunged into an agricultural crisis. And, to a certain extent, this is precisely what happened to Nicaragua.

Before the embargo, Nicaragua had relied overwhelmingly on hybrid seeds and Green Revolution inputs from the United States. The embargo instated in 1985 banned the export of these products. Even before the embargo was enacted, the Iowa-based Pioneer Hi-Bred had pulled out of Nicaragua, leaving behind a seed processing, storage and distribution facility. This facility had serviced all of Pioneer Hi-Bred's Central American markets and was far too complex and sophisticated for local needs.[41]

The Sandinistas immediately began to seek alternatives in order to minimize the impact of the pull-out and the embargo on local agriculture. Western European companies such as Switzerland's Sandoz have provided a source for new seeds. With aid from such sources as the Canadian University Service Overseas (CUSO) the Sandinistas have developed relatively small-scale seed facilities to replace the complex left behind by Pioneer Hi-Bred. The most successful of these new facilities is the National Agrarian Reform Seed Production Enterprise (ENPROSEM) on the outskirts of Managua. ENPROSEM even developed its own line of bean variety (called 'Revolution') which was exported to other Central American countries – Costa Rica, Honduras and El Salvador. ('Did you know that Nicaragua is exporting Revolution?' quipped one ENPROSEM bean breeder.) The Sandinistas recognized that to effectively continue such work towards agricultural self-sufficiency Nicaragua needs to preserve, and in some cases recover, its indigenous seed strains. Sandinista Nicaragua made more of an effort in this direction than did any other Latin American nation.[42]

Unfortunately, many such indigenous Nicaraguan varieties could be found only at the Fort Collins, Colorado facility run by the United States federal government – and their return to Nicaragua was barred by the embargo! In 1984, the Sandinistas appealed to the International Maize and Wheat Improvement Center (CIMMYT), a World Bank-funded Green Revolution research facility in Mexico, for the return of samples of native Nicaraguan maize which had disappeared from Nicaragua. (The maize had been originally collected in 1964. Nicaraguan *campesinos* had been asked for samples of local varieties and were offered a bag of hybrid maize in return.) Some of the samples were returned, but after months of silence CIMMYT officials admitted that more had long since been passed on to the US for long-term storage at Fort Collins. At the request of Sandinista Agrarian Reform Minister Jaime Wheelock, the Mexican officials at CIMMYT co-operated in requesting the return of the Nicaraguan samples from Fort Collins to CIMMYT (presumably without a truthful explanation for the request). Two years later, 64 samples finally arrived back in Nicaragua (via Mexico). Half of them were dead.[43]

Needless to say, Nicaragua's new seed facilities have been targeted by the contras. On 12 October 1984, Nicaragua's main seed storage warehouses were destroyed in a contra raid on ENPROSEM. It was most unusual for the contras to attack so close to Managua; the right-wing guerillas (or their CIA masters) clearly knew the value of their quarry. Seeds for the next season's vegetable crops and agricultural equipment were lost in the raid. That same month, the contras also attacked an agricultural research station on the Atlantic Coast, destroying the collection of banana seed varieties housed at the facility.[44]

The contras can, therefore, be seen as a weapon against Nicaragua's attempt to break the near-monopoly on indigenous Central American varieties that is maintained by the US via the Fort Collins facility, the world's largest seed storage bank. The Fort Collins resources are available to corporate researchers (frequently subsidiaries of oil multinationals such as Shell and Exxon, which also produce petroleum-derived fertilizers and other agro-inputs) and researchers funded by the World Bank and the Rockefeller Foundation, such as Mexico's CIMMYT.[45] These Green Revolution leaders claim that their work is providing a service to humanity by fighting world hunger. A somewhat different view is expressed by environmental activist Bill Hall:

One of the primary functions of the Green Revolution is to promote dependency. Underdeveloped countries are hooked into a technological package. They need loans from foreign banks to fund the importation of inputs. Then, when the price on the world market for their agro-exports crashes, they need *more* loans and the debt crisis results. The Green Revolution is a technological fix on a political and social problem. The problem of hunger is related to who controls the land. The Green Revolution intensifies the concentration of land in elite hands, because small farmers cannot afford the inputs. For small farmers, the Green Revolution equals debt and loss of land.

Indigenous agriculture supported large populations in Central America for tens of thousands of years. Today Central America is a net food importer. In Africa, systemic famines have emerged as Green Revolution agribusiness expands.[46]

Although Nicaragua has been able to turn to Western European sources for the agro-inputs upon which it depends, the US embargo has severely limited its ability to earn foreign exchange to purchase these inputs. With so many weapons of economic warfare at their disposal, it is with the utmost cynicism and hypocrisy that the Reagan and Bush Administrations have blamed Nicaragua's crisis on 'Sandinista economic mismanagement'. A cartoon, which recently appeared in the Sandinista daily *Barricada*, succinctly summed up the roots of the Nicaraguan crisis. In the first panel, a Somoza National Guardsman boots a *campesino* off a patch of land while a businessman looks on and says: 'I don't care if you're growing maize here. I need this land to grow cotton'. In the next panel, a National Guardsman boots a *campesino* off a patch of land as a businessman looks on and says: 'I don't care if you're growing maize here. I need this land to raise beef'. In the last panel, the businessman turns to the reader and says: 'There's no maize! It's the fault of the FSLN!'

That the contra war has resulted in a wave of *campesino* displacement and a shortage of basic foodstuffs is inevitable, as the contra rebel army was built on the remnants of the Somoza National Guard, which has a long history of forcing *campesinos* from their land.

A kind of Marxist arrogance

But charges of a degree of culpability on the part of the Sandinistas in the agro-economic crisis have also come from *left*-wing critics – even from within the Sandinistas themselves. On occasion, when the Sandinista government favoured turning expropriated plantations into state farms, maintained as large, centrally-managed entities rather than breaking them up into smaller plots for distribution to *campesinos*, some *campesino* leaders have defined this as a betrayal of the agrarian reform's promise to provide land to every Nicaraguan peasant. In fact, landless farmworkers were given a low level of priority in the agrarian reform process, because the government feared that by giving them their own land to farm they would be lost as a source of labour in the agro-export sector, which is so critical for foreign exchange earnings.[47]

Others charge that there is a deeper, more subtle problem in the FSLN's relations with Nicaragua's peasant population: a kind of Marxist arrogance that sees peasants as 'backward' and wage-earning 'proletarians' as inherently more revolutionary. Said FSLN Agrarian Reform Minister Jaime Wheelock;

> There have been many agrarian reforms that in one stroke have handed over the land. But this type of land reform destroys the process of proletarianization in the countryside and constitutes a historical regression.[48]

Some Sandinistas have expressed misgivings about this attitude. The following excerpt is from an interview with long-time Sandinista militant and agrarian reform worker Alan Bolt, in *Pensamiento Propio*, a pro-Sandinista Nicaraguan journal of political thought:

> Disgracefully, many of the people who are attending to political work in the countryside are from the city – Marxist manualists, so to speak . . . When they come to the countryside, they do not try to understand it, but they assume 'The *campesino* is backward, the *campesino* has a petit-bourgeois economy, we have to make the *campesino* aware, we have to educate him' . . . If the revolution is just and if it is supposedly *of*, not *for*, the *campesinos* – why are there *campesinos* who support or have at certain moments supported the counter-revolution? From confusion? From fear? . . . The contras are a terrible and bloody enemy, but there are other factors involved. There are people who have supported the contras not because they are afraid, but because of our economic errors, and because they feel resentful against our vertical dispositions . . .

Interviewer: *Could you give us some examples?*

> The imposition of laws they don't understand or accept, the imposition of prices they don't understand why they have to adhere to   The military draft, for example. I know we have a war, and the people know they have a war. But the draft is more understandable in the city. In the countryside it is different. A son is a pair of arms for the family economy . . . The propaganda, the verticalist political education, go against people's participating, reflecting, analyzing. Furthermore, people believe they cannot do anything on their own because of the great paternalism which has been created. They think that all the ills which this country suffers can be solved from above. Politically, this is a big problem because it is leading people to an attitude of passivity. There are cases in which the Somozistas of yesterday are the Sandinistas of today because Daddy Government [*Papa Gobierno*] gave them a land title or named them a coordinator of something or other or let them have a car . . .[49]

If Sandinista insensitivity at times strained relations between the revolutionary government and Nicaragua's peasant population, it meant complete disaster for relations with Nicaragua's Indian population. Nicaragua's Miskito, Sumo and Rama Indians inhabit the eastern half of the nation, which is isolated, remote and blanketed with rainforest.

The Miskito Coast was historically isolated from the rest of Nicaragua because it was governed by the British from Jamaica, who armed the Miskitos and set them up as a puppet 'kingdom' as an effective means of keeping the Spanish out. Britain only ceded its claim to the Miskito Coast in the 1850s, under pressure from the United States, then eyeing Nicaragua as a site for building an inter-oceanic canal. The Miskitos resisted annexation by Honduras, to whom Britain had ceded its claim, and accepted incorporation into the Nicaraguan department of Zelaya only on the understanding of local autonomy and non-interference with tribal government.[50]

Under Somoza, this region was exploited by foreign companies, which destroyed the rainforest with impunity and paid neither taxes nor fair wages – basically due to the fact that Somoza was getting his cut. Standard Fruit grew bananas and the US-owned Nicaraguan Long Leaf Pine Company felled mahogany, while directly paying the Somoza family a percentage of their multimillion dollar profits. In the 1970s, the region's Indians formed an organization, called ALPROMISO (Alliance for the Progress of the Miskito and Sumo), with the support of the World Council of Indigenous Peoples, to challenge the Somoza regime on issues relating to the control of land and ecological degradation in the rainforest.[51] Yet, the revolution that toppled Somoza was not fought in the Miskito region. Both the Sandinista insurgency and the Somoza repression were distant from the lives of most of Nicaragua's Indians. After the revolutionary victory of 1979, when the FSLN moved quickly to unify the entire country behind its leadership the historic isolation of the Miskito region was abruptly broken. One of their first moves in the region was to establish a Sandinista 'mass organization' among the Indians. Built on the leadership of ALPROMISO, the new organization was called MISURASATA (Sandinista Union of Miskitos, Sumos and Ramas). But friction between the Indians and the new revolutionary government was evident from the start.[52]

Much of the land which had been exploited by the Nicaraguan Long Leaf Pine Company was nationalized and the lumber industry came under the control of IRENA, the agency responsible for setting limits on deforestation and ensuring that profits are reinvested within Nicaragua. But the exploitation of precious timber on Indian land continued, without the land rights ever being clarified to a degree satisfactory to the Indian leaders. Indian leaders argued that profits from trees felled on Indian lands should be reinvested not merely within Nicaragua, but within the Indian communities. When IRENA created the Bosawas forest reserve in the Miskito region, ostensibly with the intent of protecting both the environment and indigenous communities, the Indians who lived there saw the project as part of a government plan to 'nationalize' their traditional home. It was due to land-based issues such as these that ALPROMISO had been formed in the Somoza era. Conflicts also developed because the new government literacy programmes in the region were only in Spanish rather than the Indian tongues.[53]

In 1981, MISURASATA broke with the FSLN. The Sandinistas responded by arresting several Indian leaders. Thousands of Indians fled across the Coco River to Honduras and began to arm themselves through the network the CIA was establishing for the contras. The Miskito region was instantly militarized. The situation deteriorated into an actual shooting war as the FSLN had thousands of Miskito Indians forcibly relocated away from the border zone and burned the abandoned Indian villages to prevent them from being used as bases by the rebels. In the ensuing guerrilla war, the Sandinistas applied, on a relatively small-scale, some of the same counter-insurgency methods used by the right-wing militaries of El Salvador and Guatemala on a much larger scale (and which were pioneered by the US in Vietnam on a still larger scale): forced relocations away from the guerrilla zones, aerial attack by helicopter.[54] Indian resistance was met with ground attack by tank.

The CIA, for its part, attempted to graft on the Miskito insurgency to the larger contra war and absorb the Miskito rebel groups into the (CIA-created) contra military coalition. This led to a split in the Miskito insurgency. Some factions, desperate for guns and funds, took the bait, while others resisted.[55] (This situation also has parallels in Indo-China, where the CIA manipulated indigenous tribal peoples, such as the Hmong in Laos and the Montagnards in Vietnam, into fighting against Communist insurgent forces.)[56]

The initial split was between MISURASATA leader Brooklyn Rivera, who resisted CIA pressure to unite with the contras in the anti-FSLN guerrilla struggle, and rival Miskito guerrilla leader Steadman Fagoth, who formed a splinter group called MISURA (dropping the 'Sandinista' from MISURASATA) and closed ranks with the Somozista-dominated contras. (MISURA would later change its name to KISAN, for Nicaraguan Coast Indian Unity.) By 1987, however, both Rivera and Fagoth were publicly charging the CIA, the US State Department and 'Contragate' figures such as Lieutenant Colonel Oliver North with undue intervention in internal Indian politics.[57]

The degree to which the CIA and the 'Contragate' private spy network succeeded in turning Miskitos into a 'clandestine army' (as the CIA and, before them, French intelligence, had referred to the Hmong of Laos)[58] can be assessed from the reported presence of numerous Miskito mercenaries in FLASH, the armed Panamanian exile group, which took over the Panama–Costa Rica border during the US invasion of Panama in December 1989; a war that certainly had very little to do with Indian autonomy on Nicaragua's Atlantic coast![59]

Although the warfare took a terrible toll on the rainforest, this situation did subsequently improve. Brooklyn Rivera, the principal Miskito rebel leader who has refused to accept the hegemony of the CIA/contra network, agreed to a cease-fire in 1985 to give the Sandinistas a chance to work out an autonomy plan for the Indian region. The plan, written into the new Nicaraguan constitution was ultimately rejected by Rivera as 'an ethnocidal plan which they hide behind the word "autonomy".'[60] But Nicaragua is the only country in the Western hemisphere to include *any* kind of regional Indian autonomy plan in its constitution – even if a limited, flawed and insufficient one. By 1986 the Sandinistas were freely admitting to 'errors' (if not 'ethnocide') in dealing with the Indians and began taking steps to remedy the situation.[61] The literacy programmes, for instance, were expanded to include Indian tongues as well as Spanish.[62] By 1988, under a United Nations High Commission for Refugees programme, which is part of the Central American peace plan, hundreds of Indian refugees began voluntarily returning to Nicaragua from Honduras.[63]

Revolution under pressure

One of the goals of the Nicaraguan revolution and agrarian reform was to make the nation self-sufficient in such staples as maize and beans. This was seen as a means of both freeing the country from dependency on external sources, which can be subject to political manipulation, and empowering the *campesino* population. It would also have had beneficial environmental consequences, freeing land from the environmentally destructive cotton and cattle industries. Even at the peak of the agrarian reform programme Nicaragua still had a long way to go towards this goal. The 1984–85 harvest yielded only 70 per cent of national consumption (up from the previous year's 50 per cent).[64]

The biggest obstacle to redistributing more land and growing more beans and maize for local consumption was the need to grow agro-exports to earn foreign exchange – a need made all the more critical by the war and economic crisis. For instance, one of Nicaragua's most important imports is oil. In times of war, more oil is needed for military transport, to keep army trucks, jeeps, helicopters and tanks on the move and at the ready. In any case, in order to purchase oil, Nicaragua must rely on Green Revolution-style agro-export industry which itself is highly energy-intensive and requires petroleum-based fertilizers and oil for tractors and other farm equipment.

The new national economic plan implemented by the FSLN in 1988 placed so much emphasis on increasing exports and cutting government spending that critics within the Sandinistas as well as others on the Nicaraguan left likened it to the 'stabilization programmes' and 'austerity measures' imposed on other Latin American nations by the World Bank and the IMF. In response to this comparison, one Sandinista economic planner said:

> In Nicaragua, there is a fundamental difference because the possibility exists to redistribute the wealth. In Argentina, Brazil, or Peru, for example, there are more limitations against succeeding in this because a series of political mechanisms exist that impede carrying out structural transformation.[65]

But critics contended that more cotton and coffee would mean less beans and maize in a nation already plagued by shortages of these staples.

Nicaragua's external debt is $6 billion, four times its yearly gross domestic production; the interest alone exceeds the value of Nicaragua's yearly export earnings. There was some discussion among the Sandinistas of relying on mega-scale development projects as a way out of the economic crisis – a way of thinking that also parallels the World Bank/IMF approach to such problems.

For instance, the World Bank is funding massive hydroelectric dams in the Amazon rainforest in hopes of providing Brazil with a means to generate money to service its foreign debt (to, among others, the World Bank). Similarly, the Sandinistas looked to the large-scale development of the Miskito rainforest as a way out of their economic crisis. In addition to eyeing agricultural expansion and construction of deep-water ports on the Miskito Coast to facilitate increased trade with Eastern Europe, the Sandinistas also considered turning to the Soviet Union to provide assistance in building two massive hydroelectric dams in the Miskito rainforest. By the 1990s, according to the plan, Nicaragua would be earning foreign exchange by selling surplus electricity to its Central American neighbours. Another plan under consideration was the construction of a 'dry canal' – an extensive port and rail network linking the Atlantic and Pacific coasts, which could serve as an alternative to the increasingly inadequate Panama Canal. Both of these plans would be certain to destroy large areas of rainforest.[66]

Nicaragua, with its huge lakes and east-running rivers, is an ideal location for an inter-oceanic canal, and it was to secure the rights to build such a canal that the US first intervened in Nicaragua's affairs over a century ago. Eventually the canal was built in Panama instead, but the prospect of a Nicaraguan canal remains a considerable factor in the region's politics. For instance, General John K. Singlaub, a former CIA operative and a key figure in the contra supply network, saw ousting the Sandinistas as essential, partially to enable the US to build a new canal through Nicaragua. In 1987, Singlaub told a reporter that he believed it to be essential to have a second and better canal operational 'before we pass the key to Panama in 1999' and that there is 'no question about it' that Nicaragua was the best site. He also believed that the Sandinistas need to be ousted before the Soviets got a chance to build the canal first. Said Singlaub:

> The obvious place for a second canal – ocean-to-ocean all through the isthmus – is through Nicaragua. I would not want to have [it] in the hands of the Soviets, which it would be . . . if we allow the Sandinistas to consolidate this communist revolution there.[67]

Regardless of whether such a canal was built by the US or the USSR, or, for that matter, Japan, which has expressed interest in funding such a project, it would result in destruction of farmland and rainforest – the last thing Nicaragua needs.

Sandinista plans to generate foreign exchange with mega-scale projects of the sort promoted by the World Bank have, however, remained in the planning stages. Meanwhile, small-scale, low-impact projects aimed at local self-sufficiency through the use of appropriate technology have actually been implemented. Ben Linder, a young volunteer technician from Portland, Oregon was working on a *small* hydro-power generator to provide electricity for the remote village of El Cua when he was killed by the contras in April 1987. The generator had been part of the Cua-Bocay Integrated Development Project, which aims at establishing a self-sustaining economic and technological infrastructure for this severely underdeveloped and war-torn region of Nicaragua. The Cua-Bocay project also includes the building of energy-efficient cooking stoves made from local materials such as clay and rock to replace the more wasteful metal stoves that must be imported. The project also calls for building more small hydro-generators, reforestation programmes, installing household drinking-water systems and latrines, repairing old coffee-processing equipment and introducing new small-scale industries such as ceramics and furniture making. Reducing reliance on imports and foreign technological inputs was seen by some Sandinista militants as potentially more effective in alleviating the economic crisis than was the development of mega-scale projects to generate foreign exchange. A more self-sufficient economy would take pressure off the desperate need for foreign exchange.[68]

One of the Sandinistas' challenges was to create pro-maize propaganda to counter the pro-white bread propaganda imposed on Central Americans by US corporations for decades. The Central American middle class especially, consider white bread (made from wheat, a crop ill-suited to Central America which needs to be imported from the US) as more contemporary and sophisticated than maize tortillas, the food of the *campesino*. Not only does white bread keep Nicaragua dependent on imported wheat, but it is less nutritious than corn tortillas. After the Reagan Administration cut off Nicaragua's wheat credits, the Sandinistas organized a series of maize festivals throughout the country. With a slogan of '*Maize, Nuestra Raiz*' (maize, our roots) and a symbol of Xilem, the indigenous maize god, the festivals promoted the manifold uses of maize – as tortillas, tamales, corn-on-the-cob, *pozole* (maize soup), *atole* (a maize drink which can be hot, cold, alcoholic or non-alcoholic). Maize cooking contests were held and a Managua fast-food joint produced a *tortiburguesa* – a maize tortilla hamburger.[69]

This event had a grisly parallel in 1987, which reflected Nicaragua's growing crisis. With local staples in short supply, Nicaragua was suddenly flooded with a massive donation of potatoes from East Germany. An event was held to promote various ways of preparing potatoes, and Managua fast-food joints halved the price of french fries. Potatoes were distributed instead of rice on ration cards and there were even reports that people had to buy 14 pounds of potatoes just to receive other rations, such as beans and soap. But people abruptly stopped eating the potatoes when a rumour spread that they had been dumped on the Nicaraguan market because they had been irradiated by the Chernobyl nuclear plant accident. We will never know whether the potatoes were really contaminated, whether this was a CIA disinformation campaign, or even a false rumour started independent of CIA disinformation.[70]

However, despite the pressing need for foreign exchange, in 1987 the Sandinistas began to step up the redistribution of land to small farmers – partially in response to pressure and protests from *campesinos*, and partially in response to the fact that state farms have consistently been more productive when broken up and given to co-operatives or individuals. In 1985, nearly 100,000 hectares were granted to individual farmers (compared to only 36,000 hectares from 1979 through 1984), bringing the total area redistributed to nearly 50 per cent of Nicaragua's cultivated land.[71] Of the land redistributed in 1985, nearly 60 per cent came from the state farm sector.[72] Since 1979, the total area in state-owned farms has declined from 24 per cent to 14 per cent of the country's arable land.[73]

In addition, the world cotton market has collapsed within recent years, partially due to the increasingly widespread use of petroleum-based synthetic fibres. The drop in world cotton prices greatly accelerated in 1987, and as a result, many of Nicaragua's state cotton farms were broken up and redistributed to small private owners, or turned into co-operatives, to produce staples such as maize, beans and rice. In 1987 and 1988, Nicaraguan cotton production dropped by two-thirds. If cotton prices continue to fall (as seems likely), and if the agrarian reform programme is allowed to continue (as, alas, seems less likely), Nicaragua's Leon–Chinandega cotton zone could once again be known as 'the Granary'.[74]

Sandinista National Park Service Director Lorenzo Cardenal clearly saw his country's agrarian reform in terms of ecological recovery:

> There is no environmental problem in Central America that is not connected to profound social, economic and historical factors – precisely because the history of the subcontinent has been marked by the progressive deterioration of the environment. The environment has been transformed by the patterns of land use that began in the era of the Spanish conquest, continued through the colonial era, and continue today with the system of imperialist domination. Many ecologists look at environmental problems in the abstract, without analyzing the deep roots of the origin of the problem. We hope to demonstrate that the factors which have brought about the environmental crisis in Central America are precisely the same factors which have brought about the social and political crisis in the region. It is impossible . . . to study the classical environmental problems of the region, such as deforestation, without at the same time studying and interpreting the factors which produce the poverty, the misery, the social iniquity. . . . Therefore, we have come to the rather untraditional conclusion for ecologists that one of the principal environmental problems for Central America is land tenure. For instance, the problem of deforestation, so eulogized by the world scientific community, has to do with the conditions under which the peasants have to live, which has to do with the social and economic structures of Central America. . . . We have only forty years of cotton cultivation, but these forty years have seen the most dramatic process of environmental degradation in the Pacific and central zones of Nicaragua. It's the typical process, you know – in Somoza's time the landowners took all the land and sent the campesinos to the agricultural frontier – to the humid zone, and there these campesinos have to practice slash-and-burn agriculture and destroy more forest each year. Now the agrarian reform in Nicaragua makes a big change. Now the campesinos have their own land, and good soils, and they are not in the colonization process.[75]

Similar concepts were expressed by Sandinista Minister of Culture and unofficial poet bard of the revolution Father Ernesto Cardenal in a poem called *New Ecology* and written shortly after the revolutionary victory:

In September more coyotes were seen near San Ubaldo.
More alligators, soon after victory,
    in the rivers out by San Ubaldo.
        Along the highway more rabbits, racoons . . .
The bird population has tripled, we're told,
    especially tree ducks.
The noisy tree ducks fly down to swim
    where they see water shining.

Somoza's people destroyed the lakes, rivers and mountains, too.
    They altered the course of the rivers for their farms.
The Ochomogo had dried up last summer.
The Sinecapa dried up because the big landowners
    stripped the land.
The Rio Grande in Matagalpa, all dried up, during the war,
    out by the Sebaco Plains.

They put two dams in the Ochomogo,
    and the capitalist chemical wastes
Spilled into the Ochomogo and the fish swam around as if drunk.
    The Boaco River loaded with sewage water.
The Moyua Lagoon had dried up. A Somocist colonel
robbed the land from peasants, and built a dam.
The Moyua Lagoon that for centuries had been so beautiful.
    (But the little fish will soon return).

They stripped the land and they dammed the rivers.
    Hardly any iguanas sunning themselves,
        hardly any armadillos.
Somoza used to sell the green turtle of the Caribbean.
They exported turtle eggs and iguanas by the truckload.
    The loggerhead turtle being wiped out.
Jose Somoza wiping out the sawfish of the Great Lake.
In danger of extinction the jungle's tiger cat,
    its soft, jungle-colored fur,
and the puma, the tapir in the mountains
    (like the peasants in the mountains).

And poor Rio Chiquito! Its misfortune
the whole country's. Somocism mirrored in its waters.
The Rio Chiquito in Leon, fed by streams
of sewage, wastes from soap factories and tanneries,

white water from soap factories, red from tanneries;
plastics on the bottom, chamber pots, rusty iron. Somocism
    left us that.
(We will see it clear and pretty again singing toward the sea.)

And into Lake Managua all of Managua's sewage water
and chemical wastes.
    And out by Solentiname, on the island of La Zanata:
a great stinking white heap of sawfish skeletons.
        But the sawfish and the freshwater shark could finally
        breathe again.

Tisma is teeming once more with herons
    reflected in its mirrors.
It has many grackles, tree ducks, teals.
    The plant life has benefited as well.
The armadillos go around very happy with this government.
    We will save the woodlands, rivers, lagoons.
We're going to decontaminate Lake Managua.
The humans weren't the only ones who longed for liberation.
The whole ecology had been moaning. The Revolution
also belongs to lakes, rivers, trees, animals [76]

Said US environmentalist Bill Hall of the Sandinista revolution in 1988: 'The ecological vision has respect, but it's not total – there is conflict and controversy over the role of ecological consciousness in development.' [77]

The new order

To whatever extent the Sandinistas were committed to ecological principles – or, for that matter, political pluralism or human rights – such a commitment was unlikely to come into full fruition in the atmosphere of fear and privation created by the contra war and the economic aggression.

Indeed, manoeuvring the Sandinista government into policies which would be unpopular with their own people was undoubtedly a goal of the US 'covert destabilization' effort, along with creating misery and economic chaos. In February 1990, the Sandinista party was voted out in favour of the US-backed National Opposition Union (UNO), which includes former leaders of the contras.

The consensus now emerging among the Sandinistas and their supporters is that much of the Nicaraguan populace reasoned that continued Sandinista rule would mean continued US aggression – war, hunger and misery – while an UNO victory would mean that US aid would pour in, the embargo would be lifted and the contras would be called off. In this context – nearly a decade of 'covert destabilization' – the election does not appear to have been truly 'free', despite the intense international scrutiny which verified that there had been no actual fraud or manipulation by either side.

Since the elections, most of the controversy surrounding the transfer of power has concerned the FSLN military and internal security apparatus.[78] This is tragic and ironic as, perhaps, these institutions more than any other caused popular disillusionment and discontent with the Sandinistas. The military draft, instated by the Sandinistas in 1984 in response to the contra terror, had long been unpopular – so much so that authorities had to resort to periodic unannounced raids on movie theatres and other places where youths congregate to snare evaders.[79] UNO made the smart move of promising an end to the draft if elected – a facile political strategy, since an UNO victory would certainly mean an end to Washington's support for the contras.[80] Draft age and voting age are the same in Nicaragua . . .[81]

The 'state of emergency' provisions imposed by the FSLN in 1982 which called for press censorship, also gave sweeping powers to the Sandinista secret police, the General Directorate of State Security (DGSE), allowing for indefinite and incommunicado detention without charges.[82] The domain of the FSLN's most notorious hard-liner, Interior Minister Tomas Borge, the DGSE received assistance and training from Eastern bloc nations, especially East Germany's (now ostensibly disbanded) Ministry of State Security.[83] The DGSE's 'El Chipote' detention centre in Managua became notorious for its harsh conditions.[84]

If any semblance of the agrarian reform, the most progressive and important legacy of the Nicaraguan revolution, is to be maintained, the survival of Sandinista *campesino* organizations and unions such as the ATC will prove to be far more essential than that of such unpopular institutions as the DGSE. But Sandinista leaders fear that unless the FSLN maintains some degree of control over the military and security apparatus, groups such as the ATC will have no chance under the new government.

Such fears are, alas, warranted. The new UNO president, Violeta Barrios de Chamorro, has already expressed her intentions to have lands expropriated by the Sandinista regime returned to their previous owners.[85] Chamorro, like many UNO figures, had originally been in the Sandinista government after it came to power in 1979, but subsequently broke with the regime, accusing it of 'totalitarianism'.

The Sandinistas, in turn, accused Chamorro and her fellow defectors of advocating 'Somozismo without Somoza', by which they meant the kind of oligarchical rule that exists elsewhere in Central America. Pre-revolutionary Nicaragua had been dominated by a single family: the Somozas. Other Central American countries are dominated by several elite families – such as the so-called 'fourteen families' of El Salvador or the 'Twenty Families' of Panama. The Sandinistas saw meaningful agrarian reform as the only way of assuring that such a system would not emerge in post-Somoza Nicaragua.[87]

Central America's oligarchical regimes, of course, stay in power through the repression of rebellion by state terror. *Campesino* organizers, journalists and even church workers who refuse to toe the line are singled out for 'disappearance', assassination and torture by death squads linked to the military, or secret police with links to the CIA such as Guatemala's G-2 or El Salvador's Treasury Police. Many fear that the contras may be poised to fill the vacuum that will be left in the Nicaraguan military and security apparatus by the departure of the Sandinistas – and this could be a step towards the creation of another Central American oligarchical terror state.

There are already reports that the Chamorro government has agreed to have personnel from the Israeli spy agency Mossad train and staff the new Nicaraguan intelligence apparatus, replacing the Cubans and East Germans who had been brought in under the FSLN. According to one news report, 'CIA officials are said to favor a Mossad role in Nicaragua because of the close ties between the US agency and its Israeli counterpart.' Israeli arms dealers with ties to Mossad had also been extensively used by the CIA as a weapons conduit to the contras.[88]

UNO's ties to the contras are numerous and obvious. Many of the slick technocrats who defected from the Sandinista regime in the early years of the revolution later closed ranks with the former Somoza National Guardsmen who made up the contra command for the common purpose of removing the FSLN from power. The CIA had an assigned role for both groups. The Somozista goons did the dirty work in the field, while the defected technocrats became the ostensible 'civilian leadership' of the contras, providing a 'democratic' image for public consumption in the US. Key UNO figures are among these former contra 'civilian leaders'.[89]

Balancing the egos of liberal technocrats who had opposed the Somoza regime with those of military thugs who had supported the Somoza regime was a difficult job for the CIA. To do this, it was constantly forming contra umbrella groups in an attempt to create a unified command. One such umbrella group actually had the same acronym as the electoral coalition: UNO. The contra acronym had stood for United Nicaraguan Opposition. That organization split in 1988 when members of its civilian leadership – including Pedro Joaquin Chamorro Barrios, son of the new President Violeta Barrios de Chamorro – resigned in protest of the presence of Enrique Bermudez, a former colonel of the Somoza National Guard, as UNO military commander. Bermudez had been charged with corruption and brutality.[90]

But the CIA was more inclined to juggle the 'civilian leadership' than to sacrifice a military commander, so Bermudez stayed and a new contra umbrella group was formed, the so-called Nicaraguan Resistance, for which a new director was found who would be willing to close ranks with the Somozista Bermudez – Alfredo Cesar.[91]

Cesar, a relative-through-marriage of President Chamorro, had been a US-educated administrator of the Nicaraguan sugar industry under Somoza, and later a Sandinista guerrilla, imprisoned by the Somoza regime in 1978. After the victory of the revolution, he assumed a number of high-level posts concerning the economy and finance, most notably head of Nicaragua's central bank. He broke with the Sandinistas in 1982 and was named to the directorate of the contra Nicaraguan Resistance in 1988. He returned to Nicaragua the following year to prepare for his leading role in the elections. He is today widely acknowledged to be the key power-broker behind the electoral UNO coalition and the brains behind President Chamorro.[92]

Former Miskito Indian guerrilla leaders have also assumed posts in the Chamorro government. Brooklyn Rivera, former leader of the MISURASATA guerrilla group, had been appointed chief of the newly-created Nicaraguan Institute for the Development of the Autonomous Region (INDRA), a cabinet position. Formerly leaders of the rival Indian guerrilla groups MISUARASATA and MISURA, Rivera and Steadman Fagoth are now co-operating in YATAMA, founded in 1987 when the two decided to put aside their differences. The following year, YATAMA laid down its arms and began its transformation from guerrilla army to political organization. Following the 1990 elections, YATAMA gained a majority of the representative seats from the Miskito autonomous region. Fagoth, who has a degree in biology from the Nicaraguan National University, is in the post responsible for overseeing the environmental issues in the Miskito autonomous region.[93] During his years as a guerrilla leader, Rivera had steered a more or less independent course from the contras. He had briefly allied with the renegade 'Southern Front' contras who operated out of Costa Rica and were largely led by defected Sandinistas who had opposed the Somoza regime, but had resisted CIA pressure to close ranks with the most powerful contra army, largely led by Somozistas and operating out of Honduran base camps. Fagoth's MISURA, however, had succumbed to similar pressure and joined the CIA-created umbrella group.[94]

While both UNO and the FSLN are publicly maintaining that the contras should now be disbanded, all parties concerned are obviously now faced with the 'disposal problem' – what to do with the CIA's army of hired thugs after they have served their purpose?

Many Nicaraguans were undoubtedly expecting generous quantities of US aid to pour into their country following Chamorro's ascendance to the presidency. In the year since then, however, the nation's economic crisis has only worsened. The US, itself massively in debt to Japan and Germany, has neither the will nor the financial resources to permanently underwrite the Nicaraguan economy. While the US Congress approved a post-election aid package of $300 million, the money was held up until the Chamorro government's new economic plan was fully implemented. The US even refused to release funds to fight the giant forest fire which was raging out of control on the Miskito Coast in April 1991. Chamorro's Natural Resources Ministry reported that efforts to put out the fire were hindered by lack of funds, the danger of mines remaining from the contra war, and the failure of various countries to respond to requests for help.[95] By September, some $60 million of the aid had arrived, but by then Chamorro's economic plan, calling for privatization of state industries and massive cuts in government spending, was sparking widespread protest. Sandinista militants erected barricades in the streets as they had during the 1979 uprising; factories were taken over and offices occupied by government workers. Finally, the Chamorro government was forced to modify the plan.[96]

While Nicaraguan exiles have been returning to the country from Miami, it remains to be seen how much of the land expropriated under the Sandinista agrarian reform will actually be returned to its previous owners – and what will become of the *campesinos* who have been growing *maize* on these lands for the past several years. Many Nicaraguans feel betrayed by the hold-up in the US aid. It seems that economic sabotage has merely been replaced with economic blackmail.

The embargo has been lifted, and as seeds, petroleum, fertilizers, irrigation systems, credit and trade return, Nicaragua will once again have a functioning economy, it is reasoned. But *how* will that economy function? Will the *campesinos* remain a permanent captive labour force of the agro-export sector, deprived of adequate land to feed themselves? Will the nation continue to depend on food imports from the United States and elsewhere, continue to exploit its own land and labour to pay the interest on debt to international banks? Will interminable poverty, hunger, pesticide abuse and deforestation be the norm, as is the case elsewhere in Central America?

Will peasants who attempt to organize for change face state-sponsored terror? Will the ATC and other Sandinista grass-roots organizations be suppressed or forced underground?

Will conflict over the control of the military and security forces be the justification for a US invasion to finally crush the Sandinistas altogether?

Or will the Sandinistas, who still control a minority of the seats in the National Assembly, be given enough political space to organize as an opposition party and struggle through the political process to, at least, keep some semblance of the agrarian reform alive and resist the emergence of a new oligarchy?

The answers to these questions depend, in large part, on how closely the press and the public of the US and other world powers watch the political transition in Nicaragua – and, perhaps, on whether international environmentalists as well as anti-intervention activists will recognize the importance of defending the gains of the revolution and bringing pressure against those banks, corporations and agencies in their own countries which, implicitly or explicitly, act as accomplices in the effort to reverse those gains.

12. Costa Rica: Paradise on the Brink?

With no armed forces, a long tradition of neutrality and peaceful democracy, and one of the western hemisphere's most ambitious national parks and wilderness preservation programmes, Costa Rica seems to have little in common with its impoverished and war-torn neighbours. But the explosion of the cattle industry has led to a frighteningly rapid rate of deforestation outside of (and sometimes even within) officially protected areas, and threatens to render the wilderness preservation programmes irrelevant. It has also led to the beginning of peasant unrest and, with the emergence of numerous right-wing paramilitary groups, seeds of repressive terror. The power bloc represented by these paramilitary groups also worked closely with covert US efforts to turn Costa Rica into a staging ground for the Nicaraguan counter-revolution – an effort that not only threatened to reverse Costa Rica's traditions of peace and unarmed neutrality, but also turned officially protected wilderness areas into militarized zones.

After a brief civil war in 1948 (one of the few wars in Costa Rica's history), the victorious moderate left forces came to power. One of their first moves was to disband the military, which proved to be a most effective (and, unfortunately, unique) means of avoiding a military *coup d'etat* and directing limited resources towards meeting human needs. As a result, today Costa Rica has Central America's highest literacy rate and lowest infant mortality rate, as well as the most extensive national parks programme. While tourists flock to Guatemala to see the Maya Indian culture (as it struggles to survive amidst poverty and repression), they are attracted to Costa Rica by pristine, jungle-covered mountains and tropical beaches. Its beautiful mountainous countryside and its traditional stance of neutrality and non-entanglement in the turmoil of its neighbours have won Costa Rica the title of 'The Switzerland of Central America'.

But pressures, both internal and external, are threatening Costa Rica's unarmed, democratic status and its pristine wilderness areas. The internal pressures are related to increasingly centralized control of the land, which results in both deforestation and peasant unrest. The external pressures have been related to Costa Rica's embroilment in the Nicaraguan war – specifically, the 'Contragate' scandal – and a concerted drive by the Reagan Administration to involve the country in remilitarization.

Costa Rica's stable democracy is rooted in the fact that there was more equitable land distribution there than in the other countries of the region. This was because Costa Rica never had a very large Indian population; and without a large Indian population to enslave, the Spanish colonialists could not establish the system of *latifundismo* (large-scale plantation farming) as had been done elsewhere in Central America. Instead, the Spanish colonists in Costa Rica established small farms, which could be worked by a single family. The country therefore remained an unimportant backwater of the Spanish empire, but developed a relatively equitable social order, which some historians have termed 'Jeffersonian'.[1]

A coffee oligarchy did emerge with the advent of the coffee boom in the late nineteenth century. In fact, Costa Rica led the way in switching Central American agriculture from such archaic crops as cochineal and indigo (rendered obsolete by the discovery of aniline dyes) to coffee. Peasants displaced by the coffee boom found employment on the banana plantations of Limon, in the Caribbean zone, as Costa Rica once again led the way into a new export crop that would soon be adopted by the other Central American nations; UFCo's first Central American plantations were established in Costa Rica. The first signs of landless peasant unrest emerged with a massive banana workers' strike against UFCo in 1934.[2]

By the 1940s, Costa Rica began to take on another characteristic of a Central American militarized oligarchic state, as the populist leader Rafael Calderon Guardia established control over the presidency through fraud and terror. But this consolidation of power was arrested by the crisis that shook the nation in 1948. In the presidential election of that year, Calderon was defeated by an opposition candidate and responded by declaring the results void and proclaiming a personal puppet president. Jose 'Pepe' Figueres, a rival populist with leftist leanings who had supported the opposition candidate, accused Calderon of trying to set up a political dynasty modelled after Nicaragua's Anastasio Somoza, who Calderon evidently emulated (certainly an irony considering Calderon's populist tendencies and alliance with the Communist Party). With an army of exiles from various Central American and Caribbean dictatorships, and arms supplied by the leftist regime then in power in Guatemala, Figueres launched a rebellion. The military mostly closed ranks behind Calderon and a brief civil war ensued – from which Figueres emerged victorious.[3]

After a transition period in which Figueres held the presidency and the (largely pro-Calderon) military was abolished, the first in an, as yet, unbroken chain of orderly elections was held. Figueres established the moderately leftist (but quite strongly anti-Communist) National Liberation party, while Calderon's supporters established the more conservative Social Christian party. An unofficial tradition was established whereby the presidency was alternated between the two parties, with each party winning alternate elections. Somehow, the Costa Rican citizenry could generally be counted on to elect whichever party was not in power. As National Liberation drifted to the right, however, the differences between the two parties became fairly minimal; both parties remain unwaveringly pro-US.[4]

But Figueres' rivalry with Calderon, and with Calderon's chum Nicaraguan dictator Anastasio Somoza, occasionally made for some lively escapades. During the two terms that Figueres returned to the presidency, he openly allowed Nicaraguan exiles to concoct anti-Somoza plots from Costa Rican territory. In the late 1970s, Costa Rica served as a staging ground and a conduit for smuggled arms for the Sandinista guerrillas, but in the 1980s, as the victorious Sandinista revolution moved too sharply to the left for elite Costa

Rican sensibilities, the country became a staging ground and arms conduit for the contras.

Figueres, and other Costa Rican presidents of both parties, have co-operated with the CIA in several capacities (Figueres is a member of the World Anti-Communist League, his democratic ideals notwithstanding), but the CIA, displaying a kind of political schizophrenia, has also plotted against Figueres. He would tell his biographer that the CIA-contracted US Air Force fighters which bombarded Guatemala City during the *coup d'etat* of 1954 'afterwards came . . . and machine-gunned eleven defenseless towns' in Costa Rica, where Figueres was then president. This was done as a favour to Somoza, who had co-operated with the CIA coup by allowing hired mercenaries to use Nicaraguan territory as a staging ground. If this incident took place, it is especially absurd in light of the fact that the US had just sold four Mustang fighter planes to Costa Rica in response to threats of Nicaraguan military incursions, themselves a retaliation for Figueres' pressure on Washington to drop Somoza.[5] When Figueres returned to the presidency in 1970, he again got himself in trouble by establishing diplomatic relations with the Soviet Union and eastern Europe, with an eye towards wooing them as coffee markets. 'This diplomatic recognition in no way shakes our loyalty to the United States or to the democratic cause,' said Figueres. 'People everywhere are tired of the cold war. Russia controls half of Europe, and we want to make the Russians drink coffee instead of tea.' However, a right-wing paramilitary group known as the Free Costa Rica Movement (MCRL) began to make veiled threats to launch an armed revolt against Figueres in response to the move, and rumours abounded that the MCRL was being supplied with weapons by the CIA. This time Figueres vigorously denied CIA involvement, and eventually the storm blew over. Despite Figueres' popularity, significant forces in Costa Rica would remain bitterly opposed even to his moderate and liberal brand of revolution. For instance, all three of Costa Rica's daily newspapers are controlled by conservative elements of the coffee oligarchy and maintain links with the MCRL.[6]

When Figueres came to power in 1948, his revolutionary government did not implement a far-reaching agrarian reform programme, but rather kept the social security system which had been established by Calderon, and instated price subsidies for staples such as maize, beans and rice. Under this programme, Costa Rica became the only Central American nation to achieve self-sufficiency in these basic foods. On the banana plantations, National Liberation encouraged an ethic of worker–boss co-operation and supposed mutual reciprocity known as *Solidarismo* (Solidarity) as an alternative to the class-struggle ethic of the Communist-led unions. *Solidarismo* called for employees and employers to form joint councils in which concerns could be addressed in a non-confrontational manner. Figueres did, however, claim for the Costa Rican state UFCo's schools, hospitals and railroads, and wrested a wage increase from the company.[7]

In the early 1950s, the racist laws which had barred Limon's blacks from migrating to the capital, San José, or other Ladino areas, were overturned, and women were granted the right to vote. The system of state-subsidized agriculture for domestic consumption made for a remarkably humane and efficient social order by Central American standards.[8]

Unrest and remilitarization

Cracks in this system started to emerge following the enormous growth of the cattle industry in the 1960s and 1970s. The advent of large-scale cattle ranching resulted in a serious wave of peasant displacement, yet the Costa Rican government failed to adopt an effective programme to deal with the issue of landlessness.

In the 1980s, just as the problem of the landless peasant was reaching crisis proportions, the Costa Rican government started to cut crop subsidies in response to pressure from the international lending institutions. Due to Costa Rica's relatively high public spending (derided by critics as a 'welfare state'), the IMF cites Costa Rica as an example of a country 'living beyond its means'. Yet its deficits are no higher than those of Honduras or Guatemala, where funds are directed into the military rather than a 'welfare state'. The IMF urges Costa Rica to install 'austerity measures' and cut back on social programmes.[9]

On 18 September 1986, a sight all too familiar in El Salvador and Guatemala appeared for the first time in the streets of the Costa Rican capital, San José. A thousand *campesinos*, organized by the Union of Atlantic Agricultural Producers (UPAGRA), blocked traffic on the Central Avenue for four hours in protest at the recent abolition of price supports for rice and beans. Troops of the Civil Guard – Costa Rica's small and ostensibly non-military constabulary – equipped with gas masks, shields, batons and helmets, dispersed the *campesinos* with tear-gas. The protesters took refuge in the Metropolitan Cathedral where they awaited a government decision on agrarian policy. Compromise measures were eventually reached; but Costa Ricans were shocked by the violence of the Civil Guards.[10]

It is often heard said in San José that only ten years ago the Civil Guards carried only screwdrivers, in case a parking meter was jammed; today, they carry Uzi sub-machine guns. Costa Rica still has only approximately 10,000 men under arms, as compared with 40,000 or more in the other Central American countries. But the Reagan Administration, with the co-operation of ultra-conservative elements in the Civil Guard, made a concerted effort to transform the constabulary into a full-fledged military force. Between 1980 and 1985, US military aid to Costa Rica increased from zero to $10 million as thousands of M-16 rifles, armed personnel carriers, mortars, jeeps and patrol boats poured in.[11] There has even been talk in Costa Rica that USAID, the CIA and the 'privatized' intelligence network, which came to light in the wake of the Contragate scandal, have been attempting to establish a 'parallel government' in Costa Rica.[12]

Of course, the remilitarization of Costa Rica was closely linked to the effort to depose the Nicaraguan Sandinistas. The US Army Corps of Engineers began to rebuild old bridges on Costa Rica's coastal highways. Many speculate that this was in order to have the roads ready for transporting US troops and war material from the US Southern Command in Panama to the Nicaraguan border in the event of an invasion of Nicaragua.[13]

In September 1987, UPAGRA held a one-year anniversary march in San José, despite a request from National Liberation's President Oscar Arias to refrain from marching. In contrast to the previous year's march, there was no violence. The *campesinos* chanted '*Frijoles, si; flores, no!*' (beans, yes; flowers, no!), a reference to the IMF's demands that Costa Rica increase non-traditional (and high-risk) agro-exports such as flowers. At a press conference, UPAGRA leader Carlos Campos asked: 'Who is running this country – the IMF or the president elected by Costa Ricans?' The protesters demanded that Costa Rica maintain self-sufficiency in basic grain production, reduce grain imports and reliance on US aid, and increase state support for small farms producing staples.[14]

It has been estimated that one out of six rural families in Costa Rica is *precarista*: in a 'precarious' position, on land to which they do not hold legal title – essentially squatting.[15] Especially in the north and in the Caribbean province of Limon, idle land on large holdings has been invaded by *precaristas*, or squatters. In the 1980s, right-wing paramilitary groups emerged as a potent force in Costa Rican politics, arming and training on remote ranches. Many of them first surfaced as private goon squads to remove *precaristas* from plantations and ranches. The groups are frequently led and trained by reactionary Civil Guards, and one is even made up entirely of Civil Guard reservists. The MCRL, the great-grandfather of these groups, maintains ties with Guatemalan and Salvadoran death squads, Cuban exile terrorist groups in Miami and international organizations such as General John K. Singlaub's ultra-right World Anti-Communist League. In the north of Costa Rica, these groups provided logistical and economic support for the Nicaraguan contras operating out of Costa Rican territory. The dynamic that exists in Guatemala and El Salvador of ostensibly 'civilian' (but actually military-linked) armed groups terrorizing the peasant population threatens to take hold in Costa Rica.[16] Although Costa Rica's militant *campesino* movement is non-violent, it serves as evidence of 'Communist subversion' against which defence is necessary and as a justification for the militarization. For instance, in June 1988, UPAGRA mobilized 3,000 *campesinos* to blockade the main roads and highways of the nation to press their demands for land grants for the landless and government farm credit for *precaristas*.[17] The Ministry of Public Security responded by accusing UPAGRA leadership of being 'extreme-leftist Marxists' receiving arms and training from Nicaragua's Sandinista government, but declined to present the evidence for reasons of 'national security'. In response UPAGRA leader Campos said: 'If there were any arms, they would have been found and the owners put in jail. Our strongest weapons are the arguments backing our position.'[18] The Ministry of Public Security is the office that controls the Civil Guards and is well-infiltrated by the MCRL and other paramilitary groups.[19]

UPAGRA and other *campesino* groups have actually filed libel suits against the conservative Costa Rican daily *La Prensa Libre* for reporting as fact the Public Security Ministry allegations that the groups are plotting a leftist guerrilla insurgency in Costa Rica.[20]

Father Elias Arias, a priest who was arrested in an occupation with one hundred *precaristas* in October 1987 said:

> Costa Rica urgently needs an integral land reform. But legislators will not carry out such a project because it contradicts their interests. Instead of helping the *campesino*, our public security officials protect the property of foreigners like John Hull. We've been criticized for breaking the law. But the real culprit is the legal system that permits such inequities. We believe in private property for all and within measure. Hungry peasants without land are a recipe for communism.[21]

John Hull is a US rancher and CIA operative with sprawling properties in northern Costa Rica, which he provided to the contras as a base camp for their attacks across the Nicaraguan border.[22]

In Limon province, on the Caribbean coast, where the *precarista* crisis is at its worst, much of the land is under the control of giant banana plantations. All three of the banana '*pulpos*' – Standard Fruit, United Brands and Del Monte – are active in Costa Rica. Violent strikes on Standard Fruit plantations in the early 1980s led to a concerted effort to finally supplant the last of the Communist-led unions with *Solidarismo*. Hailed by the Ministry of Labor and the Catholic Church as 'the Costa Rican road to labor peace', *Solidarismo* has largely succeeded in routing the last of the union strongholds in the banana industry. But one union leader told the press that '*Solidarismo* is like Alka-Seltzer: once the initial fizz is gone, the worker will be left with an empty glass and a flat taste in his mouth', and warned that the destruction of a legitimate trade union will force labour militants into 'underground struggle'.[23]

Pesticides proliferate

One major obstacle to quelling the traditional labour militancy on the Costa Rican banana plantations is the widespread use of dangerous pesticides on these plantations. The story is told that in 1979 then Costa Rican President Rodrigo Carazo sent a letter to a Standard Fruit banana complex in the Caribbean zone asking the company to reduce pesticide-tainted run-off which was destroying the coral reefs of nearby Cahuita National Park. When the park director of Cahuita approached the Standard Fruit plantation manager for his response, the manager asked him; 'Do you want to know what I think of this?' And without waiting for a reply, he tore up the president's letter.[24]

Obviously, the overuse of these pesticides threatens the health of banana workers as well as the local ecology. In 1987, suits were filed on behalf of 100 Costa Rican banana workers in Miami and Houston federal courts against

Standard Fruit, Shell Oil and Dow Chemical. The workers were among several hundred who had become sterile due to exposure to the pesticide DBCP (produced by Shell and Dow) on Standard Fruit plantations. Standard Fruit had continued to use DBCP on its Costa Rica plantations even after the Environmental Protection Agency had banned its use in the US in response to the 1977 sterilization of workers handling it at an Occidental Petroleum plant in California.[25] The suit against Standard Fruit in Miami is currently on appeal after dismissal. In March 1988, the suit against Shell and Dow in Houston was decided in favour of the sterilized banana workers, but the companies have appealed.[26]

In response to the outcry in the wake of the case, the Costa Rican government banned the sale of the so-called 'dirty dozen' dangerous pesticides: toxaphene, chlordane/heptachlor, chlordimeform, DDT, aldrin, dieldrin, endrin ('the drins'), ethylene dibromide (EDB), lindane (BHC), paraquat, pentachlorophenol, 245-T and, of course, DBCP.[27]

Nonetheless, pesticide exposure remains of grave concern to agricultural workers throughout Costa Rica. The issue was in local headlines once again in June 1988, when a 15-year-old farmworker died after working three days spreading a fertilizer–pesticide mixture on a sugar-cane field in south-west Costa Rica.[28] The Costa Rican Minister of Agriculture is investigating incidents in which entire vegetable crops have been contaminated by irrigation with pesticide-tainted water.[29]

In 1985, in an effort to explore the option of chemical-free organic farming, the University of Costa Rica initiated the Experimental Workshop for Alternative Agricultural Production (TEPROCA). Using natural predators, such as frogs, to kill insects, organic pesticides, like the bark of the *madero negro* tree, and organic fertilizers like chicken manure, TEPROCA maintains three farming co-operatives run by 27 *campesino* families in Cartago province producing a variety of food crops. Professor Margarita Bolanos, a TEPROCA leader said:

> We're the only people doing this. People are dying all the time here because of cancer. It may be because of these products – pesticides, chemical fertilizers, even hormones. That's why we're looking for alternative ways of agricultural production.[30]

Other insensitive behaviour on the part of banana companies has also contributed to worker unrest in Costa Rica's Caribbean zone. The banana '*pulpo*' United Brands (formerly UFCo) is in the process of pulling out of Costa Rica in the wake of a controversy stemming from the company's decision to convert its Costa Rican banana holdings to the more capital-intensive oil-palm production. This move, in defiance of a 50-year agreement with the Costa Rican government to keep a certain percentage of its lands in the more labour-intensive banana cultivation, resulted in a massive lay-off of United Brands banana workers in 1985.[31] United Brands made the decision to leave the country after 1,000 of the former employees launched a non-violent occupation of company land, demanding its immediate expropriation by the government.[32] Much of the land was transferred to the government, and a pledge was made to the former employees that it would become farming co-operatives for them to work. But this move has been held up by three years of complicated negotiations between United Brands and the Costa Rican government.[33] (Production of oil-palms rapidly expanded in Costa Rica in the 1980s, and many economists hailed palm-oil, which is used in margarine, cooking oil and cattle feed, as the crop of the future. This optimism has recently been dampened by reports in the US media that consumption of palm-oil leads to high cholesterol levels, which increase the risk of heart failure.)[34]

The United Brands' pull-out threatens to contribute to the economic instability that is fuelling the *precarista* crisis. Unfortunately, *precaristas* have not only occupied foreign-owned plantations, but also forested land, even wilderness areas ostensibly under government protection. With pressure from the World Bank and IMF to increase exports, the Costa Rican government is unlikely to have much patience with *precaristas* who challenge land which is producing bananas, coffee, beef, or new 'non-traditional' exports like macadamia nuts. Therefore *precaristas* are more likely to take chain saws to forested areas.

The conservation programme

Between National Parks, wildlife refuges, private reserves, Indian reserves and forest reserves, over 25 per cent of Costa Rica's national territory is officially protected wilderness – a higher percentage than any other country in the Western hemisphere. Yet Costa Rica also has the western hemisphere's fastest rate of deforestation. Costa Rican environmentalist Alexander Bonilla terms this situation Costa Rica's 'ecological contradiction'.[35]

Central America's first and most extensive programme of wilderness preservation was started in Costa Rica in the 1960s. The political impetus for the programme came from two unlikely foreigners. In 1955, Olof Wessberg, a retired Swedish military man, and his Danish wife, Karen Mogensen, settled in a remote corner of the country – the southernmost tip of the sparsely populated Nicoya Peninsula on the Pacific coast – in search of the simple life. They established a self-sufficient farm, mostly growing fruit trees, on the densely forested coast and lived a life of vegetarianism and a reverence for nature that bordered on the mystical, taking great joy in the company of monkeys and coatimundis. They also watched with growing unease as the pattern of deforestation, sweeping all of Central America, began to affect the Peninsula. Agricultural settlers from the fertile central plateau began arriving from across the gulf and clearing the forest for their crops. Then, after a few seasons of profuse cultivation, yields rapidly fell and the settlers sold out to the cattle and lumber interests. Olof and Karen feared the destruction of the habitat of the animals that they considered their friends. As Karen puts it today; 'We got in touch with the spirit of the wild animals – that really made us feel how terrible it

was that the last of the forest was going. What would happen to the animals?'
As the deforestation crept closer to the southernmost tip of the peninsula,
Wessberg, acting on a sudden late-night inspiration, wrote a letter to the Costa
Rican government and various international organizations, such as the World
Wildlife Fund, appealing for the formation of a wildlife reserve at Cabo Blanco
– the cape at the end of the peninsula, immediately to the south of their farm at
the village of Moctezuma. In 1965, after 20 trips to San José, Wessberg
succeeded in bringing about the establishment of Central America's first nature
reserve.[36]

By 1970, Wessberg's initiatives had led to the establishment of a national
parks programme. The first National Parks Directors were young and idealistic
and approved one park after another. With the aid of the US Peace Corps and
international environmental groups, the programme grew rapidly. But
meanwhile at the first nature reserve, Cabo Blanco, things were not going well.
One of the first wardens actually killed off the last ten remaining grey spider
monkeys – found nowhere else on earth – for their fat, which brought a high
price due to its supposed medicinal value. After several more trips to San José
to harass bureaucrats, Wessberg was finally granted authority to choose the
wardens for Cabo Blanco. He developed a questionnaire to sound out the
ecological sensitivity of prospective wardens. His method proved so successful
that he was offered a position with the National Parks Service to screen
wardens for other parks and reserves. He declined because he could not face the
prospect of relocating to San José.[37]

In 1975, Wessberg was sent by the National Parks Service on a voluntary
expedition to Corcovado, the rainforest which covers the Osa Peninsula,
another remote corner of the country on the Pacific Coast. Corcovado is the
only Pacific Coast rainforest anywhere in Central America (the rest are on the
Caribbean coast) and due to its inaccessibility it had remained forested and
home to incredibly profuse flora and fauna including crocodiles, tapirs and
jaguars. Wessberg's expedition into the quasi-unexplored interior of Corcovado
was to be an initial study for the establishment of a national park there. He had
promised Karen that he would return to Moctezuma by her birthday. He never
returned. He was killed in Corcovado by a blow with a machete while looking
at some monkeys playing in a tree. The killer, a young man he had just met who
had offered to go into the jungle with him, waited in Corcovado until he was
apprehended, then claimed he 'didn't know' why he did it. The authorities
concluded that he had acted alone, but to this day Karen maintains that the
investigation was inadequate. She speculates that 'maybe he was paid to do it' –
several economic concerns, both foreign and domestic, had had their eyes on
Corcovado for citrus plantations and lumber exploitation.[38]

Karen Mogensen continues to live at Moctezuma, which in recent years has
become an 'alternative' tourist spot for 'New Age' types. She is not bitter, but
sometimes appears closer to the monkeys and coatimundis than people. 'The
monkeys are so much happier than we are,' she says. 'We human beings are so
stupid. The wild animals are much more intelligent. They can live on the land
for thousands of years and leave it beautiful. We human beings come in and in

twenty years it is destroyed.' She observes which leaves the monkeys eat in the forest and has actually lived on these leaves alone for up to weeks at a time. 'I am sure that was our original food. I'm sure that one hectare of forest could produce as much food as one hectare of rice or beans. The monkeys have 300 different foods from the trees. The people come in and plant one crop – either rice or beans or maize, which you have to cook with lots of salt just to eat it. We can learn a lot from the monkeys.' She has harsher words still for the cattle interests. She recalls how Olof had responded to a 1960s headline in the daily *La Nacion*, 'Cattle is the Wealth of Costa Rica': 'It should have read: "Cattle is the Poverty of Costa Rica"!'[39] Well into her sixties Karen talks endlessly and animatedly about the activities of the monkeys and coatimundis in her forest home, and about how her perception changes at the times when she is subsisting on the monkey-food. 'You hear the music in the atmosphere and see more shades of colors. I feel stronger, I can climb trees without difficulty. Perhaps when young people take drugs, it is because they have an instinct for how their life should be, but they are only using a destructive substitute. Most people don't really live – they only exist. They don't hear, they don't see . . .'[40]

Karen has noticed a depletion in wildlife over the years that she has lived in Moctezuma. She attributes the decline in birds and tepuscuintles (a type of giant rodent) to the heavy use of pesticides on local ranches. She saw her last puma in 1983. She earns enough to survive now by renting out rooms to tourists, but is considering donating her land to a proposed Moctezuma National Park to prevent both incursions by peasant squatters and further tourism development such as the building of resorts. Karen has also noticed a decline in the length and wetness of the rainy season over the years which she has lived in Moctezuma. She attributes this to the deforestation and warns that Central America could become 'another Africa', referring to the Ethiopian famine.[41] Unfortunately, plans to develop tourist resorts on the Nicoya Peninsula are moving much faster than plans to develop a national park there. A Spanish conglomerate, which has built several resorts in Europe and the Caribbean, has already singled out a beach near Moctezuma for the construction of five massive new luxury hotels.[42]

Corcovado, where Karen's husband was murdered, is today one of the largest national parks in Central America, at 40,000 hectares. It is also one of the least accessible and has the fewest facilities for tourism – even by Costa Rican standards. (You really have to be dedicated to get to many of Costa Rica's national parks – it often entails hiking tens of kilometres over unpaved roads.) In recent years Corcovado has been threatened by the discovery of gold in the Osa Peninsula. In 1968, Puerto Jimenez, a small, sleepy port on the inland side of the peninsula, became a 'boom town' with new buildings springing up and a large transient population. Many of the newcomers were *oreros* – small-time individual gold-planners. Most *oreros* were landless peasants hoping to find a new means of economic survival by sifting the precious grains from the silt of the Osa's waterways. Few of the *oreros* could afford to travel to San José to apply for a permit, so most were forced to work illegally and many found their way into the rainforest interior of Corcovado.

As always, larger economic interests followed in the wake of the landless peasants. Large mining concessions were bought and sold in San José, but small property holders whose land was involved were rarely notified of the transactions. Under Costa Rican law the state owns all mineral rights and land can be expropriated if the owner and concession cannot agree on adequate compensation. Some local farmers on the edge of the forest have expressed hostility towards the large-scale gold operations. One local farmer told a reporter: 'It is a detriment to Costa Rica to mine gold. The waters dry up when you mine with machinery. Cattle and agriculture suffer. And mining companies destroy the forest.'[43]

By the 1980s, there were some 1,500 *oreros* working illegally in Corcovado National Park, while 3,500 legal mineral concessions surrounded the park. While the *oreros*, with their low-tech methods, were responsible for some small degree of deforestation in the park as they eked out a harsh existence in the fragile ecosystem, just outside the park boundary highly mechanized mining companies were using open-surface mining, which not only deforests on a massive scale but also destroys soil systems which took millennia to develop.[44]

More and more local farmers joined the ranks of the illegal *oreros* as the large-scale mechanized mining made agriculture in the area more and more difficult. In 1987, the Costa Rican government sponsored an International Gold Conference in San José in hopes of drawing more foreign investment to the Osa. The existence of vast deposits in the region had been revealed by a joint study conducted by the University of Costa Rica with the US Geological Survey and Los Alamos National Laboratories, the New Mexico-based federal nuclear research centre. Natural Resources Minister Alvaro Umana said to prospective investors at the conference:

> There exist areas in which you can't mine – like our national parks, for instance. If we're going to develop the industry, we must also protect the environment. However, the majority of the area is certainly open to exploration.[45]

Just as the government was encouraging the large-scale mining companies' wholesale environmental destruction it cracked down on the minimal environmental destruction of the *oreros*. On 2 March 1986, 200 Rural Guards (the rural equivalent of the Civil Guards) routed the *oreros* from Corcovado, destroying their makeshift shelters and confiscating their primitive mining equipment. For several weeks in 1987, the *oreros* camped out in the Central Park of San José, demanding compensation for their destroyed and confiscated property. The government, embarrassed, finally agreed to pay the equivalent of $3,800 to each of the displaced *oreros* (although the funds were held up by bureaucratic entanglements after the agreement).[46]

Since then yet another threat to the Osa Peninsula rainforests has emerged. In early 1989, approximately 750 US Army Corps of Engineers personnel arrived in the Osa to build roads and seven bridges which will strengthen the links between the isolated jungle peninsula and the Pan-American Highway.

Environmentalists, drawing comparisons with the massive deforestation that followed the construction of the Trans-Amazon Highway in Brazil, fear that the new roads and bridges will open the peninsula to yet more uncontrolled development and exploitation. Although the project is dubbed 'Roads For Peace', many note that heavily-armed personnel may have been sent to the Osa to establish a military presence and infrastructure in response to the instability across the border in Panama and the worsening relations between the US and that country. The eastern tip of the Osa Peninsula is less than 20 miles from the Panamanian border. The foreboding atmosphere of chaotic violence that prevails in this border area was especially intense in the prelude to the US invasion of Panama in 1989, with tensions rising between *campesino* squatters, *oreros*, Costa Rican Civil Guards, Panamanian security forces and armed Panamanian exile groups. Some Costa Ricans feel that the US forces may have been introduced to the Osa in response to this tension, just as the 'Roads For Peace' projects on the coastal highways may have been initiated in preparation for an invasion of Nicaragua.[47] The president of the Costa Rican Legislative Assembly even claimed that the US forces were in the country illegally, in violation of an article of the Costa Rican constitution which requires authorization from the Legislative Assembly for a landing of foreign troops. He demanded an investigation.[48]

This is not the first time such issues have been raised. In 1985 the USS *Iowa*, naval battleship, made a visit to Costa Rica's Caribbean port of Limon. This sparked off several days of debate in the Legislative Assembly. At issue was the *Iowa*'s cargo of 32 Tomahawk cruise missiles, which may be armed with nuclear warheads – it is Navy policy neither to confirm nor deny the presence of nuclear weaponry on any given ship. Many Costa Ricans felt that allowing the *Iowa* to dock in Limon constituted a violation of the 1967 Treaty of Tlatelolco which, attempting to establish Latin America as a nuclear free zone, bans nuclear weapons from the territory of signatory nations – including Costa Rica.[49]

The 'ecological contradiction'

The case of the Corcovado *oreros* clearly illustrates the rift between leftists and ecologists in Central America. Costa Rican leftists immediately came to the support of the *oreros* during their occupation without ever really addressing the ecological issues involved. Meanwhile, Costa Rican environmentalists applauded the ousting of the *oreros* from Corcovado without ever challenging the far more environmentally destructive mining operations of the large companies. The same short-sightedness is at work regarding the more common sources of deforestation. Environmentalists decry the destruction of forested areas by landless *campesinos* without ever addressing the need for agrarian reform. This has led many leftists to dismiss environmental concerns as 'bourgeois' and insignificant, or worse: another excuse devised by the ruling class to keep peasants off the land.

Yet despite this mutual distrust, leftists and ecologists in Central America face common enemies and threats, such as the multinational lending institutions, which both offend the nationalist and 'proletarian' sensibilities of leftists by imposing 'austerity measures' that hurt the poor majorities, and fund environmentally destructive projects such as mega-scale hydro-dams which flood rainforest. Furthermore, as the case of Olof Wessberg indicates, even in democratic Costa Rica it is almost as dangerous to be a Central American environmentalist as a Central American leftist – or at least the kind of environmentalist who is unafraid of confronting entrenched interests.

At least some *campesino* groups have – without in any way compromising their militancy – begun to recognize the value of wilderness preservation, even to their own interests. When the International Union for Conservation of Nature and Natural Resources (IUCN) held its 17th General Assembly in San José, in January 1988, it was presented with a paper entitled 'Declaration of the Campesino Organizations of the Costa Rican Atlantic Region'. While noting that 'conservation without development deprives us of the right to a dignified life,' the paper called for a 'sustainable development', which takes conservation into account. The document demanded that

> [T]hose ecologically and biologically critical wild areas (National Parks, aquifers and others) be consolidated under absolute state protection provided that the *campesinos* found within these areas are compensated, in as short a time as possible, with appropriate lands, to which they will be granted legal title.[50]

One Costa Rican ecologist making such connections is Alexander Bonilla. Formerly director of two National Parks (Santa Rosa and Poas Volcano), he is now attempting to form a Costa Rican Ecology Party, loosely modelled on the West German Greens, which he hopes will one day vie with the two major parties in the nation's elections – although for the moment the embryonic Party is impeded by a lack of economic resources. With Costa Rica militarizing, Bonilla's Ecology Party would promote principles of non-violence and adherence to the nation's tradition of 'permanent unarmed neutrality'. As Costa Rica is rolling back its 'welfare state' in response to pressure from the multinational lending institutions, Bonilla's Ecology Party would promote agrarian reform. In Bonilla's words: 'The problem with many ecology groups in Central America is that they fail to address the political and economic problems as a part of the environmental problems.'[51] For instance, as a solution to the problem of the *oreros* in Corcovado, he would support,

> [A] limited group of *oreros* exploiting gold in the park for artisan purposes using traditional techniques. Indigenous and traditional people must be incorporated into national parks systems. The large-scale corporate gold exploitation can only be allowed in the context of a rational plan for sustainable development, a strategy which will protect natural resources and contribute to the development of the region and Costa Rica. But what is happening now is exploitation which means only pain for Costa Rica. We

need very strict limitations on exploitation outside the national parks as well.[52]

As for the far more widespread problem of *precaristas*, to quote Bonilla again:

> This is a grave form of destruction and until there is a meaningful agrarian reform in this country, the problem will continue. Agrarian reform means not only land redistribution, but providing technology, finance and education for the *campesinos*. Until then, the problem will continue, especially as long as there are not enough funds for personnel to effectively guard the forest reserves from intruders. There are *precaristas* inside several Costa Rican forest reserves and wildlife refuges, including Osa Forest Reserve, which is adjacent to Corcovado National Park.

He cites lack of funds for maintaining vigilance as the single biggest weakness of the National Parks' programme. Many of the National Parks are surrounded by ranching, mining, slash-and-burn *campesino* agriculture, high-pesticide corporate agriculture (such as banana plantations), or timber exploitation on their borders. Not only do these activities outside the parks take a toll within the parks (as when the forests of Cahuita National Park on the Caribbean coast are damaged by pesticide run-off from nearby banana plantations), but without adequate vigilance these activities are actually threatening to spill over into the parks themselves. Bonilla sees the problems of funding the National Parks programme and ending *campesino* landlessness as interrelated:

> To end deforestation, we need to improve social and economic conditions within the country – better education, better distribution of land, better distribution of wealth. We need a total restructuring of the Costa Rican political system. We need to re-orient the development of the country, which means seeking alternative sources of energy, seeking a new solution to the problem of international relations, to the problem of the external debt. We need to negotiate a new deal with the IMF.[53]

For Bonilla, seeking 'a new solution to the problem of international relations' means refusing to allow Costa Rica to be manipulated in what he sees as a geo-political proxy war being waged over Central America. 'I support active neutrality,' he says. 'If we are to have peace in Central America, we have to induce the United States and the Soviet Union to keep their hands *out* of Central America – then we Central Americans can solve our own problems.'[54]

As for seeking a new deal with the IMF, as well as the World Bank and other multilateral lending organizations, Bonilla supports an innovative new plan which would link debt 'forgiveness' to preserving tropical rainforest zones in the debtor nations. The debt crisis and the deforestation crisis are already linked – therefore the solutions must be linked as well. Costa Rica is currently spending three-quarters of its export earnings just to pay the interest on its $3.7

billion debt. This demands ever-increasing reliance on the agro-export sector and keeps the economy depressed – which drives landless peasants to colonize forested areas. Without adequate funds to maintain effective vigilance of national parks and other protected areas, they are threatened by colonization. Furthermore, the protected areas themselves, if allowed to become isolated islands of forest in an otherwise completely deforested country, will be relatively futile – ecosystems cannot survive fragmentation. And if the current rate of deforestation continues, that is precisely the situation that Costa Rica will be looking at in another decade – by that time there will simply be *no* forest outside of protected areas.[55]

Bonilla believes that the tropical rainforests should be recognized as a common heritage of all humanity, essential for the ecological integrity of the entire planet – the lender nations as well as the debtor nations. Under Bonilla's vision, the debts of tropical countries such as Costa Rica would be cancelled in exchange for a commitment to redirect resources into effective rainforest protection.[56]

This concept has its roots in the 'debt-for-nature' swaps which are being arranged by the world's leading environmental groups. In the first such arrangement in 1987, Conservation International received a grant to purchase $100,000 of Bolivian debt at a discount rate in exchange for the creation of a rainforest protection zone in the Bolivian Amazon. In a second, the US-based Nature Conservancy is purchasing $5.6 million of Costa Rica's debt at a reduced $784,000 provided by world environmental groups and the Swedish government – with the freed funds to be used in support of the Costa Rican national parks programme, specifically the restoration of the Pacific Dry Forest at Santa Rosa National Park. The banks holding Costa Rica's debt are co-operating by selling the debt at a greatly reduced rate.[57] Critics maintain that these 'swaps' mainly serve to provide banks with a tax write-off on funds they would probably never collect. More importantly, they take land out of local control and into the control of foreign conservation groups, forcing governments to allocate resources according to a foreign agenda. But Bonilla maintains that the 'swap' approach can be a means of international *support* for a pre-existing *local* environmental agenda, allowing the wealthy nations of the North to take their share of responsibility for tropical forest restoration. He also sees it as perhaps the only way to avoid both the twin global disasters of economic collapse brought about by massive debt default and ecological collapse brought about by rampant tropical deforestation.[58]

Bonilla's Costa Rican Ecology Party (PEC) registered to participate in the 1986 elections, but was disqualified at the last minute on the grounds of incomplete paperwork.[59] The CEP's single biggest obstacle – lack of funding – is a familiar one for Bonilla. He had been the founder and president of the Costa Rican Association for the Preservation of Nature (ASCONA) which from its inception in 1972 grew to be one of the most respected and powerful environmental groups in Latin America – until its recent demise from lack of funds.[60]

ASCONA, which started as a volunteer organization, eventually began to accept funding from the USAID, which made full-time paid staff members a precondition for ASCONA's funding; volunteer membership in the organization subsequently declined.[61] In 1983, ASCONA took a stance against the construction of an ocean-to-ocean oil pipeline across Costa Rica. Bonilla was the author of a study published by ASCONA documenting that foreign corporations with economic interests in the construction of the pipeline were funding political campaigns in Costa Rica and that the project's ecological impact was being ignored. The pipeline was stopped (the developers built it in Panama instead), but AID cut off ASCONA's funding in the wake of the fray, after which the group existed 'in name only', says Bonilla.[62]

Another mega-scale development project for ocean-to-ocean transport through Costa Rica is the 'Dry Canal' – a four-lane highway and series of pipelines with newly-constructed port facilities at either end and 'free trade' (that is, tax-free, low-wage) zones which would (according to its promoters) make Costa Rica a new epicentre of global commerce. The massive transport system would cut across the north of the country, from north of the Caribbean banana port of Limon to north of the Nicoya Peninsula on the Pacific coast.[63] But with foreign construction firms still trying to sell the idea to the Costa Rican government, the 'Dry Canal' has already been shaken by scandal, with various promoters of this 'eventual replacement for the Panama Canal' embezzling from each other.[64]

When asked whether he would be willing to organize to fight the 'Dry Canal' should it prove necessary, Bonilla says:

> An idea is not good or bad in itself. The problem is when decisions are hidden, made by economic interests without public discourse or consideration of factors concerning the preservation of natural resources. That was the case with the oil pipeline. We will see if it will be the case with the Dry Canal.[65]

The Costa Rican government has recently taken steps to crack down on illegal exploitation of wilderness areas. In 1988, on orders of the Ministry of Natural Resources, the Rural Guards started conducting surprise checks of logging trucks in an effort to stop illegal felling. According to Natural Resources Minister Alvaro Umana, loggers often bury illegally felled lumber under a layer of agricultural goods in their truck beds, or have forged logging permits. They often work at night to fell trees in such protected areas as Corcovado National Park.[66]

In 1988 the Costa Rican Department of Forestry actually appealed to the Executive Branch to declare a national state of emergency in response to the deforestation crisis. Enacted the following year, this state of emergency grants the Forestry Department power to suspend all permits to fell trees outside tree plantations, prohibit the export of unfinished wood products, and frees funds to enforce the measures.[67] In response, the lumber industry – which contributes an estimated $20 million per year to the Costa Rican economy – has bought space in local newspapers to denounce the move.[68] Most editorials and commentaries, however, supported the move.

Costa Rica has laws prohibiting the export of exotic wildlife, but there is a thriving illegal traffic in wild creatures. This traffic is also prohibited by international agreements banning the unauthorized trade of endangered species. There are many species which are indigenous only to small areas of Costa Rica, and their habitats are frequently threatened or destroyed. In October 1987, a routine baggage inspection of an outgoing flight at Costa Rica's international airport revealed several hundred small frogs and lizards and seven big snakes. The snakes were presumably destined for laboratories; the frogs and lizards for European pet shops. The airport inspector estimated that there were 100 of the colourful little frogs, but 'it's hard to count so many active small frogs'.[69]

It is encouraging that *desarrollo sostenido* ('sustainable development') is virtually a household term among educated Costa Ricans today. One example of *desarrollo sostenido* currently very popular in Costa Rica is nature tourism, sometimes even called 'eco-tourism'. By attracting North American and European travellers (and the vital foreign exchange currency they bring with them) to the country, Costa Rica's remaining pristine rainforests, beaches and volcanoes can be made to 'pay their way' rather than being sacrificed on the altar of foreign debts. But some sceptical ecologists wonder just how profound the concept of 'sustainable development' really is. Even tourism, while certainly preferable to logging or ranching, is not without its ecological impacts. For instance, tourism is beginning to take a toll on the National Parks and nature reserves of Kenya, as vehicles trample the veldt in search of lions and cheetahs.[70] Furthermore, if the growing instability and militarism in Costa Rica continues, tourists could be scared away. Costa Rica's tourism industry is currently growing by leaps and bounds, but that could rapidly change if the right-wing paramilitary groups were to metamorphose into death squads.

Other plans to make the forests 'pay their way' and contribute to the national economy include harvesting indigenous flora and fauna, such as wild iguanas, which can then be exported as expensive delicacies to North America and Europe. This plan is contingent on idealistic Madison Avenue minds succeeding in making iguana pâté fashionable among yuppies with a taste for the exotic.[71]

Contragate's environmental connection

Rarely has the link between militarism and ecological destruction been so clear as in the recent case in which a secret airstrip linked to the contra resupply effort was discovered on land which was projected to become part of a new Costa Rican national park. The contested area is in the Santa Elena Peninsula, a finger of land stretching out into the Pacific just a few miles south of the Nicaraguan border. The fate of the Santa Elena Peninsula can be seen as a case study in the conflict between the official Costa Rican government, with its tradition of peace, neutrality and conservation, and the US-controlled 'parallel government', with many of the same players and objectives as the US 'shadow government', which ran a secret foreign policy campaign out of the basement of the White House during the 'Contragate' operations.

In 1984, with both the contras and right-wing paramilitary groups arming in the north of the nation and military aid from the US rapidly beefing up the Civil Guard, then Public Security Minister Angel Edmundo Solano publicly warned that for the first time since the disbanding of the army in 1948 a *coup d'etat* was possible in Costa Rica. Border skirmishes between Civil Guards and Sandinista troops were becoming alarmingly frequent, and Solano maintained publicly that these clashes were being instrumented by the contras and the CIA as a means of derailing Costa Rica's neutral status. Mere days after Solano's ominous warning, it was then President Luis Alberto Monge himself who staged a bloodless 'soft coup' – he fired his entire cabinet, then rehired them all again the next morning – minus Solano and his supporters.[72]

Then US Ambassador to Costa Rica Curtin Winsor, Jnr would later admit to the press that he had been trying to get Solano fired as a means of squelching investigations into the illegal contra resupply operation, in co-operation with the CIA and the White House's 'shadow government' operative Lieutenant Colonel Oliver North.[73] Such meddling prompted the directorate of Costa Rica's National Liberation party to issue a formal statement accusing Ambassador Winsor of 'unheard of' interference in domestic affairs.[74] Early the next year, Winsor was called home by Washington, apparently for insufficient subtlety, after he had called Nicaragua in a public address 'an infested piece of meat that attracts insects from all over.'[75]

Solano was replaced as Public Security Minister by Benjamin Piza – one of the original founders of the MCRL, the patriarch of Costa Rica's right-wing paramilitary movement and member of the World Anti-Communist League.[76] Piza immediately began to make arrangements with US officials for Civil Guard units to be trained by the US ultra-elite Army Special Forces division, the 'Green Berets'. A site for the training to take place was chosen – conveniently and ominously – close to the Nicaraguan border: the Santa Elena Peninsula.[77]

Much of the Santa Elena Peninsula is covered with tropical Dry Forest – some of the best examples anywhere in Central America of this vastly depleted habitat. The southern part of the peninsula includes one of Costa Rica's most popular national parks – Santa Rosa. Its popularity is due to the fact that it is an historical site as well as a magnificent Dry Forest reserve. It was at Santa Rosa that Costa Rican forces repulsed William Walker in 1857. Walker was a gringo adventurer with financial backing from Cornelius Vanderbilt, the US railroad baron who was then seeking to secure a monopoly over ocean-to-ocean transport through Nicaragua. In one of the most bizarre chapters in Central American history, Walker briefly took over Nicaragua with a private army, declared English the official language, reinstituted slavery (which the Spanish had abolished centuries earlier) and then proceeded to invade Costa Rica. The date of his defeat at Santa Rosa is a Costa Rican national holiday. It is, then, appropriate that more than a century later the Santa Elena Peninsula would once again be the scene of a drama involving gringo meddling in Central America.[78]

On the northern side of the peninsula, at a place called Murcielago, the Nicaraguan dictator Anastasio Somoza (ousted by the revolution in 1979) had had a vacation hacienda. Minister Piza had this hacienda converted into a base camp where 1,000 Costa Rican Civil Guards received training from a team of US Green Berets in counter-insurgency warfare, riot control, border patrol and jungle survival in ten two-week sessions. Minister Piza had arranged the training programme with CIA and Pentagon officials, without the knowledge or consent of his own president, Luis Monge. When Monge found out, he was reportedly furious – but by then the training was already underway and he had little choice but to accept it.[79] With training from Israeli and West German advisors as well as the Green Berets, Murcielago gave birth to an elite Civil Guard unit known as the Relampago Battalion (Lightning Battalion). This Battalion would go on to train, in turn, other Civil Guard units, thereby accelerating the militarization of Costa Rica's police force.[80]

The Civil Guards were still technically a police, not a military force, and US training of foreign police forces had been barred by the Carter-era human rights campaign. Just as the Murcielago training programme had been conceived, the US Congress approved the Foreign Aid Authorization Bill of 1985, which made an exception in the law to allow for training of police personnel in 'a country which has a long-standing democratic tradition, does not have standing armed forces and does not engage in a consistent pattern of gross violation of internationally recognized human rights.' Costa Rica is the only country on earth that fits that description.[81]

Many Costa Ricans apparently feared that the gradual transformation of the Civil Guard into a full-fledged military force is a threat to their country's human rights record. In the 1986 presidential elections, Costa Rica broke its long-time tradition of always electing the party that was out of power. Oscar Arias ran on a peace platform and was elected even though he, like Monge before him, was the National Liberation candidate. Arias' Social Christian opponent Rafael Angel Calderon had favoured the remilitarization of Costa Rica. (He is also the son of the Rafael Calderon Guardia who led the conservative government that was overthrown in the revolution of 1948 by the forces that subsequently disbanded the army and formed the National Liberation Party.)[82]

The Arias election was even more significant in light of the fact that his opponent Calderon had made a deal with US intelligence officials whereby he would receive their financial support in return for allowing Costa Rica to be used as a base for the contras after his election. The 'Contragate' private spy network secretly funnelled funds from private right-wing organizations in the US into the Calderon campaign.[83]

President Arias began making plans to convert the entire Santa Elena Peninsula into a national park, expanding on the already-existing Santa Rosa National Park. The new park, to be called Guanacaste (after the name of the province and Costa Rica's national tree) would actually extend inland from the peninsula to include two volcanoes of the central mountain chain. The logic behind this is to protect both of the habitats of migratory animals, which seasonally alternate between the Pacific Dry Forest of the peninsula and the cooler highland forest of the volcano slopes.[84]

In September 1986, however, (the same month that the Civil Guards had a chance to try out their new 'riot-control' techniques by roughing up *campesino* protestors in the streets of San José), it was revealed that yet another clandestine operation was underway on the Santa Elena Peninsula. In response to reports from locals that large military transport aircraft were flying into a remote spot on the peninsula at unusual hours, Guardsmen raided a clandestine 6,500-foot airstrip only ten kilometres away from the Green Beret facility at Murcielago. Lieutenant-Colonel Oliver North, and Lewis Tambs, then US ambassador to Costa Rica, would later testify to the Tower Commission (the US government-appointed team which made the initial investigative report into the 'Contragate' scandal) that they immediately decided to threaten Arias with a cut-off of USAID assistance to Costa Rica if he made the discovery of the airstrip public. Undaunted, Arias held a press conference at which he announced the existence of the airstrip, and its closure.[85]

With the Contragate scandal just breaking in Washington, journalists on the Central America beat flocked to the story of the secret airstrip. In the subsequent investigations it was revealed that the land on which the strip was built was controlled by Udall Research, one of the Panama-incorporated 'dummy corporations' which had been established by Richard Secord, Albert Hakim and other members of the so-called 'Project Democracy' – the private spy network established by Colonel North to keep the contras alive, in violation of US law. Udall Research had secured the co-operation of the local Civil Guard commander to build the airstrip under the guise of a 'tourism project'.[86] The local commander had pressured Santa Rosa park officials to let workers and equipment pass through the park on their way to the airstrip, and had even loaned several Guardsmen under his command to the construction effort. Investigations would later reveal that the Guardsmen had been setting forest fires, dining on endangered turtle eggs and deer meat, and on at least one occasion killed a tapir for sport.[87]

In 1987, the local commander was indicted by a Costa Rican court for his role in the project. Also indicted was ex-Public Security Minister Benjamin Piza (who had been replaced by a more moderate figure when Arias took power). Piza had instructed the local commander to co-operate with Udall Research and CIA Costa Rica Station Chief Joe Fernandez (alias 'Tomas Castillo') in building the airstrip. Piza did *not*, however, advise the Costa Rican cabinet or Civil Aviation Authority, which approves the construction of airfields.[88] Lewis Tambs shortly resigned as US Ambassador to Costa Rica as rumours mounted that the Embassy had pressured then President Monge into approving construction of the clandestine strip by threatening an aid cut-off (or promising an aid increase as a 'reward').

Monge would later tell reporters that he had agreed to the airstrip scheme after early 1985 visits from 'officials from Washington' who warned of an imminent Sandinista 'invasion' of Costa Rica and claimed that the strip would be used to airlift in military supplies to defend the Costa Rican border.[89] In June 1988, CIA Costa Rica Station Chief Joe Fernandez would be indicted by US independent counsel Lawrence Walsh for overseeing construction of the strip.[90] Speculation that Monge had been 'bribed' with increased US aid into supporting the airstrip and other contra operations in northern Costa Rica is supported by the fact that in 1986, the year Arias took office, the inflow to Costa Rica from USAID (an agency with known ties to the CIA) dropped from $180 to $120 million; in 1987 the sum dropped to $85 million.[91]

At a time when US law prohibited aid to the contras, the strip had served as a stop-over for the contra's air supply organized by Project Democracy, a trans-shipment point for weapons and cocaine (which became a major source of funding after Congress barred further aid to the right-wing guerrillas).[92] With all these heads rolling, Arias decided to postpone the creation of Guanacaste National Park because he did not want to appear as if he had been 'pressured' into claiming Udall's land.[93]

Local environmentalists feared that the Guanacaste project might be a lost cause; but almost a year after the discovery of the airstrip, in summer 1987, President Arias announced the annexation of the Udall land into Santa Rosa National Park. Negotiations for the purchase were underway with the land's actual owner – a group of US investors from whom Udall had been renting the land.[94] In addition to absorbing the airstrip into Santa Rosa National Park, Arias also declared a large forested area west of the peninsula across the Pan-American highway the Guanacaste Protected Zone, which includes the two highland volcanoes. The entire contiguous protected area may someday become Guanacaste National Park, if all goes well.[95] The largest area of the peninsula which remains unprotected is the Somoza hacienda-turned-Civil Guard training base at Murcielago, which seems to have become a permanent military school. Although the Green Berets may no longer be there, the Civil Guard units they trained are currently training other Civil Guard units.[96]

Despite the survival of the military school, environmentalists and peace activists alike see the Santa Elena Peninsula as a victory. Vast areas of the Honduran border with Nicaragua have become militarized zones, where contra supply strips were frequently in close proximity to training camps established by elite US forces such as the Green Berets. Just a few years ago (1986) the Santa Elena Peninsula seemed in danger of developing in a similar direction. Now it seems destined to become the site of so far the most extensive project for ecological recovery of tropical Dry Forest.

In the meantime, five key Contragate figures – Oliver North, Major General Richard Secord, former National Security Advisor John Poindexter, former US Ambassador to Costa Rica Lewis Tambs, and former CIA Costa Rica Station chief Joe Fernandez – have been barred from returning to Costa Rica after a special investigative commission of the Legislative Assembly concluded that the contra resupply network they had established doubled as a cocaine-smuggling operation.[97]

Since nearly all of the Santa Elena Peninsula has been turned into pasture at one time or another, the task of the Guanacaste project is primarily recovery rather than preservation. Its aim is to return the peninsula to the thriving Dry Forest that greeted the Spaniards when they first arrived nearly 500 years ago. Funding is coming in from international organizations such as the Nature Conservancy and the World Wildlife Fund (WWF). A major source of WWF's funding for the project is the Exxon corporation[98] (which strikes many as ironic, considering how much Exxon has done to degrade local ecology in Central America and elsewhere). Funds from Costa Rica's recent 'debt swap' are also earmarked for Guanacaste.[99] The restoration project's mastermind, University of Pennsylvania tropical biologist Daniel H. Janzen, is hoping to secure enough money to buy out local ranchers who still maintain pastureland in the protected areas. Dry Forest is far easier to reclaim than rainforest. According to Janzen, once a few trees have been replanted in the pasture, natural seed-carrying agents such as wind and animals like bats, monkeys and tepuscuintles will do the rest – in only ten years new Dry Forest can encroach several hundred metres into an old pasture.[100]

Janzen also envisions a park which can incorporate the local human population. Former ranch workers can be employed managing and reforesting the park, or staffing its educational and research facilities after receiving professional training.[101] He also believes that a degree of concentrated and more efficient cattle raising can be accommodated and that, if it is done correctly, cattle and horses can even play a role in seed-distribution in areas being restored. In contrast to most ecologists in the region, Janzen was vocally critical of the Burger King boycott, maintaining that it would economically hurt Costa Rica, a country in his view already committed to preserving its forests. Some sceptics speculate that Janzen's position was motivated by a political need to remain on good terms with his Guanacaste neighbours – almost all of whom are cattle ranchers.[102]

Yet, despite the victory on the Santa Elena Peninsula, the threat that militarism represents to Costa Rica's wild areas and national parks still remains. In August 1989, a naturalist and two North American tourists were hiking in the Cloud Forest of Braulio Carrillo National Park when they stumbled on a detachment of Civil Guards and ten US Green Berets dressed in camouflage with paint on their faces. The soldiers summarily escorted the hikers from the area. One of the tourists would later tell a reporter; 'We didn't understand why Americans in camouflage uniforms were throwing us out of a national park in Costa Rica. We thought it was outrageous.'[103] After the story hit the press, it was revealed that the Green Berets were in Costa Rica at the request of the Public Security Ministry to train Civil Guards in anti-narcotics tactics. The Braulio Carrillo park director told the press that the soldiers did not have permission to be there, pointing out that Costa Rican law prohibits weapons and military manoeuvres in national parks.[104]

Whither sustainable development?

If the Santa Elena Peninsula clearly demonstrates the link between militarism and ecological destruction, there is another place in Costa Rica which clearly demonstrates the link between peace and ecological preservation. This is Monteverde, a pristine Cloud Forest straddling the continental divide in the north of Costa Rica's central mountain chain. In the early 1950s, after Costa Rica disbanded its armed forces, a group of Quakers from the United States decided to settle in the country so that they could pay taxes and contribute to a local economy without their efforts supporting a war machine. After searching the country for the most suitable location, they settled on 3,000 acres on the slopes of Monteverde. Two thousand acres of the mountainside were divided among them for farmland while the 1,000 acres at the peak were left as a watershed and forest reserve. Their rural community soon grew prosperous producing cheese – Monteverde cheese is today consumed throughout Costa Rica, and the administration of the cheese factory has been turned over to Costa Ricans.[105]

In the 1970s, the San José-based Tropical Science Center began buying forest adjacent to the Quakers' watershed reserve, expanding it into a 10,000 acre refuge which is still growing today and is the most popular eco-tourism attraction in Costa Rica. The Monteverde Cloud Forest reserve is by far the best place in Central America to see quetzals, and as such it attracts bird-watchers from all over the world. In addition to providing a habitat for an amazing diversity of species, (some of which, like the intensely bright golden toads, exist nowhere on earth outside a small area of the reserve), the forest also protects much of the watershed for Costa Rica's largest hydroelectric dam, Arenal.[106]

Yet Monteverde is in danger of becoming an ecologically isolated island. The forest area currently protected covers only 16 square miles. The surrounding forest, an area of 150 square miles, is increasingly threatened by the encroachment of land speculation and cattle interests. The Tropical Science Center, with the assistance of the Nature Conservancy and the WWF, is attempting to raise funds to buy as much of the surrounding forest as possible and annex it to the reserve. They are also trying to convince the Costa Rican government that an Arenal National Park should be created which would be contiguous with the Monteverde reserve.[107]

A lesser problem is actually presented by eco-tourism, itself created as a strategy to save tropical wilderness by making it 'pay for itself' with a functioning niche in the modern economy. Monteverde now receives around 20,000 visitors annually, and a recent Tropical Science Center study found that many animals migrate away from the most-visited areas during the high tourist season – an obvious problem in an area that people visit to see wildlife. Some Monteverde residents view the supplanting of an agricultural economy with a tourism economy sceptically, and the issue of whether or not to have the road leading up the mountainside paved has been an item of debate in the community. Most residents, however, are optimistic that, if efforts to arrest deforestation and insensitive forms of tourism prevail, their community will continue to provide an example of sustainable, ecologically sound development.[108]

The Quakers also maintain a Peace Center in San José – the only one in Central America. It serves as a meeting place and focal point for activists working to support Costa Rica's threatened policy of 'unarmed neutrality'.[109]

While in other Central American nations, school children are marched around in formation carrying mock rifles in preparation for future military service, in Costa Rica the government-supported National Youth Movement enlists student volunteers in the protection and maintenance of national parks during school vacations. As a result, these young people frequently become advocates of tropical forest conservation.[110] Pepe Figueres, the aging patriarch of the 1948 revolution who originally disbanded the military, recently said in response to his nation's resurgent militarism: 'Somebody seems to be losing sight of Costa Rica as a small, unarmed neutral democracy, a heritage which Costa Rica offers the entire world as a political asset.'[111]

Such fears seemed to lose their urgency under the presidency of National Liberation's Oscar Arias, who won the 1987 Nobel Peace Prize for authoring the Central America peace plan and actually took certain measures to reverse Costa Rica's trend towards remilitarization, such as abolishing military-style uniforms and ranks from the Civil Guard.[112]

But with the February 1990 presidential race, Costa Rica returned to its tradition of electing the opposition, and after three consecutive attempts Rafael Angel Calderon – son of Rafael Calderon Guardia and godson of Anastasio Somoza – finally won the presidency. By all accounts, it was a 'dirty' campaign, with Calderon and his National Liberation opponent accusing each other of complicity in drug trafficking. In fact, Calderon's campaign manager was none other than Roger Ailes, the mastermind of the 'negative' campaign that helped George Bush win the White House in 1988 by playing on racist fears and portraying his opponent as soft on the (by strong implication, black) criminal element. But Calderon also strongly appealed to the populist sentiments of the peasants, accusing National Liberation (perhaps with some justification) of concentrating on dabbling in external politics, such as promoting the Arias peace plan, while ignoring worsening domestic conditions.[113]

When Calderon ran against Arias in the 1986 election, he had openly favoured abandoning Costa Rica's 'unarmed neutrality'.[114] In the 1990 race this was no longer a part of his rhetoric, but as I write it remains to be seen whether Costa Rica's remilitarization will enter another period of escalation under Calderon. It also remains to be seen whether Calderon will make any moves to challenge the 'parallel state' that critics in National Liberation have accused the US of building in Costa Rica. This 'parallel state' comprises private organizations funded by the USAID which duplicate public organizations of the Costa Rican state ranging from agro-export investment agencies to schools for the study of tropical biology.[115]

Although it certainly took a back seat to drug-related corruption, environmental concerns were also an issue in the campaign. A stir was created, when ASCONA, recently reformed as an environmental watchdog under mostly new leadership, claimed to have received numerous phone calls from unidentified residents of Puerto Jimenez on the Osa Peninsula who said that Calderon's Social Christian collaborators in the area had promised local *oreros* a free hand to extract gold in forested areas, even within Corovado National Park. Calderon denied the charges, accusing National Liberation of 'trying to hide the failure of the [Arias] administration to find a solution to the socioeconomic problems which confront the communities surrounding the Park.' But the charges were supported by the Corcovado park director, who said; 'We've identified these people as Calderon people, and they were telling the goldminers that Corcovado National Park would be given to them.'[116]

Nonetheless, the Calderon camp may well be voicing some legitimate objections to the Arias administration's approach to problems in the Osa, and peasant colonization of Costa Rican rainforest in general. As Calderon's chief ecological advisor, Mario Boza, told the press, '. . . in any place so humid and rainy, neither agriculture nor cattle-raising is a viable activity . . . the ground is so acidic and poor that agricultural activities are good for a year or so, and then you have to move on. The fact that the IDA [Costa Rica's Agricultural Development Agency] hands out parcels to the *campesinos* there does not solve anything – they will never leave their misery.'[117] Yet it seems unlikely that Calderon's administration will provide a workable solution if it means stepping on the toes of agro-export industries.

With US-backed forces consolidating power in Nicaragua, the key justification for Costa Rica's remilitarization has lost most of its potency. But with drug-related violence and corruption escalating in Costa Rica, to crackdown on smugglers may be poised to fill the propaganda void left by the defeat of the Sandinistas.[118] The circle of militarists, which revolves around groups such as the MCRL and pervades the Civil Guard and the daily newspapers, may have been dealt a blow by the ripples from the 'Contragate' scandal that prompted Benjamin Piza's indictment, but not a mortal one. The fact that many of the paramilitary groups maintain links with the death squads of El Salvador and Guatemala, and that many of them have participated in the forced ejection of *precaristas* from private ranches, points to the ominous possibility that the burgeoning *campesino* movement may be a future target for violence.[119]

The world environmental movement sees Costa Rica as something akin to a living laboratory. Cutting-edge concepts for saving tropical forest, such as eco-tourism and debt swaps, are being implemented in Costa Rica as a possible model for other developing countries with threatened tropical forests. The world environmental movement injects an unusually large amount of money into Costa Rica proportional to its size. This is because the Costa Rican government has demonstrated its concern to save the nation's wild areas and remarkable diversity of species; and the tradition of stable democracy provides a political climate conducive to experimental strategies. Yet this political climate is now threatened, and the experimental strategies may prove fruitless without meaningful agrarian reform.

While environmentalists in North America and Europe frequently take a keen interest in Costa Rica, activists in the movement against US political and military intervention in Central America frequently overlook Costa Rica, their attention drawn by the repression of revolutionary movements in El Salvador and Guatemala, or the drama of the struggle in Nicaragua. But these activists may also have an important role to play in support of peace and social justice in Costa Rica as well – namely injecting some political content and grassroots sensitivity into the world environmental movement's agenda for that nation.

13. Panama: Canal Trouble Again

On numerous occasions the United States has used military intervention to secure, build and protect an inter-oceanic canal through Central America. Today that canal is the base for the Pentagon's Southern Command, bristling with elite military facilities. Now, however, the threat to the canal is less a military one than an ecological one – Panama's rampant deforestation, which is depleting the watersheds that feed the canal's massive locks. Deforestation is therefore contributing to the potentiality of yet a second canal being blasted through Panama – which would almost certainly mean more ecological destruction, as well as posing a threat to the autonomy of the nation's Kuna and Choco Indian peoples.

Panama is not one of the traditional 'Five Republics of Central America' (Guatemala, El Salvador, Honduras, Nicaragua and Costa Rica). In the era of Spanish colonialism, Central America was administered from Guatemala while Panama was under the administration of Lima, along with the Andes region of mainland South America. After independence, Panama became part of Colombia. Yet, in the twentieth century Panama has been drawn into the politics and turmoil of Central America by virtue of sharing the narrow isthmus with the traditional Central American nations – an isthmus which is the ideal site for an inter-oceanic canal. At the turn of the century United States and European interests abandoned the idea of building a canal through Nicaragua, their original choice, because General José Santos Zelaya's nationalist regime was demanding control of the canal zone. Efforts to depose Zelaya by sponsoring conservative rebellions in Nicaragua (aided by US mercenaries) ultimately succeeded – but too late. By the time Zelaya was finally ousted, intrigues in Panama had already paid off. When the Colombian government had proved to be no more co-operative than did the Nicaraguan in granting the US control of the canal zone, the US began to promote and arm a movement for Panamanian 'independence'. In 1903, US troops and warships prevented Colombian troops from reaching the Panamanian isthmus; the state of Panama was born and the canal was built. President Theodore Roosevelt proudly proclaimed; 'I took the canal zone and let Congress debate.'[1]

Actually, Panama remained an official protectorate of the United States until 1936. The US policed Panama City and the Caribbean port of Colon, and claimed the right to appropriate lands and water at will. Before the canal could be built, a modicum of stability had to be reached, not only between the US and Colombia, but also between the US and the French company which had been bidding with Colombia's government to build a canal through Panama. The French company was paid $40 million for its rights, Colombia was paid $25 million as compensation, while Panama, safely under virtual US military occupation, received a mere $10 million. In 'exchange', Panama 'agreed' to grant the United States the Canal Zone *for ever*. The US eradicated malaria from the zone, to facilitate the construction of the canal, but by the time it was completed in 1914, its construction had nonetheless claimed thousands of lives – mostly of black labourers imported from the Caribbean islands. Racial discrimination pervaded the construction effort: canal zone authorities classified US workers 'gold' and everyone else 'silver', with the 'golds' receiving much higher salaries. Service windows in Canal Zone post offices were marked 'gold' and 'silver'.[2]

Even today, Panama's only currency is the US dollar. President William Taft declared in 1912:

> The day is not far distant when three Stars and Stripes at three equidistant points will mark our territory: one at the North Pole, another at the Panama Canal, and a third at the South Pole. The whole hemisphere will be ours in fact, as by virtue of our superiority of race, it already is ours morally.' [And that US foreign policy] may well be made to include active intervention to secure for our . . . capitalists profitable investment.[3]

This legacy led, of course, to an anti-US backlash. In 1959, riots erupted on the streets of Panama City as the US authorities refused to accede to demands that the Panamanian flag be raised over the Canal Zone alongside that of the US. President Eisenhower finally conceded on the issue; but riots erupted again in 1964 as US residents of the Zone attempted to renege on Eisenhower's agreement and tore a Panamanian flag to shreds. Panamanians responded by rising in anger and tearing down the fence separating Panama City from the Zone. The US Marines were called out as fighting and looting spread across the country. Over the next three days, 18 Panamanians were killed.[4] The Panamanian national guard played no part in these disturbances – they were confined to their barracks under command of the President. The Panamanian presidency was traditionally under the control of the nation's conservative oligarchy – the so-called 'Twenty Families'.

By the late 1960s, nationalist elements in the military were growing increasingly impatient with the presidency's perceived subservience to the United States. During the reshuffling following the riots, one Dr Arnulfo Arias assumed the presidency. He was a member of one of the leading families of the oligarchy, had served as Panama's ambassador to Mussolini's Italy, and had met with Hitler in 1937. In the early months of World War II he had been ousted from the first of his three presidential terms by a *coup d'etat*, organized with US connivance, because of his pro-Fascist leanings. He was ousted from a second term after the war when the military decided that it could no longer tolerate his notion of Panamanian nationalism – which was to insist that the nation's English-speaking Caribbean blacks be sterilized and racially segregated from the Spanish-speaking majority; and that Chinese businessmen sell out to native-born Panamanians. His third term, beginning after the riots, yet again ended with his ousting by a military *coup d'etat* – but this time the *coup* was to prove to be a turning point in Panamanian history.[5]

In 1968, the charismatic populist and nationalist General Omar Torrijos seized power and put President Arias on a plane to Miami. Torrijos was a man with a mission. He was determined to wrest control of the Canal Zone from the *norteamericanos*. Despite his dictatorial rule, he soon became a hero to many of Panama's workers and peasants, who saw him as the defender of their interests against those of the United States and the local oligarchy.[6]

In 1977, after years of negotiations, the Carter–Torrijos Treaty was signed, mandating a return of the Canal Zone to Panamanian control by the year 2000.[7]

In 1981, General Torrijos was killed in an air accident. Many Panamanians questioned exactly how 'accidental' the crash had been, and rumours of CIA involvement abounded. After a period of reshuffling, Torrijos' chief of intelligence – General Manuel Noriega – assumed power.[8]

Noriega had a history of both brutality and corruption. As intelligence chief under Torrijos he had been assigned with the task of snuffing dissent by the same ugly methods common to military regimes everywhere. Such methods ill-became Torrijos' populist image, so Noriega was granted a high degree of autonomy in this area. *Campesino* leaders were among those murdered on the probable orders of Noriega's secret police, known (like its far bloodier counterpart in Guatemala) as G-2.[9]

The canal and the free trade zone in the Caribbean port of Colon attracted international capital, and in the 1970s Panama City became a centre for world banking, encouraged by the institution of policies of strict secrecy rivalled only by those of Geneva. This made Panama a magnet for intrigue and dirty deals. In the late 1970s and early 1980s, a cocaine economy exploded throughout Latin America. The coca leaves are grown by exploited Indian labour in the mountains of Bolivia and Peru, then smuggled to Colombia to be chemically refined into the addictive white powder in the secret laboratories of the increasingly powerful 'cartels'. The powder is then filtered through a network of contacts and secret airstrips throughout Central America and the Caribbean to US ports of entry such as Miami, New York, Houston, Brownsville and San Francisco. Profits from this lucrative market have to be 'laundered' before they can be reinvested in real estate, aircraft or weapons – that is, circuited through so many labyrinthine channels of financial trickery that the money becomes untraceable. After his rise to power, Noriega, who had been wheeling and dealing with drug and arms smugglers extensively as G-2 chief, allowed Panama City to become a key laundering centre for the cartels.[10]

As US military installations established in the Canal Zone were gradually turned over to Panamanian control, in accordance with the 1977 Carter–Torrijos Treaty, right-wing politicians in Washington DC grew more and more uneasy – especially as it became increasingly evident that Noriega had no loyalty to the United States, or, for that matter, anybody else. He was playing ball with every conceivable power-broker in the region, from the CIA and the contras to the Colombian cocaine cartels to Cuba's Fidel Castro and Nicaragua's Sandinistas to leftist guerrillas in El Salvador and Colombia to Israeli intelligence. Although Noriega had been on the CIA payroll for several years[11] and had proved a valuable asset in the CIA's covert war against Nicaragua,[12] it was obvious that in the final reckoning he was a wild card who could not be depended on. His involvement in drug smuggling served as a useful propaganda device for the US campaign to unseat him, which was launched in 1986 and finally culminated in the US invasion of Panama in the final weeks of 1989. But the fact that the Reagan Administration's 'shadow network' had been more than willing to use drug profits as a means of funding the contras indicates that the real motives behind the invasion had little to do with fighting a 'war on drugs'. Indeed, the new government installed by the US has nearly as many links to dirty drug money as had the Noriega regime.[13] The invasion, which according to some sources claimed 4,000 Panamanian lives,[14] was a decisive means of re-establishing US control over the Canal Zone – treaty or no.

The wrong enemy

In addition to its strategic geopolitical importance for the United States' globe-spanning military empire, the canal is the centre of Panama's internal politics and the lifeblood of its developing economy. Around 11,000 ships pass through its three locks every year, providing $340 million in direct revenues and 17 per cent of the national income. The US military's Southern Command, based in the Canal Zone, is defended at all times by a minimum of 10,000 troops. All three branches of the US armed forces have barracks in the Canal Zone and it also frequently hosts US National Guard reserve units. In addition, the US runs military training schools in the Canal Zone, such as the Small Wars Operations and Research Directorate (SWORD), which serves as a think-tank and planning centre for US-sponsored military operations throughout Central America.[15] Air bases in the Canal Zone are the launching point for US surveillance flights over Nicaragua. When the Sandinistas were in power the US forces in the Canal Zone were poised to attack Nicaragua by air, land and sea at the command from Washington.[16] Despite the fact that Panama is part of the Latin American Nuclear Free Zone, established by the 1967 Treaty of Tlatelolco, the US bases a number of strategic communications and electronics facilities in the Zone, making it a key link in the Pentagon's nuclear weapons command and control structure. The Zone also serves as a testing ground for aircraft, small missiles and nuclear artillery.[17]

Yet, for all the money and energy expended on militarily defending the Canal from perceived enemies, it appears that the most serious and immediate threat comes not from an external hostile power but from the ecological degradation of Panama. In the words of one journalist; 'like the human race that created it, the Canal is dependent on fresh water for its survival.'[18] About 50 million gallons of fresh water are needed to lift each ship through the series of locks over Panama's mountainous backbone. The water for these gravity-powered aquatic elevators comes from two huge man-made reservoirs – Lake Gatun to the west of the Canal and Lake Madden to the east. Lake Madden is also important as a source of hydroelectricity. Today the watershed that feeds these two lakes is being rapidly depleted.[19]

In March 1987, a sudden power blackout hit parts of Panama City, the nation's capital, and Colon, its second city. The source of the problem was traced to sedimentation in Lake Madden – soil had washed down the steep slopes surrounding the reservoir, displacing water needed for hydroelectric generation. The source of this sedimentation is erosion and the source of the erosion is uncontrolled deforestation. The problem threatens not only Panama's electricity grid, but also the continued operation of the Canal.[20]

While the Canal itself is administered by the joint US–Panamanian Panama Canal Commission, the responsibility for maintaining the watersheds essential for the Canal's functioning is the Panamanian government's. Only two months before the blackout, a Panamanian government panel headed by the nation's most outspoken environmentalist, Dr Stanley Heckadon Moreno, had revealed chilling findings that launched a controversy over the canal's future. At the time of writing, 70 per cent of the watershed had been deforested according to Heckadon. He warned that at the current deforestation rate of up to 2,000 acres per year, siltation will drastically reduce the Canal's cargo limits, and therefore revenues, by the year 2000. This is the year that, under the Carter–Torrijos Treaty of 1977, Panama is scheduled to take over the Canal from the US.[21]

Heckadon's findings have been confirmed by other studies. Ecologist Frank Wadsworth, former director of the US Institute of Tropical Forestry, says that 'only forests can restore and stabilize the capacity of the Canal', and predicts that if deforestation continues, by 1999 the Canal will be 'a worthless ditch, a colossal monument to resource mismanagement'.[22]

The causes of deforestation in Panama are the same as in the traditional Central American nations – logging, peasant colonization and cattle ranching. As elsewhere, these three activities are part of a single linear process by which the forests are converted to cheap pasture land. And, as elsewhere, the whole process is fuelled by an agro-export economy chasing its own tail to service a foreign debt. At $3.8 billion, Panama's foreign debt is one of the highest in the world, proportionate to the country's small population.[23] However, while it is cattle ranching and United Brands' banana operations that dominate much of the country's land, the Canal is a vital pillar of Panama's economy. In addition to collecting tolls on all traffic through the Canal, the international trade attracted by the Canal has spawned the secondary economy of international banking in Panama City and the Free Trade Zones in Colon, where foreign industries operate with immunity from taxation and minimum wage laws.

Conservation programmes

Having recognized deforestation as a threat to the Canal, the Panamanian government has taken very serious measures to arrest it. In 1987, the Panamanian Institute of Renewable Natural Resources (INRENARE) enacted Forestry Law 13, which prohibits cutting any virgin forest and any secondary growth more than five years old. In recent years, the rate of deforestation has been decreasing. Says Dr Heckadon: 'Ten years ago, Panamanians didn't care about forests. Pastures equalled progress. Today, most realize that [deforestation] generates poverty rather than progress.'[24]

But the problem continues and much more needs to be done. Heckadon has been urging the bi-national Panama Canal Commission to raise the Canal's current toll rate of $1.83 per ton by a few cents which would be used for watershed management. He claims that this measure would contribute $7.5 million per year to the struggle against deforestation. The Commission has resisted this idea, claiming that its rates make the Canal competitive and that any increase would lose Canal customers to pipelines, rail and other forms of land transport. The Panamanian INRENARE has, however, responded to the watershed crisis by creating two national parks – Soberania in 1980 and Chagres in 1984. Together they cover almost half of the Canal's watershed area.[25]

With the formation of Soberania, Chagres and Parque Amistad (Friendship Park) on the Costa Rican border adjacent to the Costa Rican national park of the same name, Panama's national parks programme has, over the 1980s, progressed from virtually nil to one of the most extensive on the Central American isthmus. There is also Darien National Park, which covers an enormous expanse of rainforest along the Colombian border and has been designated a United Nations Biosphere Reserve.[26] Yet, all these parks are threatened. Soberania and Chagres were formed only in response to extensive deforestation already underway; to simply declare the areas national parks has not meant an immediate halt to the destruction.[27] The recently completed oil pipeline and parallel highway, which run from Chiriqui on the Pacific to Bocas del Toro on the Caribbean, cut dangerously close to Amistad and for the first time have opened the area to logging, peasant colonization and cattle ranching.[28] The rainforest of Darien is sometimes referred to as the 'Darien Gap' because it is the one missing piece in the Pan-American Highway that runs from Alaska to Chile. The gap in the highway has never been filled because the Darien rainforest serves as a natural barrier to prevent a particular cattle disease spreading north from South America into Central and North America. If this missing section of the highway is ever completed, it will clearly be bad news for the Darien rainforest. Darien National Park stretches from coast to coast and lies right in the Pan-American highway's path.[29]

There is another large protected area along the Caribbean coast in the province of San Blas known as Kuna Yala – which, in the language of the region's Kuna Indians, means 'Kuna Earth'.[30] The Kuna were never conquered by either the Spanish or the Panamanians due to the inaccessibility of their remote rainforest homeland. In 1925, in response to escalating incursions by banana plantations and Panamanian government forces into their territory, the Kunas revolted. After several days of fighting, the Panamanian government conceded to a peace agreement which granted the Kuna almost complete autonomy over their territory in return for a commitment of allegiance to Panama. In the ensuing decades, Panama honoured its agreement; the Kuna language, culture, lifestyle and subsistence economy remained intact.[31] In the

1970s, however, offshoot roads from the Pan-American Highway began snaking towards Kuna territory, bringing with them peasant colonists and the cattle ranchers that inevitably follow in their wake. Prior to this, much of the Kuna lands could be reached only by boat or small plane. Fearing the destruction of the rainforest upon which their traditional lifestyle depends, Kuna leaders began organizing in Panama City to have a forest reserve declared along the border of the Kuna's autonomous reservation, which stretches more than 100 miles along Panama's Caribbean coast. The forest reserve would serve as a buffer zone to help keep outside economic interests out of the Kuna reservation. The result is Kuna Yala.[32] Managed and patrolled by trained Kuna tribesmen, the reserve has already meant higher levels of rainfall and reduced soil erosion by halting and reversing deforestation.[33] The Kuna are attempting to obtain United Nations recognition of Kuna Yala as a Biosphere Reserve.[34]

Prospects look less bright for the Kuna who inhabit the Bayano region, in Panama's interior, to the south of Kuna Yala. Forced to resettle after their traditional lands were flooded by the construction of the Bayano Hydroelectric Complex in 1976, their new lands have since been subject to incursions by the timber and cattle interests. Negotiations for the demarcation of their new territory had been going well under the government of General Torrijos, but were relegated to the back burner after his death in 1981.[35]

Evidence that Noriega was considerably less popular among the Kuna than Torrijos had been was also demonstrated by the small skirmishes which had been breaking out between Indians and Panamanian troops patrolling San Blas archipelago in the final months of the Noriega regime, with many Kuna leaders charging that government-recognized Kuna chiefs had become cronies of the Noriega regime and were eroding Kuna autonomy.[36] Many Kuna also had little love for Noriega's anti-US propaganda, as the 1925 autonomy agreement had actually been worked out with US mediation on board a US warship introduced into the archipelago in response to the unrest.[37] Torrijos had also had strong anti-US tendencies, but was perceived as having greater sensitivity to Indian autonomy.

There are also Kuna and Choco Indians in Darien, and their culture will be seriously threatened if work is ever resumed on completing 'the Gap' in the Pan-American Highway.[38]

On the other side of Panama, in Chiriqui province not far from the Costa Rican border, a huge development scheme threatens the culture of the Guaymi Indians. The scheme, known as the Cerro Colorado Copper Project, is financed by the World Bank and IDB and calls for the construction of a hyrdroelectric dam to power copper mines, pipelines and smelters. The Cerro Colorado project would result in the relocation of several entire Guaymi communities and would seriously degrade the environment of their traditional homeland.[39]

A new canal?

Another project which seems to be on the horizon is the construction of a second canal through Panama to either replace or complement the old one. This new canal would be at sea-level and would therefore require no water-consuming locks. Panama is engaging in ongoing discussions to secure funding for this project with the US and with Japan, a major user of the present Canal.[40]

For all its importance to world trade, the Panama Canal is outdated – it is too small to accommodate modern supertankers. When this first became apparent in the 1960s, the US Atomic Energy Commission (AEC) proposed using nuclear explosives to blast a second, larger canal through Panama – a so-called 'Panatomic Canal'. The site chosen for the project was Panama's lowest point – which also happened to be one of the Central American isthmus' last remaining vast stretches of virgin tropical rainforest: the Darien.[41]

The AEC actually undertook a feasibility study for the project in the Darien rainforest between 1965 and 1970, contracting a huge staff of biologists and geologists to conjecture the effects of radioactive fallout on the local environment and population. Drilling rigs were hoisted into position by helicopters in order to obtain rock samples from thousands of feet underground. Ecologists studied the diet of the local fauna and the agricultural methods of the local Kuna and Choco Indian population to trace the possible paths of radioactive isotopes through the food chain. In 1970, however, the AEC conceded that 'prospective host country opposition to the nuclear-canal excavation is probably . . . greater than estimated in 1964' when the idea was first hatched. Rather than risk a replay of the anti-US riots that shook Panama in 1959 and 1964, the AEC dropped the project. But other mega-scale development projects which threaten rainforest and Indian land would emerge in the ensuing decades.[42]

While the World Bank and the IDB continue to fund projects such as Cerro Colorado, which are extremely damaging to Panama's forests, USAID has recently moved away from such projects, recognizing the threat to the Canal. AID has even gone so far as to invest $40 million in reforestation and watershed management projects, provide funds to strengthen INRENARE's staff and technical expertise and assist in such ecologically sound projects as the Kuna Yala reserve.[43]

Sadly, however, AID underwent this profound shift of policy in Panama just before the Reagan Administration launched its drive to destabilize the Panamanian government of General Noriega. In retaliation for the imposition of US economic sanctions against Panama as a tool to force Noriega out of power, in December 1987 the General ordered AID out of the country.[44]

The World Bank and IDB – which are multinational, rather than exclusively US controlled – remain in Panama, funding environmental destruction, while USAID, the only major foreign lending agency in Panama which had switched to a more environmentally sound policy, was given two weeks to close up shop. By January 1988, AID's Panama City office was closed and all its Panama workers were back in the US.[45]

Of course, AID returned to Panama following the US invasion of December 1989. After prolonged economic warfare aimed at destabilizing the Noriega regime, including a limited trade embargo, a suspension of the monthly $6.5 million payments for the use of the Canal and a freezing of Panamanian assets in US banks, Panama's economy needs to be rebuilt. Like the more drastic economic warfare that was levelled against Nicaragua, this programme was aimed at increasing common citizens' level of daily privation and suffering, as a means of sparking internal unrest. To a degree, the strategy succeeded. Such measures, of course, devolve most harshly on the poor. By 1989, poor families in Panama City were being fed by church organizations, if they were lucky enough to be eating at all. Yet Noriega proved amazingly tenacious, claiming a certain degree of support among the poor by playing the card of Panamanian nationalism, claiming for himself the Torrijos legacy.[46]

To the extent that Noriega gained support by portraying himself as a heroic figure standing up to US imperialism, the economic sabotage actually backfired. The new government installed by the US invasion is made up of precisely the kind of people that, in his efforts to rally Panama's poor, Noreiga was able to effectively use as convenient enemies – oligarchs, technocrats and representatives of the 'Twenty Families'. The new President, Guillermo Endara, a wealthy corporate attorney, has represented companies run by big-time cocaine-smuggler Carlos Eleta, who has been indicted on drug-related charges in the US. Endara is also a political protégé of the late Arnulfo Arias, the conservative populist who was ousted by Torrijos in 1968. Vice President Guillermo 'Billy' Ford is a co-founder and part-owner of the Miami-based Dadeland bank, which has been named in federal court testimony in the US as a depository for money laundered by Colombia's Medellin Cartel.[47]

Therefore, it seems unlikely that the new regime will seriously affect Panama's drug-smuggling financial infrastructure. It also seems unlikely that the envisioned economic future built around high finance and an eventual second canal will be altered, or that any meaningful land redistribution will be considered.

The 1989 invasion of Panama provoked little outcry of protest in the US, even from anti-intervention activists. Obviously, few leftists saw any idealistic revolutionary movement to rally around in Noriega's corrupt, if still vaguely populist, regime. But certainly, the invasion claimed hundreds and perhaps thousands of Panamanian lives, in addition to those of 23 US servicemen, and represents an effort to reconsolidate firm US control over Central America and the Caribbean. It is, perhaps, significant that the invasion of Panama was launched just as a popular revolution in Romania was overturning the last of the East European bloc's Communist dictatorships. Now that the Soviet threat seems to be dissolving, US elites need a new scapegoat to justify their longstanding tradition of what, in a less euphemistic age, was termed 'gunboat diplomacy'. The so-called 'war on drugs' may fit the bill.

The rainforests of Darien and Kuna Yala, which protect sloths, jaguars, tapirs and giant ant-eaters, are a meeting place for the distinct biological realms of South and Central America. As industrial civilization encroaches on to

Indian land, they are also becoming a meeting place for two distinct world-views with widely disparate ways of perceiving the human race's relationship to the Earth. Norman Myers of the National Wildlife Federation recently wrote:

> The Kuna tell the story of an occasion in 1980, when Panama's former strongman, General Omar Torrijos, visited a number of Indian leaders at an island village. Torrijos, having flown in by helicopter over the rainforest, asked, 'Why do you Kuna need so much land? You don't do anything with it. And if anyone else cuts down so much as a single tree, you shout and scream.' To which Kuna leader Rafael Harris responded, 'Suppose I go to Panama City and stand in front of a pharmacy, and because I need medicine but have none of your money, I pick up a rock and break the window. You will take me away and put me in your jail. For me, the forest is my pharmacy. If I have sores on my legs, I go to the forest and get the medicine I need to cure them. We Kuna need the forest, and we use it and take much from it. But we take only what we need, without having to destroy everything as your people do.'[48]

If the geopolitical needs of globe-spanning financial and military empires are insensitive to and destructive of local sovereignty and self-determination, they are equally insensitive to and destructive of ecological integrity. Geopolitical needs resulted in both the creation of Panama in 1903 and the invasion of Panama in 1989. In the near future they may lead to the sacrifice of more Panamanian rainforest for new canals, mines and hydro-dams. Both those who seek to end interventionist military excesses and those who seek to save rainforests and other wild areas would do well to keep watch on US – and Japanese and European – finance, intrigues and meddling in Panama.

14. Belize: The Forgotten Corner

The least populous and least developed of the Central American nations has thus far been spared both unchecked ecological destruction and unrestrained militarism. But recent development proposals indicate there may be changes for Belize in the near future.

In 1934, British author Aldous Huxley, travelling through Central America and the Caribbean, wrote:

> If the world had any ends British Honduras would certainly be one of them. It is not on the way from anywhere to anywhere else. It has no strategic value. It is all but uninhabited, and when Prohibition is abolished, the last of its profitable enterprises – the re-export of alcohol by rum-runners, who use Belize as their base of operations – will have gone the way of its commerce in logwood, mahogany and chicle. Why then do we bother to keep this strange little fragment of the Empire?[1]

Fifty years later, little seems to have changed. British Honduras was renamed Belize upon being granted nominal independence from the Crown in 1981, but the sparsely populated country is still almost entirely reliant upon British imports and has very little economic infrastructure of its own. Indeed, since the abolition of prohibition, cultivation and export of another illicit substance – marijuana – has become the most lucrative activity in Belize. This has recently prompted the US Drug Enforcement Administration to begin a programme of aerial herbicide spraying over the Belizean rainforests. Aerial spraying of the herbicide paraquat was a political issue in Belize's first post-independence presidential elections. In 1983, Belize discontinued the spraying programme due to concern that the chemical was killing honey-bees and other economically beneficial life forms. The United States has since pressured Belize to resume spraying with supposedly safer herbicides, such as glyphosate.[2] Some of these flights have continued across the border into non-marijuana-producing Guatemala, where the actual target of the sprayings may be leftist guerrillas. (See chapter 8.)

In the colonial era, the British attempted to carve out territory in the Spanish-dominated Central American isthmus by populating its Caribbean coast with rebellious slaves and other blacks from Jamaica and other British-controlled Caribbean islands. In Nicaragua and Honduras, the British armed the Miskito Indians and set them up as a puppet 'kingdom' to resist Spanish control of their region. At the turn of the century, Britain came under pressure from the US to cede its ambiguous claims to Central American territory, in order to facilitate political negotiations with the region's governments for building an inter-oceanic canal. Belize was the one possession Britain did not relinquish. Neighbouring Guatemala agreed to recognize Britain's claim in return for the building of roads which would grant Guatemala access to Belizean ports on the Caribbean. The roads were never built and for generations thereafter Guatemala's military leaders would threaten to take over Belize.[3]

Belize is today the most ethnically heterogeneous nation in Central America, as well as by far the least populous at 40,000. It is made up primarily of English-speaking black Creoles with a large and growing minority of Spanish-speaking *mestizos* from Guatemala and smaller minorities such as Mennonite immigrants who work collective farms, and Garifuna and Maya Indian groups, which are barred by law from owning land but communally work the land on government 'reservations' with more or less undisturbed autonomy.[4]

Guatemalan maps still show Belize as a department of Guatemala, although since Belizean independence and Guatemala's return to ostensibly civilian government in the 1980s, relations between the two countries have been normalized. Britain, however, still maintains 1,500 troops in Belize – just in case. Belize's own armed forces number only 700, by far the smallest in Central America.[5]

The agribusiness threat

It was also in the 1980s that the US began eyeing this forgotten corner of Central America as a suitable site for building military bases and investing in agribusiness. Many recognize this type of development as a threat to the lush tropical forests which still cover much of Belizean territory. The eastern extent of the once-vast tropical rainforest that starts in southern Mexico (where it has been decimated) and stretches across Guatemala's northern department of El Peten still covers much of Belize. The first significant threat that US investment posed to the Belizean rainforest was in 1985 when Minute Maid, a subsidiary of Coca Cola, purchased nearly 200,000 undeveloped acres in Belize. In such a small country, this is a significant proportion of the national territory. Attracted by Belize's guaranteed duty-free access to US markets (a provision of the 1983 Caribbean Basin Initiative economic development plan), Coca Cola purchased the land from a developer, who is probably the wealthiest man in Belize and who owned nearly 13 per cent of the entire country before the sale to Coca Cola. He sold the holdings because the Belizean government had balked at plans to finance a huge wood-burning power plant he had hoped to construct on the land. Coca Cola moved in with plans to turn the forest into citrus plantations to serve the ever-expanding US market for frozen orange juice.[6] As Coca Cola announced its purchase the London *Financial Times* commented: 'A vast forest with 90-foot high trees and some of the finest wildlife in Central America is about to become the focus of an exciting agribusiness venture.'[7] However, Coca Cola was also to run into problems on the land. To begin with the plan to turn rainforest into citrus plantations was immediately assailed by Friends of the Earth (UK) and even the Belize Audubon Society (whose entire budget is less than the salary of the executive director of the Sierra Club).[8]

Another problem surfaced when Coca Cola attempted to procure political 'risk insurance' against nationalization, without which no corporate operations abroad dare proceed in this unstable era. The federally-funded US agency, which usually provides such insurance, the Overseas Private Investment Corporation (OPIC), gave in to lobbying by domestic economic interests that stood to lose from Coca Cola's Belize operation: the Florida citrus industry. OPIC denied insurance to Coca Cola.[9]

In 1988 Coca Cola announced that it was placing the Belize operation on indefinite hold and began to break up its enormous land holding. Thousands of acres were turned over to the Belize Audubon Society and the Belizean government for a national park, and Coca Cola even provided a $50,000 grant to get the park started. A smaller area was turned over to the Belizean government for distribution to small farmers. Another area will remain in Coca Cola's hands, but the company seems in no rush to clear it and has pledged it will not do so without an environmental impact report. The largest area will, however, simply be sold to the highest bidder regardless of development intentions. This area is home for many species nearing extinction, such as jaguars, tapirs and howler monkeys.[10]

Coca Cola is obviously sensitive about the public relations image of its Central American operations. The company came under attack by environmentalists for its purchase of the Belize holdings just as it was recovering its image from leftist criticism, and even a boycott, in response to both substantial investments in South Africa and union-busting at its Guatemalan bottling plant – in which labour organizers at the plant were kidnapped, tortured and killed by death-squads.[11] Environmentalists are hoping that continued public pressure could induce Coca Cola to hold over sale of the Belize holdings for a bidder with ecologically sound development plans. Hopefully, Belize will be able to develop the economic infrastructure it so desperately needs to provide basic human services to its small, poor population without succumbing to deforestation, ecological degradation, agro-export dependency and the consequent militarization that prevail elsewhere in Central America.

Mixed signals

The signals since Belize achieved independence have been mixed. The first president following independence in 1981 was George Price of the leftist People's United Party, who had been leading the movement against Belize's colonial status since his party emerged in the 1950s with the support of the leftist regime of Jacobo Arbenz across the border in Guatemala. Price's leftist and nationalist sympathies notwithstanding, in 1983 several US oil companies began exploratory drilling in Belize.[12] The following year's elections brought to power Manuel Esquivel of the conservative opposition United Democratic

Party. The nation subsequently moved closer the US which accounts for nearly half of Belize's imports and exports (with the UK accounting for most of the other half). That year, the US Drug Enforcement Administration rated Belize as the world's fourth largest exporter of marijuana.[13] In 1986, the IMF proclaimed as successful the austerity programme it had imposed on Belize with the co-operation of the Esquivel government, which, like most such schemes, called for slashing public spending and increasing exports. Citrus, banana and sugar production expanded, while gold was discovered in the country's small and mostly forested range, the Maya Mountains. Sugar had been the nation's fastest growing export crop when the world sugar market collapsed, prompting further expansion of the citrus industry.[14] (Another explanation for the balance tilting in favour of citrus may have been related to the fact the former US Ambassador to Belize, Malcolm Barnaby, went to work for Coca Cola in Houston, Texas after leaving the foreign service.)[15] Charging Esquivel with being 'soft' on the drug trade, the US began proposing military aid and even installations in Belize to crack down on marijuana growing.[16] Progress on these plans has at least slowed down since the 1989 elections, which returned George Price and the People's United Party to power. Sugar remains the top (legal) agro-export, but manufacturing is the fastest growing industry and tourism is also growing faster than any agro-export.[17] Apart from the remains of a Mayan pyramid, natural beauty is what Belize has to offer the tourist. With aid from international environmental groups, Belize has established a few wildlife sanctuaries, including Cockscomb Basin Jaguar Preserve, the world's only refuge managed specifically for the jaguar.[18]

Neither wholesale deforestation nor unbridled militarism have yet taken hold in Belize. Pressure from international environmentalists may have played a significant role in the substantial modification of Coca Cola's plans for the nation. A watchful eye from international environmentalists and anti-intervention activists alike could help ensure that ecological sanity and self-determination will prevail as Belize develops its economy – and, if need be, help call a halt to such potential near-future disasters as irresponsible agro-export development, continued herbicide spraying and anti-marijuana militarization.

Part 3:
Towards a Solution

15. Ecological Preservation as a Pillar of Peace

As we have seen, ecological destruction has been a major underlying cause of strife in Central America, and the militarization which has been introduced in response to the strife has itself become a form of ecological destruction. It is, therefore, logical that plans to bring peace to the region include plans for ecological restoration.

Central America's environmentalists have been developing an ecological component to the regional Peace Plan which was drawn up by Costa Rica's President Oscar Arias and signed by the four other regional presidents in the summer of 1987 at Esquipulas, Guatemala. In May 1987, a few months prior to the Esquipulas summit, the region's environmentalists held their own summit at Managua, Nicaragua. Entitled the First Central American Conference on Environmental Action, it was organized by the Nicaraguan Association of Biologists and Ecologists (ABEN) and the US-based Environmental Project on Central America (EPOCA), and attended by representatives from environmental groups in every Central American nation – including a delegation of Kuna Indians from Panama. Many facets of Central America's ecological crisis were addressed: pesticide abuse; agro-export dependency; deforestation; militarism; scorched-earth warfare; defoliant spraying. The Conference also marked the inception of a new organization dedicated to international co-operation on Central America's environmental problems: the Regional Network of Environmental Non-governmental Organizations for Sustainable Development in Central America (REDES).[1]

Many of the Conference organizers are promoting a programme that would simultaneously foster peace and ecological protection by establishing parks straddling international borders in forests and watersheds which are shared by neighbouring nations. The programme is known as the International System of Protected Areas for Peace, and its Spanish acronym of SI-A-PAZ translates as 'Yes to Peace'. Four areas are being proposed for incorporation into SI-A-PAZ. One of them has already been designated as an international park – La Amistad, on the Costa Rica–Panama border. Another, to be called El Trifinio, would expand on El Salvador's tiny Montecristo Cloud Forest reserve to incorporate both Honduran and Guatemalan territory in the area where the three nations meet. This three-nation park would be quite close to Esquipulas, the Guatemalan town where the Arias Peace Plan was approved, which is also an important religious centre and annually receives thousands of pilgrims from all over Central America. In November 1987, the vice presidents of the three nations declared the common border area a reserve.[2]

The proposed international parks bordering on Nicaragua have been experiencing the most difficulty, due to the militarization and warfare along both of Nicaragua's borders. One of the proposed parks would expand on the Bosawas reserve in the Nicaraguan Miskito rainforest to incorporate Honduran territory across the Coco River. The creation of this international park faces serious obstacles because the area is both extremely remote and a militarized zone.[3]

The SI-A-PAZ organizers have been concentrating most of their efforts on the creation of an international park in the basin of the San Juan River, which forms the eastern part of the Nicaragua–Costa Rica border. This area of dense rainforest has recently been a hotbed of contra activity. Much of the rainforest in this region is virtually unexplored and uninhabited; more than half its species have never been taxonomically identified. However, only a few months after Nicaragua's President Daniel Ortega publicly expressed his support for the creation of an international park in the San Juan basin, Nicaragua's State Forestry Corporation signed a contract with a Costa Rican lumber concern granting logging rights to 3,200 square kilometres of forest surrounding the San Juan for the next twenty years, with the Nicaraguan government receiving $25 million per year. This accounted for more than half the rainforest on the Nicaraguan side of the San Juan basin, or 2.5 per cent of Nicaragua's territory. Both ABEN and Costa Rican environmentalists, as well as SI-A-PAZ organizers in the US, immediately began protesting against the contract. ABEN maintained that the contract violated the new Sandinista Nicaraguan constitution, which states, 'defense of our natural resources is an inalienable right and sovereign duty of the Nicaraguan people'. Speculating on the motives behind the lumber deal, Costa Rica's English-language weekly the *Tico Times* wrote:

> [M]ost Nicaraguans believe that the Sandinista government would never have signed a contract so similar to those signed in past years by strongman Anastasio Somoza (wherein he sold most of Nicaragua's primary forests to international corporations at rates very favorable to them) if it were not being pressured by the drawn-out war with the contras. The Sandinistas desperately need foreign exchange to import goods, and $25 million per year would help a great deal, they say. In addition, critics of the project note the Sandinistas may hope deforestation of the southern jungles will destroy cover for rebels operating in that area.[4]

The motives of the Costa Rican lumber concern in moving to Nicaraguan territory are obvious – it wishes to continue its lucrative activity, and Costa Rica is rapidly running out of forest which can be legally felled. Despite the concern's pledge to exploit the Nicaraguan forest in a 'rational and technical fashion' and assertion that 'what happened in Costa Rica won't happen here',

Costa Rican ecologist Alexander Bonilla warned that the firm would undoubtedly 'clear-cut Nicaragua, just as they have done in Costa Rica'.[5]

When ABEN gave an extensive interview opposing the lumber deal to the Nicaraguan daily *Nuevo Diario*, it was axed by government censors. ABEN responded with a campaign to pressure for its publication, and the censorship actually resulted in widespread coverage of the issue in the Nicaraguan news media, including a front-page story in *Neuvo Diario*. In a response in the government daily *Barricada*, the State Forestry Corporation stated that the deal would not be cancelled and would not be environmentally destructive. But ABEN continued to organize against the deal, besieging government workers in the natural resource sector with questions about it at their public appearances. In support of ABEN's efforts, US-based groups such as EPOCA launched a letter-writing campaign to President Ortega.[6]

The continued pressure paid off. In June 1987, President Ortega cancelled the lumber deal.[7] ABEN continued to press for official protection for the San Juan basin, and in February 1988, the Nicaraguan and Costa Rican natural resource ministers met in the Costa Rican capital to sign a statement of intent to create an international peace park across their common border.[8]

The entire park could total as much as 6,000 square kilometres, especially if Costa Rica goes ahead with plans to create a 'corridor' of protected rainforest connecting Barra de Colorado National Wildlife Reserve (which borders Nicaragua and would be incorporated into the international park) with Tortuguero National Park, about 25 kilometres to the south. However, the proposed 'corridor' is threatened by another massive lumber concession, recently granted by the Costa Rican government to a domestic firm which exports hardwood products to US retailers such as Sears. The huge area opened to exploitation under the concession borders on both Barra de Colorado and Tortuguero. This is, of course, the subject of vehement protest by Costa Rican environmentalists.[9]

In the meantime, a new threat to the San Juan basin Peace Park has emerged in Nicaragua. With the ascendance to power of the US-backed government of Violeta de Chamorro in Nicaragua, the contras are being compelled to lay down their arms and an effort is being made to find a niche for the former troops of the mercenary army in Nicaraguan society. One plan proposed by contra leaders is the establishment of a semi-autonomous 'development pole' which would be administered and policed by the former contras in the rainforests of the San Juan basin. This would certainly mean increased population pressure and commercial exploitation of the remote region – and, with easy access to smuggled weapons from across the Costa Rican border, possibly increased militarization as well. Top contra military commander Israel Galeano ('Commander Franklin'), a proponent of the plan, has already expressed his interest in entering the timber industry. Others speculate that the contras who are eyeing the San Juan basin as a 'development pole' may be looking forward to the eventual construction of an inter-oceanic canal through the zone, which would put them in a position to profit from the secondary development and industrialization the new canal would stimulate.[10]

ABEN and Nicaraguan environmentalist Jaime Incer are also considering a peace park in the Gulf of Fonseca, which would be jointly administered by Nicaragua, Honduras and El Salvador – three nations whose past relations have often been stormy.[11] Among the Gulf of Fonseca islands being considered for incorporation into the park is Tiger Island, a Honduran territory which is the site of a high-tech electronic eavesdropping post run by the Pentagon's highly secretive National Security Agency.[12] In 1986, the pro-Sandinista Nicaraguan daily *Nuevo Diario* ran a story picked up from the Soviet paper *Izvestia* alleging that Tiger Island is the site of Pentagon experiments in meteorological warfare, aimed at creating droughts in Nicaragua both to sabotage agriculture and allow the contras freer movement through the remote northern areas of Nicaragua, which are normally impassable during the rainy season.[13]

Although the Arias Peace Plan has been moving along somewhat unsteadily, SI-A-PAZ organizers are optimistic about the growing realization in Central America that any peace plan must take ecology into account and that creating a lasting peace for the region will mean creating a new model of development. Says Costa Rican ecologist Alexander Bonilla: 'The unity of social and ecological crises with the war needs to be investigated more. Vietnam is an obvious example of this theme. Millions of refugees, deforestation, health problems, sanitary conditions in the cities, especially Managua and San Salvador – all of these problems are linked to the war.'[14]

In a 1988 interview, Nicaragua's Sandinista National Parks Director Lorenzo Cardenal stated that ecology activists have a responsibility to be peace activists as well.

> The scientists and people in general who are concerned with the environmental crisis in Central America have an important role to play: to stop the war – now. Precisely because peace is the first prerequisite which needs to be achieved in order to develop a rational plan for conservation of the region's natural resources.

On the aims of SI-A-PAZ, Lorenzo Cardenal says:

> We have a dual objective of promoting both scientific study and environmental protection, and demilitarization and international co-operation. However, we have the problem that many environmental groups in the U.S.A. are very conservative and when we state the problem in these terms, they are afraid that we are trying to 'politicize' science. There *is* no apolitical science – much less the science of conservation in Central America![15]

One environmental group in the US that represents a radical break with the tendency that Cardenal describes is EPOCA, a project of the San Francisco-based Earth Island Institute. (Earth Island Institute is also the parent organization of Rainforest Action Network, the group which spearheaded the

Burger King boycott.) EPOCA is working to link the environmental movement and anti-intervention movement in the US. Many US environmental groups active against tropical deforestation in Central America have remained silent on the issue of US military intervention in the region. Conversely, the peace groups opposing aid to the contras and the Salvadoran military have rarely participated in campaigns against deforestation, such as the boycott of fast-food chains that serve Central American beef. EPOCA is attempting to bridge the gap.

In the 1980s, the US and European anti-intervention movement organized volunteer brigades to go to Nicaragua, to pick coffee and build schools and clinics as a gesture of solidarity and an effort to reverse some of the destruction wrought by the contras. They drew inspiration from historical precedents such as the Venceremos Brigade, which went to Cuba to help harvest sugar cane in the 1960s, and the Abraham Lincoln Brigade which went to Spain to help fight the fascists in the 1930s. EPOCA organize volunteer brigades to assist in Nicaraguan reforestation programmes and sea turtle conservation projects.[16]

Another solidarity group with an ecological consciousness is the Boston-based Bikes Not Bombs. Ramshackle buses, decrepit roads and scarce petroleum – all results of the war and economic sabotage – have turned Nicaragua's transportation system (both within and between the cities) into an inefficient, chaotic, unreliable and basically unworkable nightmare. Bikes Not Bombs donated thousands of bicycles to the Sandinista government's health workers and teachers, 'enabling them,' in the group's words, 'to spend more time fighting illiteracy and disease and less time walking or waiting for overcrowded buses that often never come.' Bikes Not Bombs also periodically sends mechanics to those Nicaraguan towns that have received their donated bicycles, to ensure that they are still in working order. The group also runs a workshop in Managua where bicycle skills are shared, and has also worked with the Sandinista government towards the development of an alternative transportation policy which maximizes self-sufficiency and ecological sanity.[17] Bicycles now account for 50 per cent of all vehicular traffic on the streets of Leon, another Nicaraguan city where Bikes Not Bombs has established a workshop – up from less than ten per cent just five years ago. Bikes Not Bombs' Nicaragua workshops are now mostly run collectively by the Organization of Revolutionary Disabled, made up of veterans of the contra war. This response to Nicaragua's transport crisis is especially appropriate given that the Central American nations must spend scarce foreign exchange to import 100 per cent of their petroleum, and can afford only the highly polluting variety which has not been unleaded. Smog is already a serious problem in Managua, Guatemala City and Tegucigalpa.[18]

The emergence of groups such as EPOCA and Bikes Not Bombs points the way towards a new brand of politics that merges concerns of ecology and peace – a brand of politics that could be most effective in the United States and among other world powers where so much of the war and ecological plunder in the developing world is masterminded.

16. Overpopulation as a Propaganda Device

Population is one of the most important issues on which environmentalists and leftists tend to differ, and this difference is one of the primary reasons why the two groups frequently view each other with mutual suspicion – or worse – in Central America. To what degree is population pressure a root cause of the conflict and ecological degradation in Central America? Too often, leftists tend to simply dismiss issues of ecological degradation, while environmentalists have looked exclusively to sheer human numbers and failed to explore the link between ecological degradation and social injustice.

When the ruling elites of the 'First World' – the leaders of the massive corporations, banks and governments of the industrialized North – address ecological issues at all (as they are increasingly forced to do by the ever more frequent droughts, floods and other signs of ecological breakdown), their first response is almost invariably to promote population control. Almost never do they speak of a need for radical restructuring of land use patterns. As a consequence, much of the Latin American left is almost as puritanical about birth control as the Catholic Church. Leftists widely view family planning as a neo-colonialist conspiracy, or even inherently genocidal.

The views of many Latin American leftists are eloquently summed up by the Uruguayan writer Eduardo Galeano in his classic book *Open Veins of Latin America* (1973). It is worth quoting at length:

> In the eye of this hurricane 120 million children are stirring. Latin America's population grows as does no other; it has more than tripled in half a century. One child dies of disease or hunger every minute, but in the year 2000 there will be 650 million Latin Americans, half of whom will be under fifteen: a time bomb. Among the 280 million Latin Americans of today, 50 million are unemployed or underemployed and about 100 million are illiterate; half of them live in crowded, unhealthy slums. Latin America's three largest markets – Argentina, Brazil and Mexico – together consume less than France or West Germany, although their combined population considerably exceeds that of any European country. In proportion to population, Latin America today produces less food than it did before World War II . . .
>
> New factories are built in the privileged poles of development . . . but less and less labor is needed. The system did not foresee this small headache, this

surplus of people. And the people keep reproducing. They make love with enthusiasm and without precaution. Ever more people are left beside the road, without work in the countryside, where the *latifundios* [plantations] reign with their vast extensions of idle land, without work in the city where the machine is king. The system vomits people. United States missionaries sow pills, diaphragms, intrauterine devices, condoms, and marked calendars, but reap children. Latin American children obstinately continue to get born, claiming their natural right to a place in the sun in these magnificent lands which could give to all what is now denied to almost all . . .

The human murder by poverty in Latin America is secret; every year, without making a sound, three Hiroshima bombs explode over communities which have become accustomed to suffering with clenched teeth. This systematic violence is not apparent but is real and constantly increasing: its holocausts are not made known in the sensational press but in Food and Agriculture Organization statistics . . . [T]he Imperium is worried: unable to multiply the dinner, it does what it can to suppress the diners. 'Fight poverty, kill a beggar!' some genius of black humor scrawled on a wall in La Paz. What do the heirs of Malthus propose but to kill all the beggars-to-be before they are born? Robert McNamara, the [then] World Bank president who was chairman of Ford and then Secretary of Defense, has called the population explosion the greatest obstacle to progress in Latin America; the World Bank, he says, will give priority in its loans to countries that implement birth control plans. McNamara notes with regret that the brains of the poor do 25 percent less thinking, and the World Bank technocrats (who have already been born) set computers humming to produce labyrinthine abracadabras on the advantages of not being born. 'If,' one of the Bank's documents assures us, 'a developing country with an average per capita income of $150 to $200 a year succeeds in reducing its fertility by 50 percent in a period of twenty-five years, at the end of thirty years its per capita income will be higher by at least 40 percent than the level it would have otherwise achieved, and twice as high after sixty years.' Lyndon B. Johnson's remark has become famous: 'Let us act on the fact that $5 invested in population control is worth $100 invested in economic growth'. Dwight D. Eisenhower prophesized that if the world's inhabitants continued multiplying at the same rate, not only would the danger of revolution be increased, but there would also be a lowering of living standards for all people, including his own.

The United States is more concerned than any other country with spreading and imposing family planning in the farthest outposts. Not only the government, but the Rockefeller and Ford foundations as well, have nightmares about millions of children advancing like locusts over the horizon from the Third World. Plato and Aristotle considered the question before Malthus and McNamara; in our day this global offensive plays a well-defined role. Its aim is to justify the very unequal income distribution between countries and social classes, to convince the poor that poverty is the result of the children they don't avoid having, and to dam the rebellious advance of the masses. While intrauterine devices compete with bombs and machine-guns salvos to arrest the growth of the Vietnamese population, in Latin America it is more hygienic and effective to kill *guerrilleros* in the womb than in the mountains or the streets. Various U.S. missionaries have sterilized thousands of women in Amazonia, although this is the least populated habitable zone on our planet. Most Latin American countries have no real surplus of people; on the contrary, they have too few. Brazil has thirty-eight times fewer inhabitants per square mile than Belgium, Paraguay has forty-nine times fewer than England, Peru has thirty-two times fewer than Japan. Haiti and El Salvador, the human antheaps of Latin America, have lower population densities than Italy. The pretexts invoked are an insult to the intelligence; the real intentions anger us. No less than half the territory of Bolivia, Brazil, Chile, Ecuador, Paraguay, and Venezuela has no inhabitants at all . . .[1]

We must admit that Galeano fails to acknowledge that most of the uninhabited areas of Bolivia, Brazil, Ecuador, Paraguay and Venezuela are covered with rainforest and had best *remain* uninhabited. They cannot sustain large populations and they are not appropriate for land use patterns other than those of the indigenous peoples who have adapted their culture to the rainforest over a period of millennia. Yet the survival intact of these areas is essential for maintaining a healthy ecological balance which *can* support larger populations in the fertile highland areas upon which they border. In fact, since these words were written these areas have *become* inhabited. Landless peasants have migrated there as they have been pushed from the fertile areas by the advent of centralized, mechanized, capital-intensive export agribusiness. The result has been a disaster which, by now, has gone beyond the borders of these countries and become global. However, the culprit in this disaster is not an over-abundance of Latin American babies. The expansion of the kind of agriculture, which is pushing the peasants into the rainforest, has been encouraged and funded by the ruling elites of the Western world (termed by Galeano 'the Imperium') – the technocrats of such organizations as the World Bank.

The accuracy of Galeano's portrayal of 'the Imperium' is betrayed by its own words. In 1970, US Assistant Secretary of State for Population, Philander Claxton, presented a paper to the Latin American Conference in which he tied the impending political instability to the population explosion.

Insurrection . . . is one of the grave dangers threatening public safety and stability . . . Waves of people who pressed into slums are beginning to realize their power to make trouble . . . These people are easy prey . . . for all the irresponsible demagogues . . . and for the agents of world revolution . . . The fundamental cause of this threat to public safety and stability . . . is the excessively rapid growth of population.[2]

But why have these 'waves of people' been 'pressed into slums'? In Central

America, each introduction of agro-export industry – coffee, cotton, beef – has resulted in a wave of peasant landlessness, and consequent 'pauperization'. This process began with the Spanish conquest and the introduction of indigo for export to Spain. Over the centuries it has transformed the pre-Hispanic economy of ecologically-sound, self-sufficient, communal agriculture into an economy of abject dependency, which breeds urban shantytowns and needs to import wheat from the United States. The growth of Central America's population has not been steady. In the first century after the Spanish conquest the population decreased by nearly seven-eighths as the Indians fell to diseases, introduced by the Spanish, to which they had no immunities; as water was diverted from Indian communities by Spanish aqueducts; as Indians were enslaved on plantations or exported to wealthier regions of the Spanish empire to be worked to death in gold and silver mines. It took centuries for the population of Central America to return to its pre-conquest level. Yet, only *after* the conquest were massive numbers of people denied access to land – which means denied ability to feed themselves.

Today, of course, Central America's population far exeeds pre-Hispanic levels and there is also far more hunger and poverty there than ever before. But that does not necessarily imply a cause-and-effect relationship; there are factors at work other than population growth. The 'pauperization' process, which began with the Spanish conquest, has accelerated horrendously in the twentieth century. There is obviously a link between overpopulation and poverty, but to say that the former is the cause of the latter is a dangerous over-simplification. In fact, the reverse can be argued just as persuasively: almost invariably, fertility rates drop as the standard of living rises. Those nations which are approaching or have reached zero population growth – the USA, USSR, UK, West Germany, Japan – are those which first achieved a high standard of living.[3]

There are many reasons for this phenomenon, known as 'demographic shift'. With a more secure economic situation, couples no longer feel pressured to have more children to assure that at least one or two will survive and be around to support them in their old age. (For many poor families, especially peasants, it is actually more expensive *not* to have many children – each child provides another pair of arms to plant, harvest, fetch water, watch after younger children and free adults for other productive work. Children can maintain a small subsistence farm, allowing adults to work elsewhere and earn some cash to buy essentials such as seeds and machetes – or to buy food if the plot is too small to support the family alone.) With better education, the religious strictures against the use of contraception are loosened and women begin to question their male-defined role as child-bearers and rearers.[4] Therefore, a more equitable land distribution and better services for poor peasant communities can be seen as a first step towards a natural, spontaneous and inevitable decline in the rate of population growth. Elite global planners should take note that the Latin American country with the lowest birth rate – only one point higher than the United States – is Cuba. Since the 1959 revolution, Cuba's birth rate has fallen by more than half. This decline in the rate of population growth has occurred simultaneously with Latin America's most far-reaching agrarian reform programme.[5] Acknowledging the achievements of Cuba's land reform does not mean overlooking or apologizing for the authoritarianism and militarism of the Cuban revolution – even keeping in mind that these unfortunate tendencies have been fuelled by the ever-present threat of US intervention, even CIA attempts to sabotage Cuban agriculture with biological warfare.[6]

In the Central American nations, by contrast, the rates of population growth remain the highest in the world and land distribution is grossly inequitable. Central America's population is growing so rapidly that it will double in 24 years and, paradoxically, those areas where the population is growing fastest are those least capable of sustaining large populations – the polluted urban centres and the ecologically fragile rainforests. In a 1984 report, even the World Bank was forced to admit that 'Fertility is consistently and inversely related to household income and to education.' The facts speak for themselves:

- In Guatemala, 2.1 per cent of the landowners control 80 per cent of the agricultural land. Over 80 per cent of the rural farmers live on plots too small to support a family. Guatemala's population is growing by 3.5 per cent every year.

- In El Salvador, less than 2 per cent of the population owned almost all of the arable land and nearly 60 per cent of the national territory prior to the 1980 land reform (which changed things only marginally). Between 1961 and 1975, landless peasants increased from 11 per cent to 40 per cent of the rural population. Sixty per cent of Salvadoran estates of over 500 hectares remain uncultivated.

- In Honduras, 44 per cent of the rural poor are landless and (according to a 1982 AID report) more than two-thirds of the population 'are barely capable of a subsistence existence'. The population is growing by 3.5 per cent every year.

- In Nicaragua, before the revolution the Somoza family alone owned 23 per cent of the agricultural land. Nicaragua's population is growing by 3.4 per cent every year.

- In Costa Rica, 3 per cent of the landowners own 54 per cent of the land. One in six rural families are without legal title to land. The population is growing by 2.7 per cent every year.

- In Panama, two-thirds of the farmers are squatting in ostensibly 'protected' forest lands, such as Darien. The population is growing by 2.0 per cent every year.[7]

Yet, such factors are consistently overlooked by much of the world environmental movement. In the United States (where, incidentally, the population grows by 0.7% every year),[8] while church workers and activists in the anti-intervention movement have formed a 'Sanctuary' network, risking their own liberty to shelter illegal Central American refugees, many voices from the environmental movement are calling for closed borders, augmented by immigration enforcement and mass deportations. In the dangerously over-simplified equation of some environmentalists, hunger, poverty, war and environmental degradation are simply the result of overpopulation, and the US environment should not have to pay for the failure of Central Americans to practice birth control. A 1976 Environmental Fund statement, endorsed both by 'Imperium' spokesmen such as Zbigniew Brzezinski and figures, such as Paul Ehrlich and Garrett Hardin, hailed as overpopulation 'experts' by much of the environmental movement read:

> World food production cannot keep pace with the galloping growth of population . . . The problem is too many people. The food shortage is simply evidence of the problem . . . Some nations are now on the brink of famine because their populations have grown beyond the carrying capacity of their lands. Population growth has pushed the peoples of Africa, Asia and Latin America onto lands which are only marginally suitable for agriculture.[9]

Has population growth pushed the poor of Central America into the rainforests of El Peten and the Miskito Coast? Or the cotton and cattle industries? Elsewhere, Paul Ehrlich has written in horror that 'El Salvador, a country about the size of Massachusetts, has 4.5 million people today'.[10] Yet Massachusetts itself has a population of 5.8 million![11]

A recent article in the *Washington Post*, reporting on a conference concerning rainforest destruction, stated:

> The current mass extinction . . . is mainly the result of the world's developing countries working hard to produce food for their expanding populations. The bulldozers of large corporations and the axes of peasants are clearing forests to grow crops and graze livestock.[12]

But these same countries are producing massive quantities of luxury cash crops, such as coffee, for export. The beef from the livestock is not consumed domestically, but exported. It is not 'food' to feed 'their expanding populations', but a means of earning foreign exchange to buy tractors and pesticides and chemical fertilizers and sub-machine guns and helicopter gunships, and to service a foreign debt.

Furthermore, grazing livestock is an incredibly illogical, wasteful and inefficient means of producing protein to feed local populations. A single hectare used as grazing land will produce little more than a score of pounds of beef. The same hectare in the same year could produce tens of thousands of pounds of corn, root crops or vegetables.[13]

Obviously, the problem is more complicated than sheer numbers. Eventually the interrelated problems of ecological degradation and population growth fuelled by poverty, if they continue unchecked, could generate a situation in which it will be simply impossible for Central America to feed itself. Deforestation will decrease rainfall and worsen erosion, thereby diminishing the productive capacity of the land just as greater human numbers are demanding *more* productive land. The horn of Africa has certainly gone farther in this direction than Central America, yet Ethiopia continues to export coffee. It is still possible to break the cycle before deterioration reaches this point – but to do so requires a profound redistribution of land. The current US policy of aggressively promoting birth control in the region while sponsoring a military build-up as a means of blocking any meaningful agrarian reform is certain to back-fire as more and more Central Americans come to see family planning as a part of a foreign-backed agenda which works against their own interests.

In fiscal year 1985, Central America and the Caribbean accounted for two-thirds of USAID's population control budget for all of Latin America, with Guatemala and El Salvador the two biggest recipients. US population control aid to El Salvador doubled between 1984 and 1985 as part of AID's new concentration on Central America in response to the unrest in the region.[14] The Salvadoran Health Ministry is implementing a sterilization campaign with AID money and assistance from the International Planned Parenthood Federation, which sponsors a Salvadoran Demographic Association.[15] The programme has been rife with accusations of abuses. Relief workers in El Salvador have charged that in some areas food aid is offered to poor women as an inducement to undergo sterilization. There have been accounts of women being refused treatment in government health clinics unless they agree to sterilization; and even accounts of women being sterilized without their knowledge or consent after having given birth in hospitals.[16] The head of the Salvadoran Demographic Association told one reporter: 'We expect each nurse in the field to sign up one woman for sterilization a day, and if a nurse doesn't find 300 women a year for sterilization, she falls below what we consider average.'[17]

Based on its own surveys, the Costa Rican Demographic Association currently estimates that sterilization is second only to the pill as a birth control method in Costa Rica – even though it is technically illegal. A doctor can receive a gaol sentence of three to ten years for performing a sterilization in Costa Rica; but no doctor has ever been tried under the law and there is currently a campaign for its repeal. A recent piece in the Costa Rican daily *La Nacion* warned that the Costa Rican Demographic Association wanted to use the 'force and coercion of the State to impose sterilization on fertile women'. Such fears have been fuelled by consistent rumours of local doctors sterilizing women without their consent.[18]

It is overwhelmingly women who are targeted for sterilization. While 17 per cent of the women surveyed by the Costa Rican Demographic Association had been sterilized, only half of one per cent said that their husbands had been sterilized.[19]

In the 1950s, Costa Rica had the world's highest birth rate and this news prompted the nation's leaders to start encouraging birth control, despite the protestations of the highly influential Catholic Church. Today the Costa Rican Social Security Institute distributes contraceptives free of charge. The methods offered are pills, condoms and injections of Depo-Provera. With many men unwilling to use condoms, substantial numbers of Costa Rican women have turned to the injections.[20] Depo-Provera is a synthetic hormone which inhibits ovulation and must be administered every three months. This contraceptive device has not been approved for sale in the US because there have been too few tests to satisfy federal Food and Drug Administration requirements (although it is being administered by the federal government on US Indian reservations anyway).[21] It has been found to cause menstrual irregularities, depression, and loss of sex drive, and there is some evidence linking it to cervical cancer. Nonetheless, both the International Planned Parenthood Federation and the World Health Organization have approved Depo-Provera for widespread use.[22]

The Costa Rican Social Security Institute also used to distribute free of charge, an intrauterine device – the Dalkon Shield – but suspended distribution when the producers of the device, the A. H. Robins Company of Virginia, were successfully sued in the US after it was revealed that the product causes infections which can lead to sterility. In 1987, a suit was filed in the US against the A. H. Robins Company on behalf of 100 Central American women from Costa Rica, El Salvador and Guatemala. The suit maintains that the company information about the dangers of the Dalkon Shield was deliberately withheld from Central American consumers.[23]

Central America *does* need birth control. But if birth control is administered under coercion and without regard for women's health, as is frequently the case in Central America today, it will come to be seen (and quite accurately) as a means of social manipulation. US-funded birth control programmes in Central America have accelerated, along with the US-funded militarization of the region. The militarization is primarily a means of suppressing the one element capable of breaking the vicious cycles which are drawing Central America ever deeper into crisis – profound land redistribution. The militarization only aggravates the problem and accelerates the downward spiral.

Although the notion is virtually heresy for much of the mainstream environmental movement, from an ecological viewpoint a case can be made that population control is more essential in the United States than Central America. This assertion will at first seem illogical to many because of the obvious reality that hunger is a bigger problem in Central America than in the United States (although it must be recalled that there is hunger in the United States as well – in the inner cities, in southern Appalachia, on the Indian reservations). But the hunger in Central America may have far more to do with land use patterns than human numbers. We will never know to what extent this is the case until after the choicest land, which now makes up the agro-export zones, is returned to cultivation of basic foods for domestic consumption.

In the meantime, the citizens of the United States consume far more resources per capita than the people of Central America. While US households typically own cars, televisions, and frequently more sophisticated 'home entertainment' products such as CD players and VCRs, Central American families are privileged if they have running water, flush toilets or electricity. A few comparisons vividly clarify the disparity:

- The money the typical North American spends on alcoholic beverages in one year could cover the total living expenses of one Honduran for half a year.

- The cost of one Sears VCR could cover the total living expenses of a Salvadoran family for over ten months.

- Nabisco earns more in sales each year than the combined gross domestic products of El Salvador, Honduras, Nicaragua, Costa Rica, Panama and Belize.

- The US spends as much on cosmetics, hair care, and disposable diapers as the combined gross domestic products of El Salvador, Honduras, Nicaragua, and Costa Rica.

- If US military aid to El Salvador in 1984 were instead divided among the poorest 20 per cent of the Salvadoran people, their average annual income would quadruple.[24]

As long as this glaring disparity in per capita consumption levels remains intact, and as long as the planet's limited resources are being plundered to produce consumer goods, which society is in the most dire need of population control – the United States or Central America?

17. Towards Revolutionary Environmentalism

The ecological implications of the chasm between the industrialized North and the developing South were explored by former East German dissident exile Rudolph Bahro in his 1982 book *Socialism and Survival*, one of the seminal works of Europe's Green movement:

It has become indisputably clear . . . that the gap between North and South cannot be narrowed by any kind of 'development aid' in the context of the capitalist world economy, whether it is 0.3 per cent or 0.7 per cent of the gross national product. The reality is that every advance made in the kind of standard of living we enjoy here drives humanity as a whole deeper into its contradictions and makes these still harder to resolve. As long as we do not appreciate this basic failure of solidarity, we are only shedding crocodile tears when we talk about how we want to oppose our involvement in colonialism.

It is the model of our civilization as a whole that most decisively bars the way to the rest of humanity. Let us imagine what it could mean if the raw material and energy consumption of our society were extended to the 4.5 billion people living today, or to the 10 to 15 billion there will probably be tomorrow. It is readily apparent that the planet can only support such volumes of production and their implications for the environment for a very short time. On the other hand, the peoples of the Third World are being continually exposed to the standard set by our civilization. Can we maintain this civilization in its existing form while we know that humanity as a whole will have difficulty living according to such a pattern? And while we can only hope that it will not even attempt to do so?

The type of industrial civilization which has spread out from Europe is leading the whole of humanity into an inescapable dilemma. We know that the number of people that can be fed and provided for on a certain territory depends on their mode of production. For example, all calculations according to which the earth could supply bread for an ever-growing world population assume an agriculture that is pursued industrially and supported by the massive application of fertilizers. Apart from the destruction of the soil's fertility that threatens even in the medium term, the fertilizers are also finite resources. If the whole enterprize of expanding industrial production is continued as long as it is still possible, with ever greater consumption of ever weaker concentrations of raw materials, we shall be faced at the end of the day with a production machine that is grinding to a halt for want of supplies of materials, yet without whose operation the given population cannot be maintained.

A resolution of the North–South conflict in the spirit of solidarity requires as an indispensible condition that our production machine here is no longer expanded, but rather diminished, that it is reconstructed and reprogrammed so that the sum of things that everyone needs to have no longer grows beyond the limits drawn by the finite extent of the earth . . .[1]

Otherwise, Bahro envisions 'a terrible end in the form of . . . civil wars, forced rationing and eco-facism.'[2]

Critics of the environmental movement on both the right and the left point out that it is arrogant for industrialized nations such as the US and those of Western Europe, which have destroyed and continue to destroy much of their own forests to facilitate massive industrialization, to urge 'Third World' nations to preserve their forests. It is a disturbingly valid point. It is similarly arrogant for these same industrialized nations, often with higher population densities than the underdeveloped nations, to tell the underdeveloped nations that they must control their numbers in order to combat hunger – especially as the industrialized nations are consuming luxury crops grown on the best land in the underdeveloped nations.

The 'Pax Americana' of the post-World War II era has created an almost hopelessly contradictory world situation. For decades US propaganda has boasted of a nation with 'the world's highest standard of living', and used this boast as evidence of the inherent superiority of the Western corporate capitalist system over the communist rivals in the east. As a result, almost all the world today – from the villages of Guatemala to the shipyards of Poland – aspires to achieve this standard of living. Yet, if we live in a world where six per cent of the population consumes over 40 per cent of the resources, simple mathematics demonstrate the impossibility of peoples of the entire planet sharing the standard of living enjoyed by many (but no means all) US citizens. To be perceived as having any legitimacy whatsoever, US environmentalists may have to start by asserting that the US mode of development has been grossly flawed from the start and that the artificially inflated standard of living it has produced is unsustainable. Far from seeing the US mode of development as a model to be emulated, underdeveloped nations should seek to learn from the mistakes of the US and of Western Europe.

Some US environmentalists are approaching such a view. Said Randy Hayes of the Rainforest Action Network at a 1987 conference in New York City on rainforest destruction:

We're here to figure out how to be more effective at saving tropical Rain Forests. Essentially, I think what we need is to get our foot off the throat of the Rain Forests . . . I think our central philosophy needs to be 'Physician, heal thyself!' . . . Our tax dollars and our capital are financing a lot of destructive projects. Our corporations are cutting down the forests, and the overconsumption and the waste of our society and ourselves as consumers are all a part of that problem.

I think there needs to be a radical shift in our analysis of ourselves as activists around this issue to focus more on here at home and less on what needs to be done in India or Malaysia or Indonesia or Brazil . . . Regarding the banks, I don't think we should be talking so much about 'forgiving' foreign debt . . . These debts have been paid and repaid over and over again in the genocide of tribal cultures and the exploitation of their resources . . . Essentially, we have robbed these countries blind and now they owe us money. We cannot rely on economic growth to solve this crisis . . . I just don't buy it. It's kind of like trying to sober up by drinking martinis.[3]

Another speaker at the 1987 Rainforest Conference in New York was Vandana Shiva, who works with indigenous peoples in India who are resisting their relocation by a World Bank-funded hydro-dam project. She is also an outspoken critic of the World Bank's new and highly touted plan to save tropical rainforests. She said:

In the Rain Forest crisis, the immediate response of the northern countries is to twist the arms of the southern countries, violating the sovereignty of nations as well as native peoples. They do not examine their own role in the crisis. Aluminum exploitation, beef production and other activities which result in deforestation and cultural destruction exist for corporate profits and the convenience of First World city-dwellers.[4]

Clearly, development *is* desperately needed in Central America, as elsewhere in the impoverished South. But if Central America can move beyond dependency on an agro-export economy, development need not mean destruction of the rainforests. If we are to achieve a sustainable world, the development of such places as Central America may have to be concomitant with a *scaling back of overdevelopment* in such places as the United States.

This scaling back seems to be inevitable in any event. Today it generally takes two incomes for a US and European family to maintain the same standard of living that only required one income a generation ago. In the Reagan era, the United States not only underwrote an intense militarization of Central America (and other troubled regions), but also built up its own military machine to unprecedented levels. Contracts for the Trident, MX, Cruise and Pershing missiles, experimental stealth bombers and new submarines have proliferated. Having over-extended its military commitments beyond its economic resources, the United States, despite massive cuts in domestic social programmes, has had to turn to prosperous foreign sources – principally Japan – to finance this military build-up. As a result, in the 1980s, the United States has become by far the world's biggest debtor nation. The corporate and military elites have largely been shielded from the impact of this development – in fact their wealth and power increased dramatically during the Reagan era, while many of the USA's urban poor were effectively disenfranchized from the increasingly centralized economy and driven into homelessness.

In order to repay its astronomical debt to Japan and West Germany, the US is depending on the underdeveloped nations of the south to repay their debts to the US government, private US banks and largely US-funded multilateral institutions such as the World Bank. If the five Central American nations were to collectively default on their debts, it would seriously disrupt the world financial system – as would the default of any one of the seven biggest 'Third World' debtors (Brazil, Mexico, Argentina, India, the Philippines, Indonesia and Malaysia).[5] Collective default of the big seven would cripple the world financial system. It would mean that the United States would be unable to pay back its own debt to Japan – which, with the subsequent collapse of the US dollar, would lose the US as a market for its VCRs and Toyotas. The result would be a worldwide economic disaster.

Thus far, the response of the multilateral banks has been to pressure the debtor nations to increase exports, cut domestic spending and open up the rainforests to industrial development and peasant colonization. Such a strategy only threatens to compound the global economic crisis with a global ecological crisis, as tropical deforestation accelerates the Greenhouse Effect. Many scientists believe that the Greenhouse Effect has already taken a toll on agricultural production in the Great Plains, North America's bread basket.[6] Simply to bleed Central America and other Third World debtor nations dry is not a solution. Planet Earth's biosphere is not divisible: it pays no heed to national borders. In the 1930s, the United States suffered the twin cataclysms of economic depression and the agricultural disaster known as the 'Dust Bowl' – the latter largely due to domestic deforestation. With the Greenhouse Effect compounded by such local forms of ecological mismanagement as aquifer depletion and over-reliance on pesticides, petro-chemical fertilizers and genetically-altered seed stock, a similar disaster could currently be in the making in the US mid-west bread basket, which today is a source of grain for much of the planet.

Effective conservation of vital wilderness areas in Central America and other rainforest regions will entail radical restructuring of local economies and land use paterns. It is to avoid precisely this restructuring that the US has introduced a military build-up into the region. In the words of Mexican ecologist Arturo Gomez-Pompa:

> It is totally wrong to ear-mark an area as a 'nature reserve: keep out', and have it policed, while multitudes of starving peasants in the vicinity are looking for a suitable spot to plant next season's crop. This colonialist approach to conservation is doomed to failure.[7]

Despite the antipathy that frequently exists between revolutionaries and environmentalists, neither of their agendas is complete without the other.

Revolutionary movements which fail to profoundly reevaluate modern industrial civilization's obsession with mega-scale development and top-down planning, may find themselves depleting their nations' resource bases and alienating their own populace to the same degree as the repressive oligarchies they sought to replace. Similarly, environmental movements which fail to confront the root causes of environmental destruction and instead merely adapt to repressive power structures will eventually lose any semblance of legitimacy or effectiveness. In order to succeed, revolutionary movements must become ecological and ecological movements must become revolutionary.

For over a century, United States policy in Central America has been based on 'making Central America safe for United States interests'. Perhaps it is time that some energy was devoted to making the United States safe for Central American interests. This means calling a halt to military interventions and CIA escapades. It means seeking and implementing a new solution to the debt crisis in which 'austerity' will be imposed not on the poorest in the poor nations but on the wealthiest in the rich nations, the corporate elite who can best afford it. It means restructuring the North American (and European) economy so that consumers are not dependent on globe-spanning corporations for food and employment. Such a transformation would mean changes in the lifestyle of all North Americans. Coffee may have to become a special treat for rare occasions rather than the psychic fuel that wakes us up in the morning and gets us through the workday. Bananas will be less plentiful and more expensive. Hamburgers will be consumed less frequently, and will be made from domestic beef. Such a change would undoubtedly affect our lives in far more serious ways as well. But we needn't be gloomy about the prospect. Coffee and beef take a negative toll on human health when consumed in excess. Food which is transported from thousands of miles away loses many nutrients in transit and is frequently treated with artificial preservatives. To facilitate easy shopping, export bananas are not allowed to ripen on the tree but are picked when they are still green and hard and are then chemically treated to induce ripening upon arrival in the US – this adversely affects both nutrition and flavour.

Making the United States (and Europe and Japan) safe for Central America may mean decentralizing our intensely centralized system of food production. The same Central American banana *pulpos*, like Del Monte and Castle & Cooke, are also among the corporations that own agricultural land in southern California and elsewhere in the US south-west. These holdings, which produce an inordinate amount of the fruits and vegetables consumed throughout the United States, make intensive use of large-scale irrigation, pesticides and petro-chemical fertilizers. Not surprisingly, even these domestic holdings are frequently worked by migrant labour from Mexico and even Central America. Western states like California and Arizona are fighting over the right to divert water from common rivers such as the Colorado, in part to irrigate massive agribusiness holdings in areas that would otherwise be desert. Such practices are depleting our vital watersheds, and ecologists warn that the rivers will simply be unable to continue satisfying the growing demands of south-west agro-industry.[8]

Therefore, looking to local farmers rather than multinational corporations to put dinner on our tables would serve to preserve our watersheds and give us more nutritious, healthy and flavourful food. (Of course, achieving this kind of localized food production system might necessitate a degree of land redistribution in the United States.) Similarly, by halting the production and export of dangerous pesticides, we would free ourselves from the fear that traces of these pesticides will return to us in imported food.

Making the United States safe for Central America may mean redefining our concept of a 'high standard of living' in terms other than sheer quantity of material consumption. We may find that in making the United States safe for Central America, we can also make the United States a healthier, more humane and ecologically sound place to live.

Such sweeping structural changes, however, are unlikely to arise from the mainstream environmental movement which is underwritten by many of the world's most powerful corporations, especially oil companies – or philanthropic organizations funded by oil profits, such as those of the Rockefeller family. To cite but one example, corporate donors to the National Wildlife Federation's multi-million dollar annual budget include oil companies Amoco, ARCO, Mobil and the Rockefeller flagship Exxon, nuclear and military contractors DuPont, General Electric, Boeing, United Technologies, Monsanto and Westinghouse, food and agribusiness giant Coca-Cola, computer monolith IBM, chemical colossus Dow, steel mainstay USX, toxic handlers Waste Management, financial titans Citibank and Chemical Bank, and oil-funded philanthropic organization the Rockefeller Group.[9]

In the 1980s, as the corporate world has come to play an ever larger role in the mainstream environmental movement, an alternative 'radical' ecology movement has emerged, with a greater sense of urgency and impatience, and a more decentralized and loosely knit structure based on autonomous 'affinity groups' instead of rigid hierarchies. Groups such as Earth First! (the exclamation point is part of the name), Sea Shepherd and the somewhat less strident Greenpeace have used direct action tactics – physically interfering with the destruction of wilderness, the slaughter of wildlife or the pollution of ecosystems – rather than the more mainstream and elite tactics such as lobbying and funding nature reserves.

Such human blockades of the corporate bulldozers, chain-saws and whaling ships may be long overdue. At times, however, the radical ecology movement has demonstrated right-wing and even overtly racist tendencies. Voices within Earth First!, for instance, have hailed AIDS and the African famines as the Earth's salvation, ridding the planet of a particularly destructive life-form (human beings). Taking the 'life-boat ethic' of such figures as Garret Hardin one step further, some Earth Firsters have called for withholding food aid from the starving Ethiopians, seeing the problem of African starvation as merely a question of human numbers moving beyond the carrying capacity of the land, and seeing the solution as just a population crash.[10] This analysis is utterly bereft of any political content, any acknowledgement of how the Sahel's carrying capacity has been systematically diminished by decades of centralized agribusiness and generations of colonialism, any attempt to address the paradox of starvation in a nation which is a major exporter of the non-food cash-crop coffee. Willingness to let Africans die in the name of restoring the ecological balance without acknowledging the substantial role that colonialism has played in the destruction of the ecological balance is at best indicative of lazy and sloppy thinking and, at worst, betrays arrogant racism.

The late Edward Abbey, whose eloquent writings on the beauty of the United States' south-west deserts and the desperate need to defend them from corporate rape have been a major inspiration to Earth First!, has also been one of the most strident voices calling for sealing the US–Mexico border against Central American refugees and Mexican economic refugees in the name of protecting the USA's resources, gene pool and culture. Wrote Abbey:

> There are a good many reasons, any one sufficient, to call a halt to further immigration (whether legal or illegal) into the U.S. One seldom mentioned is cultural: the United States that we live in today, with its traditions and ideals, however imperfectly realized, is a product of northern European civilization. If we allow our country – *our* country – to become Latinized, in whole or in part, we shall see it tend towards a culture more and more like Mexico.[11]

This would result, according to Abbey, in a 'less efficient and far more corrupt economy' and 'greater reliance on crime and violence as normal instruments of social change.'[12] Abbey wrote these words just as church workers and others in the US, especially the south-west, were risking prison sentences to aid illegal Central American refugees in the Sanctuary movement, dubbed by many as the USA's 'second underground railroad'. When taken to task for these remarks, Abbey claimed to 'cheerfully acknowledge being a "cultural chauvinist"'.[13] This frightening tendency harks back to Rudolph Bahro's warning of 'eco-fascism'.

While more moderate environmentalists accuse them of going too far, this trend may indicate that the self-proclaimed '*radical* environmentalism' of groups such as Earth First! fails to go far *enough*. As the name implies, '*radical* environmentalism' merely takes the views of the mainstream environmental movement to a more extreme conclusion. 'Radical environmentalism' purports to part company with the mainstream movement by profoundly rejecting the self-appointed managerial role of the human race. But 'radical environmentalism' does not question many of the mainstream movement's underlying assumptions – that the root cause of ecological destruction is too many people, that wild areas can somehow be saved in a sort of political vacuum without addressing the social issues which are so inextricably involved.

Perhaps what is needed is less 'radical environmentalism' than '*revolutionary* environmentalism'. Revolutionary environmentalism would not merely take the mainstream movement's assumptions to a more radical level, but dispense with them completely in favour of a view that sees profound social and political transformation as both a principal instrument and an inevitable result of preserving wild areas and restoring the ecology.

Similarly, the anti-intervention movement may need to learn that calling a halt to political and military meddling, by the USA and other industrialized nations of the North, in Central America and other developing regions of the South, may entail profound transformation of the lives of those in the industrialized North, including redrawing their own countries' political map. Unless anti-interventionists are content with the prospect of an indefinite future of eternally raising a marginal voice of opposition as the US continues to promote counter-revolutions and invade small countries, while the mass media openly glorify these same things, they may have to join with ecologists and others to create a vision of a new political and economic order in their own countries.

National boundaries are frequently arbitrary from the standpoint of human cultural identity and bio-regionalism. This is largely due to the fact that these boundaries were formed during the long eras of colonialism and imperialism, in which political and economic 'metropolises' grew wealthy off the exploitation of human labour and natural resources in political and economic 'satellites'. This process began within the nations which eventually became the imperial powers, as Spain absorbed Catalonia, Galicia and Asturias; as England absorbed Ireland, Scotland and Wales; as Russia absorbed the Ukraine; as the United States absorbed the traditional lands of the Iroquois Confederacy, the Lakota, Navajo and Shoshone.

The US–Mexico border, the same that 'Deep Ecologist' Edward Abbey saw as a potential barrier to keep brown-skinned Latins from over-running a 'northern European' society, cuts right through the centre of the bio-region known as the Sonoran Desert, and exists at that apparently random spot on the map only because the United States beat Mexico with superior firepower in the war of 1848. (Many US environmentalists seem quick to forget that their own inspiration, Henry David Thoreau, was imprisoned in Massachusetts in protest against that very war.)

As imperialist expansion continued overseas, this model was exported. The Spanish, for example, established their Central American seat of power in Guatemala City, and generally in the central highlands of the isthmus. The British played for power on Central America's low-lying Caribbean Coast, but the British Empire was ultimately forced by political circumstances to cede its tenuous claim to this region. Today, therefore, the vast rainforest regions of El Peten and the Miskito Coast are under the political control of national capitals in the central highlands such as Guatemala City, Tegucigalpa and Managua. In a form of 'internal colonialism' which mirrors international colonialism, the indigenous inhabitants of these rainforest regions are deprived of a voice in the development of their own homeland. Those development decisions are, rather, made by those who understand little (and frequently care even less) of the ecology of these regions or the cultural sovereignty of their inhabitants. This is also reflected in the internal racism which allows Guatemalan Latinos to viciously exploit Guatemalan Indians, much as international racism allows US multinational corporations to exploit Guatemala as a whole.

Writes Venezuelan anthropologist Elisabeth Burgos-Debray:

> We Latin Americans are only too ready to denounce the unequal relations that exist between ourselves and North America, but we tend to forget that we too are oppressors and that we too are involved in relations that can only be described as *colonial*. Without any fear of exaggeration, it can be said that, especially in countries with a large Indian population, there is an internal colonialism which works to the detriment of the indigenous population. The ease with which North America dominates so-called 'Latin' America is to a large extent a result of the collusion afforded it by this internal colonialism . . .
>
> In Guatemala and certain other countries of Latin America, the Indians are in the majority. The situation there is, *mutatis mutandi*, comparable to that in South Africa, where a white minority has absolute power over the black majority. In other Latin American countries, where the Indians are in a minority, they do not have even the most elementary rights which every human being should enjoy. Indeed the so-called forest Indians are being systematically exterminated in the name of progress.[14]

As we have seen, an element of 'internal colonialism' was even demonstrated by Nicaragua's Sandinistas in their dealings with the Miskito Coast, even as they so forcefully rejected the 'external colonialism' to which Nicaragua has so long been subject. But it must be kept in mind that these two forms of colonialism reinforce each other.

The Central American national capitals do not act unilaterally in their decisions to plunder the Caribbean rainforests, but under direction, and sometimes pressure, from such institutions as the World Bank and USAID, and the dictates of the world economy. Even the Sandinistas' desire to consolidate political control over the Miskito Coast was driven by the quite valid fear of US military intervention – the need to secure the coastline and harbours against possible invasion by the US Navy's Caribbean Fleet, and to maintain contact with Cuba as a possible source of military assistance.

The structures of 'internal colonialism' are held in place by the structures of international colonialism: the multilateral lending institutions, the aid and development agencies, and the military machines of the industrial and post-industrial North.

This pattern repeats itself throughout the developing world. In Brazil, the Portuguese settled the fertile south, then established political control over the vast Amazon rainforest to the north. The military regime installed by a CIA-instrumented coup in 1964 saw the Amazon merely as a convenient dumping ground for disenfranchised peasantry, as a source of foreign exchange from strip-mining and hydrodams, even as a suitable place to test nuclear weapons. The World Bank was all too willing to supply funds for the colonization projects and hydrodams, while the US space agency, NASA, was happy to sell satellite photographs indicating the location of mineral deposits below the jungle floor to the highest corporate bidder. Fortunately, civilian power was restored before Brazil's first nuclear weapon could be developed. But the plunder of the rainforest is only now starting to slow due to the resistance of the Amazonian Alliance of the Peoples of the Forest, a coalition of the rubber tappers and the indigenous peoples for whom the deforestation means cultural extermination. The Alliance has blockaded the bulldozers and chainsaws with their bodies, provoking the violence of the Rural Democratic Union (UDR), a right-wing paramilitary organization tied to the wealthy cattle interests. While the famous rubber tapper Chico Mendes paid for his leading role in the Alliance with his life, his concept of 'extractive reserves' may point the way out of the holocaust now raging in the Amazon. Extractive reserves would allow sustainable economic activity which depends on the forest, such as rubber tapping, while barring destructive activities, such as ranching and mining, which devour the forest. Developed by the people who actually *inhabit* the Amazon, the extractive reserve concept represents the beginnings of a reversal of colonialism and a return to bio-regionalism.[15]

In Indonesia, the Dutch settled the central island of Java, then established political control over the outer rainforest islands of Borneo, New Guinea and Sumatra. Colonial structures remained intact after Indonesia won independence in 1949. The Suharto dictatorship, installed by a CIA-instrumented coup in 1965 and still in power today, has likewise seen the rainforests of Borneo and Sumatra as a dumping ground for peasants uprooted from their traditional lands by the explosion of coffee and sugar interests on Java and Bali. The 'Transmigration' programme, which has relocated hundreds of thousands of peasants, has been underwritten by the World Bank to the extent of $800 million. The rainforest has been largely destroyed, and its indigenous peoples, such as the Dani and Yali, have been forced into the new settlements and become despised minorities in their own land.[16]

Lest we assume that this pattern applies only to the tropical 'third world', it is instructive to take a brief look at the Canadian province of Quebec, where the French, and later the British, established colonies in the fertile valley cut by the St Lawrence River, and only later established political control over the vast regions of tundra and sub-arctic forest which lie to the north. Today, Quebec's Premier Robert Bourassa views this wilderness much as Brazil's elites have viewed the Amazon: as a harsh, vacant, expendable wasteland to be plundered for its resources. In his 1985 book *Power From the North*, Bourassa actually refers to the region as 'a vast hydro-electric plant in-the-bud'. The James Bay hydro-complex currently under construction in Quebec's far north is perhaps the biggest ever contemplated, and calls for damming almost every river that flows through the region, flooding 40,000 square kilometres. Ecologists are protesting against the construction of the complex, because it will flood much of the last remaining caribou habitat in North America, and destroy vital feeding grounds for migratory birds. The Cree Indians and Inuit ('Eskimo') peoples who inhabit the region are also protesting against it because it will flood their hunting grounds and end their way of life. The Cree and Inuit had not even been notified when the first phase of the project was built in the 1970s. In the interim, toxic mercury, leached from the rock below the floodplains by bacteria from the decay of the submerged forests, has contaminated the region's fish, an ancient staple of the native peoples' diet. The Cree and Inuit have pledged to resist the much larger second phase of the project. Quebec's internal colonialism is also a part of the larger neo-colonialist macrocosm: much of the power from the James Bay complex is to be exported to the United States, and the project is being underwritten by such globe-spanning investment firms as Merrill Lynch and Citicorp.[17]

Throughout the planet, peoples whose national identities have been suppressed or persecuted by colonial structures are growing restive, and many hope that these structures can be overcome in the new order which is emerging following the end of the Cold War. But the events of the first months of 1991 clearly indicate the nature of the 'New World Order' proclaimed by US President George Bush. The cataclysmic high-tech war against Iraq claimed 200,000 lives and a devastating ecological toll. The very resource being fought over – oil – actually became a weapon of the war, intentionally poured into the Persian Gulf and set afire to create a soot cloud extending north to Turkey and east to Iran. Iraq's entire infrastructure was destroyed in the most extended aerial bombardment campaign the world has yet witnessed. In the midst of the war, the Bush administration released its proposed energy plan for the 1990s, calling for increasing oil output, sacrificing Alaska wilderness area to Exxon and ARCO, and even reviving the nuclear power industry. While the energy plan called for hastening the licensing process for new atomic plants, another administration proposal released during the war called for loosening the federal regulations on recombinant DNA research and the bio-technology industry. Significantly, the administration is also pressing for the creation of a 'free trade' bloc with Canada, Latin America and the Caribbean, to counterbalance a newly united Europe, and Japan's 'co-prosperity sphere' in east Asia and the Pacific. Canada has already signed a Free Trade Agreement with the US, and, as I write, it seems increasingly likely that Mexico will be the next to sign. The Free Trade Agreements entail eliminating 'unfair trade barriers', but trade unionists and environmentalists fear that standards for worker health and safety and environmental protection could be among those 'barriers'.

A study by the Canadian Environmental Law Association has already written that '[b]y limiting the rights of governments to regulate the development of natural resources or to control that development to accomplish environmental objectives, the trade deal has undermined critical opportunities to accomplish goals that are necessary to abate global warming.'[18]

The Bush administration is also attempting to have 'Free Trade' principles instated worldwide through the rewritten version of the General Agreements on Tariffs and Trade (GATT). The new GATT regulation that Bush is pushing would set *maximum* toxicity standards for pesticide imports, below which no signatory nation would be able to block importation. The new GATT would also limit the ability of nations to restrict importation of hybrid or genetically-engineered seeds, artificial growth hormones for cattle, and other biotechnology products. Multinational corporations would be granted easier access to resources in the developing world. Nations which refused to sign on would be risking a trade cut-off potentially even more devastating than that which ravaged Nicaragua in the 1980s. Thus far the new GATT has been blocked, mostly by the pressure of European farmers who fear that their jobs would be lost to cheaper labour in the 'third world'. But Bush has launched a high-pressure campaign to push through the revised GATT.[19]

Whether it is being done through the overt military means, as in the war with Iraq, or through the somewhat more subtle economic means, as in the 'Free Trade' Agreements, it is clear that Bush's 'New World Order' is one in which the nations of the industrial and post-industrial north will have unrestrained access to labour and natural resources anywhere on the planet; an order that will cement and even intensify the old colonial structures. Despite Bush's campaign pledge to be the 'environmental president', and the endless lip service paid to environmental issues during 1990s Earth Day celebrations, his new order will only accelerate the rape of the planet, either through ecocidal war, or an almost equally ecocidal 'peace' of 'Free Trade' economics.

Yet, simultaneous with this tendency towards greater centralization of power is a reverse tendency, as large nation-states are beginning to splinter. Environmental issues are a driving force behind this trend. Separatist sentiment in Lithuania, Latvia and Estonia is fuelled by the fact that Moscow has long used these republics as a dumping ground for toxic wastes and some of the Soviet Union's most polluting industries. The movement to liberate Tibet from Chinese occupation is given greater urgency by Beijing's testing of nuclear weapons and dumping of nuclear waste in the Himalayan plateau. Nor are these tendencies confined to the East. Canada also seems to be on the verge of splintering, and the anger behind the 1990s Mohawk uprising in Quebec had much to do with the pollution of traditional Mohawk land and water with industrial wastes, causing poverty by destroying self-sufficiency. Throughout Canada, and, to a lesser extent, the United States, native nations are demanding sovereignty throughout their traditional territories. In the US inner cities, Black nationalism is arising in response to the dumping of sewage plants and municipal waste incinerators in Black communities, as well as to police brutality and the closing of hospitals and fire stations. It seems that everywhere around the planet, localities are reasserting their identities and feeling more and more that the distant bureaucracies of the 'metropolises' are antithetical to local interests.

If the balance of power in the North were to shift away from the elite corridors of Washington DC, New York, London, Bonn, Paris, Tokyo and Moscow to local communities, the empires with 'interests to defend' in Central America, Indo-China and Southern Africa could not only be reined in, but eventually effectively dismantled.

The separatism currently emerging in the Baltic states could spread to the West as the long-submerged identities of Scotland, Wales, Brittany, Galicia, the Basque country and Catalonia reappear. As we have seen recently, this development carries the threat of xenophobic nationalism – but it may also carry the hope of returning economic and political structures to the human scale.

In the United States since the late 1960s there has been much talk of the Pacific coast, from northern California to Seattle, seceding from the union to form an environmentally extremist 'Ecotopia' – but it is questionable how realistic this scenario is, given that this area is the nerve centre of the US corporate–military power grid, hosting sprawling military bases, the University of California and its attendant federal nuclear weapons' laboratory at Livermore, and military contractors such as Lockheed and Boeing. Perhaps more realistic prospects for secessionist movement exist in the much smaller area of the state of Vermont, where activist environmental and anti-intervention movements are growing, as are pro-independence sentiments.[20] One of the few major exponents of the corporate–military complex in Vermont is a General Electric plant outside Burlington, which manufactures the heavy machine-guns used on the helicopters of the Salvadoran air force; this plant has been the target of a sustained citizen's campaign to convert it to peaceful purposes, including occupations of the gun testing range.[21] The independence sentiment is growing in the state precisely in response to such outside economic interests operating on Vermont soil.

If a new kind of politics is to emerge from the global upheavals with which the 1990s have begun, perhaps the first step to calling a halt to your own country's domination of 'spheres of influence' in the developing world will be knowing and thinking about where your own food, water and electrical power comes from, where your domestic and industrial waste goes – and what, to begin with, you can do about *that*.

Where I live, on New York City's Lower East Side, local residents are waging their own land-based struggle – against the real estate developers who are pushing up local rents ever higher, thereby driving older low-income residents (including many Puerto Ricans, Dominicans and other Latinos) out of the neighbourhood and contributing to New York's agonizing homelessness problem. This struggle has included squatting in empty tenement buildings, and the ongoing occupation of the local Tompkins Square Park with encampments for the homeless in defiance of a City-imposed curfew. Some Lower East Side activists have been making the international connections to this local struggle. A Food Co-op has been organized to provide members with affordable organic foods produced outside the centralized petrochemical-intensive agro-industry, which exploits land and labour both in Central America and the United States. Some squatters and other local residents have reclaimed a degree of self-suficiency by turning empty lots into community gardens to grow fruits and vegetables, converting the rubble of destroyed tenements into soil with vegetable clippings and other organic waste. Local residents are organizing recycling programmes which are moving far faster than the city government's own glacier-paced and overly bureaucratized programme, recognizing that the city's solid wste crisis may eventually prompt moves to export New York's garbage to some impoverished area, perhaps in Latin America or the Caribbean. Like many cities and communities throughout the US, the Lower East Side has adopted a 'Sister City' in

Nicaragua – Bluefields on the Caribbean coast – and has exchanged delegations and offered both political solidarity and material support. This is direct people-to-people contact between North Americans and Central Americans waging similar struggles for control of their own land and self-determination against similar enemies – or, in the case of the US federal government, different tentacles of the *same* enemy: the Central Intelligence Agency in Bluefields, the corrupt Department of Housing and Urban Development on the Lower East Side.

Unless progressive-minded thinkers and activists begin to seriously address concerns of ecological responsibility and local autonomy, emphasizing their links to concerns of social justice, these issues are likely to be exploited by those with agendas of extreme right-wing nationalism or 'eco-fascism'. This is especially relevant in light of the fact that the centralized Stalinist model of socialism has now been almost universally discredited. The collapse of the 'socialist world' we are currently witnessing, could trigger a long-overdue re-evaluation of the libertarian and decentralist currents which are also a part of the heritage of the political left, but have been submerged or ignored in recent decades. These currents may point the way towards a new politics that stands opposed to exploitation and degradation of the land, as well as of human labour – and, in fact, recognizes these two forms of oppression as indivisible. In the American anarchist publication *Fifth Estate*, George Bradford wrote:

> . . . Anarchists and Marxists who reject the land connection and defend industrialism while blaming only the fragmentary 'economic' factors of capitalism for the crisis are as much an obstacle to liberation as the most reactionary misanthrope. They want a petrochemical industry that is 'worker-owned and operated'; they want the chain saw that is presently shredding the basic planetary life supports to be managed or 'appropriated' by a workers' state, or perhaps workers' councils . . .[22]

One of the simplest but most hopeful epitaphs for the Cold War was written by atmospheric physicist Michael Oppenheimer in a *New York Times* piece in May 1989, mere months before the explosion in Eastern Europe:

> One era, dominated by East–West confrontation, [is] ending and another, focused on preserving the planet, [is] dawning . . . These issues reach beyond the environment to questions of international relations, the structure of the world economy, the future of technology and trade and nuclear proliferation. It is no exaggeration to say that global environment may become the overarching issue for the next 40 years in the way the cold war defined our world view during the last 40 years.[23]

One of the challenges that lies ahead for activists on the cutting edge of forging a positive vision of the new global order is to forcefully make the connections in our organizing efforts that will demonstrate how the preservation of the planet and averting global ecological holocaust will necessarily entail the dismantling of colonialism and spheres of influence.

Notes

Notes ((A) = Article (journal etc); (M) = Monograph – otherwise citations are from books or as indicated.)

Part 1
Chapter 1
1. Dixon & Jonas, 1984, p. iii–v.
2. Nesmith (A).

Chapter 2
1. McNeill, 1982, p. 180.
2. Browning, 1971, p. 54.
3. Wolf, 1959, pp. 195–210.
4. Ibid., p. 189–91.
5. Barry, 1987, p. 71; Handy, 1984, chapter 4.
6. Terdre, 1988. (A)
7. Barry, 1987, p. 72.
8. *New York Times*, 18 April 1990; 18 September 1989.
9. Ibid., 19 May 1989.
10. Lappe & Collins, 1978, pp. 279, 307, 349.
11. Ibid., p. 313.
12. Browning, 1971, p. 73.
13. LaFeber, 1984, pp. 54, 70.
14. Quoted in Durham, 1979.
15. Armstrong & Shenk, 1982, p. 30; Galeano, 1973, p. 126.
16. Armstrong & Shenk, 1982, p. 28.
17. Ibid., p. 5.
18. Quoted in Durham, 1979.
19. Chapin, 1989 (A); Armstrong & Shenk, 1982, p. 30.
20. Hodges, 1986, p. 73.
21. Moore, 1985–86. (A)
22. Ibid., and Hodges, 1986, p. 151.
23. Ibid.
24. Nations & Leonard, 1986.
25. Ibid.
26. Ibid.
27. Ibid.
28. Williams, 1986.

Chapter 3
1. Williams, 1986.
2. Sweezey, et al, 1986. (A)

3. Lappe & Collins, 1978, p. 62.
4. Ibid.
5. Barry, 1987, p. 100.
6. Ibid.
7. Ibid.
8. Karliner & Faber, 1986b. (M)
9. Sweezey, et al, 1986. (A)
10. Ibid.
11. Barry, 1987, p. 97.
12. *Tico Times* (San Jose, Costa Rica) 14 August 1987.
13. Barry, 1987, p. 92.
14. Ibid., p. 101.
15. Karliner & Faber, 1986b. (M)
16. Sweezey, et al, 1986. (A)
17. Weir & Schapiro, 1987, p. 13.
18. Karliner & Faber, 1986b. (M)
19. Ibid.
20. Ibid.
21. Weeks, 1985.
22. *Tico Times*, 27 March 1987; *This Week* (Guatemala City) 2 February 1987.
23. Quoted in Williams, 1986.
24. *This Week*, 24 November 1986.
25. Collins, 1986, p. 107.
26. Armstrong & Shenk, 1982, p. 3.

Chapter 4
1. Mohawk, 1987 (A); and interview with author, *Downtown*, New York City, 6 January 1988.
2. Barry, 1987, p. 123.
3. Ibid., pp. 123, 124.
4. Nations & Leonard, 1986. (A)
5. Ibid.
6. Postel, 1988. (A)
7. Author's interview with Michael Oppenheimer, atmospheric physicist, Environmental Defense Fund, New York, in *Downtown*, (New York) 19 October 1988.
8. Wurster, 1988; Myers, 1985. (A)
9. Barry, 1987, pp. 123, 124.
10. Nations & Leonard, 1986. (A)
11. *Tropical Deforestation in Central America: Ten Questions Answered*, Rainforest Action Network, Earth Island Institute, San Francisco.
12. Ibid.

Chapter 5
1. Williams, 1987.
2. Nations & Leonard, 1986. (A)
3. 'La Mosquitia en la Revolucion' Centro de Investigaciones y Estudios de la Reforma Agrario (CIERA) (Managua), 1981. Quoted in Nations & Leonard, 1986. (A)
4. Nations & Leonard, 1986. (A)

5. Barry, 1987, pp. 123, 124.
6. Williams, 1987.
7. Blum, 1986, p. 264.
8. Ibid., p. 262; and Barry, 1987, p. 140.
9. Williams, 1987.
10. Ibid.
11. Ibid.
12. Ibid.
13. Leonard, 1985.
14. Hopfensperger, 1986. (A)
15. Alexander Bonilla (Costa Rican environmentalist) in interview with author, San Jose, Costa Rica, March 1988.
16. Leonard, 1985, p. 214.
17. Quoted in Nations & Leonard, 1986. (A)
18. Durham, 1979.
19. Nations & Komer, 1987. (A)
20. Williams, 1987.
21. Ibid.
22. Nations & Komer, 1987. (A)
23. Ibid.
24. Nations & Leonard, 1986. (A)
25. Nations & Komer, 1987. (A)
26. Anonymous, cited in *Tropical Deforestation in Central America: Ten Questions Answered* Rainforest Action Network, Earth Island Institute, San Francisco.
27. *New York Times*, 4 July 1972; cited in Lappe & Collins 1978, p. 291.

Chapter 6

1. Brown, 1987, p. 86.
2. Brown, 1988, p. 86.
3. 'IDB and Central America: Deforestation Threatens Big Hydro' *World Rainforest Report*, Earth Island Institute, San Francisco, March–May 1988.
4. Ibid.
5. Reed, 1988. (A)
6. Nations & Leonard, 1986. (A)
7. *World Rainforest Report*, op. cit.
8. Billes, 1983. (A)
9. *The Tico Times* (San Jose, Costa Rica) 6 March 1987.
10. Ibid., 1989 Review, 26 August 1988.
11. *This Week*, (Guatemala City) 17 March 1986.
12. Ibid., 29 September 1986; 19 May 1986.
13. Ibid., 9 February 1987.
14. Cited by Goldsmith, 1987. (A)
15. Ibid.
16. Ibid.
17. 'World Bank Renounces Tribal Policy', News release, Survival International USA, 1986.

Chapter 7

1. Lambdin, 1988. (A)
2. Ibid; and Iwobi, 1988. (A)

3. Hall, Karliner & Whitney, 1987. (A)

4. Pat Costner, Greenpeace activist, in telephone interview with author, August 1988.

5. Hall, Karliner & Whitney, 1987. (A)

6. *This Week* (Guatemala City) 1 December 1986.

7. *The Tico Times* (San Jose, Costa Rica) 2 September 1988.

8. *Barricada* (Managua) 26 May 1990.

9. Steif, 1987. (A)

Part 2
Chapter 8

1. Handy, 1984, chapter 4; Woodward, 1976, chapter 8.

2. Ibid.

3. Wasserstrom, 1975. (M)

4. Luis Cardoza y Aragon, quoted in ibid.

5. Ibid.

6. Schlesinger & Kinzer, 1982.

7. Wasserstrom, 1975. (M)

8. INTA (National Institute of Agrarian Transformation) official, quoted in Williams, 1987.

9. Williams, 1987.

10. 'Guatemala: The Terrible Repression and its Roots in the U.S. National Security State.' *Green Revolution*, (School of Living, York, PA.) Late Winter 1981.

11. Ibid.

12. Ibid.

13. Maxwell, 1984. (A)

14. Stephen & Wearne, 1984. (M)

15. Davis, 'Social Roots of the Guatemalan Resistance' in Wright & Ismaelillo, 1982.

16. Stephen & Wearne, 1984. (M)

17. Quoted by freelance journalist Clare Maxwell in interview with author, Guatemala City, January 1987.

18. Armstrong Wiggins of the Indian Law Resource Center, Washington DC, in interview with author, New York City, April 1986.

19. Wolf, 1959, p. 105.

20. Ibid.

21. *This Week* (Guatemala City) 13 October 1986.

22. Ibid., 12 January 1987; 21 July 1986; 19 May 1986.

23. Ibid.

24. Ibid.

25. Robert Rosenhouse, editor, *This Week* in interview with author, Guatemala City, January 1987.

26. Jeffrey, S. & Wilkerson, K., 'The Usumacinta River: Trouble on a Wild Frontier', *National Geographic*, October 1985; and Rohter, Larry, 'A Threat Is Seen to Two Maya Sites', *New York Times*, 26 March 1987.

27. Rossdeutscher, 1987 and 1988. (A)

28. Ibid.

29. Ibid.

30. Handy, 1984, pp. 198, 199.

31. *This Week*, 21 July 1986.

32. Ibid., 8 December 1986.

33. Ibid., 21 July 1986.

34. 'Guatemala Vows to Aid Democracy', *New York Times*, 6 December 1982.

35. *El Diaro–La Prensa*, (New York) 24 August 1990.

36. Hunter, 1987, p. 17 (M)

37. Confidential sources in interview with author, Guatemala City, Spring 1987.

38. Karliner & Faber, 1986b. (M)

39. Bradt & Rachowiecki, 1982, p. 109.

40. 'Guatemala Enacts Landmark Conservation Law' in *The Nature Conservancy* (Arlington, VA.) May–June 1989.

41. Bradt & Rachowiecki, 1982, p. 109.

42. Ibid.

43. Interviews by author with students who wish to remain anonymous, San Carlos National University, Guatemala City, January 1987.

Chapter 9

1. Armstrong & Shenk, 1982, chapters 5–7.

2. Seeley, 1986, pp. 196, 197.

3. Pilger, 1987. (A)

4. Armstrong & Shenk, 1982, p. 157.

5. Quoted in Latin America Bureau, 1985, p. 40.

6. Ibid.

7. Barry, 1987, p. 114.

8. Armstrong & Shenk, 1982, p. 156.

9. Quoted in Barry, 1987, p. 113.

10. Barry, 1987, pp. 113, 114.

11. Ibid.

12. Ibid.

13. AID consultant, Dr Norman Chapin, quoted in Barry, 1987, p. 118.

14. Laurence Simon, Oxfam America, quoted in Barry, 1987, p. 118.

15. Armstrong & Shenk, 1982, p. 144; Barry, 1987, p. 117.

16. Marion Brown, Land Tenure Resource Center, quoted in Barry, 1987, p. 118.

17. AID, 'El Salvador: Agrarian Reform Accomplishments', 20 June 1985; quoted in Barry, 1987, p. 121.

18. Armstrong & Shenk, 1982, p. 68.

19. Wright, Frank, 'Salvadorans Don't Believe Propaganda on "Success"' *Scripps Howard News Service*, 8 March 1987.

20. *New York Times*, 26 December 1985, LeMoyne, James, 'How Rebels Rule in Their Corner of El Salvador'.

21. Ibid.

22. 'El Salvador: "Scorched Earth" Campaign Targets Civilians', *Riverside* newsletter, New York, February 1986.

23. Billard, Annick, 'El Salvador: Making Up for Lost Time' *Refugees*, United Nations High Commission for Refugees, December 1987.

24. US House Committee on Government Operations, *US Assistance Program in Vietnam*, Hearings, 92nd Congress, 1st session, 15 July–2 August 1971, p. 183.

25. Smyth, Frank, 1987. (A)

26. *This Week* (Guatemala City) 15 February 1986.

27. *New York Times*, 1 April 1987.

28. *Riverside* newsletter, New York, February 1986.

29. *Sunday Times* (London) 15 December 1985.
30. Ibid.
31. Quoted in Smith, Gar, 'The Invisible War' *Not Man Apart*, Friends of the Earth, San Francisco, July–August 1985.
32. *El Mundo* (San Salvador) 24 February 1988; reprinted in *Earth Island Journal*, San Francisco, Summer 1988.
33. 'Environmental Directory for Central America', *World Rainforest Report*, Earth Island Institute, San Francisco, March–May 1987.
34. Bradt & Rachowiecki, 1982, p. 126.
35. Mohawk, John 'Salvador: Profile of a Tortured Land', in Wright & Ismaelillo, 1982.
36. Lamb, Sidni, 'El Salvador: Next Stop Home' *Refugees*, United Nations High Commission for Refugees, August 1987.
37. *New York Times*, 12 February 1990.
38. Ibid., 20 March 1989.
39. *Alert!*, Committee in Solidarity with the People of El Salvador (CISPES), New York, July–August 1989.
40. Colhoun, Jack, 1989.
41. Armstrong & Shenk, 1982, p. 160.
42. *Alert!*, Committee in Solidarity with the People of El Salvador (CISPES), Washington DC, December 1989.
43. Uhlig, Mark A., 'Salvadoran Security Forces Raid Episcopal Church, Arresting 17' *New York Times*, 21 November 1989.
44. Gruson, Lindsey, 'Court in El Salvador Indicts 8 Soldiers in Jesuit Slaying' *New York Times*, 19 January 1990.
45. Ibid.

Chapter 10
1. to 4. Durham, 1979.
5. LaFeber, 1984, p. 62.
6. Weeks, 1985.
7. Faber, Daniel R., Bill Hall, and Scott Norris, 'Honduras Roots of Environmental Destruction' *Honduras Update*, Honduras Information Center, Somerville, MA, November/December 1987.
8. *Honduras: The Real Loser in U.S. War Games*, Food First Action Alert, Institute for Food & Development Policy, San Francisco, 1987.
9. Ibid.
10. Ibid.
11. McDonald, Marci, 1987. (A)
12. Gardner, Florence, 1987. (A)
13. New York Times, 16 November 1985, LeMoyne, James, 'Rid Us of the Contras, Farmers in Honduras Ask'.
14. *New York Times*, 5 October 1988, 'Honduran Seeks U.N. Patrol to Evict Neighbors' Rebels'.
15. UPI, Tegucigalpa, Honduras, 10 May 1986. Cited in Karliner & Faber, 1986c. (M)
16. *Washington Post*, 5 April 1986. Quoted in Karliner & Faber, 1986c. (M)
17. Karliner & Faber, 1986c. (M)
18. Padilla, Alejandra, 1988. (A)
19. Ibid.

20. Ibid.
21. Coburn & McKean Moore, 1987. (A)
22. Kolankiewicz, Leon, 1989. (A)
23. Ibid.
24. 'Environmental Directory for Central America', *World Rainforest Report*, Earth Island Institute, San Francisco, March–May 1987.
25. Barry, 1987, pp. 71, 72.
26. Huss, Doug, 1986. (A)
27. Alavarado, 1988.
28. *Amnesty International Report, 1988*; *1987*, Amnesty International, London.
29. *Honduras: Desaparecidos, Jucio y Condena*, Americas Watch, Washington DC, 1988, p. 195.

Chapter 11
1. Woodward, 1976, chapter 5.
2. Ibid., chapter 6.
3. Ibid., chapter 7.
4. Hodges, 1986, p. 265.
5. Blum, 1986, chapter 49.
6. Karliner & Faber, 1986a. (M)
7. Sweezey, et al, 1986. (A)
8. Nolan, 1984.
9. Alexander Bonilla in interview with author, San Jose, Costa Rica, March 1988.
10. Nicaraguan Institute of Statistics and Census (INEC), 1988.
11. *New York Times*, 27 January 1989.
12. to 16. Karliner & Faber, 1986a. (M)
17. *Tico Times* (San Jose, Costa Rica) 15 April 1987.
18. Karliner & Faber, 1986a. (M)
19. *New York Times*, 1 July 1986, Kinzer, Stephen, 'U.S. Agency to Decide A Claim on Nicaragua'.
20. Collins, pp. 162, 163.
21. Ibid., pp. 81–3.
22. Ibid., chapter 10.
23. Rice, Paul, 1987. (A)
24. *This Week* (Guatemala City) 12 January 1987.
25. Sweezey, et al, 1986. (A)
26. Ibid.
27. Ibid.
28. Sean Sweezey in telephone interview with author, August 1988.
29. Ibid.
30. Bill Hall in telephone interview with author, August 1988.
31. Barry, 1987, pp. 102, 103.
32. *New York Times*, 17 June 1987, LeMoyne, James, 'Sandinistas Uproot Villagers to Limit Support for Contras'.
33. Wright, Frank, 'People Suffer During Dispute Over Nicaragua' Scripps Howard News Service, 8 March 1987.
34. Lappe & Collins, 1978, p. 132.
35. Ibid., p. 163.
36. Nyle Brady, quoted in Doyle 1985.
37. Pat Mooney, Rural Advancement Fund International seed specialist, in telephone interview with author, August 1988.

38. Biotechnology Working Group, New York, 1990.

39. Ibid.

40. Lappe & Collins, 1978, p. 159.

41. *International Genetic Resources Programme (IGRIP) Report* Rural Advancement Fund International, Pittsboro, NC, October 1984.

42. Ibid.

43. Pat Mooney in telephone interview with author, August 1988.

44. *IGRIP Report*, op. cit.

45. Doyle, 1985, pp. 157–9.

46. Bill Hall, in telephone interview with author, August 1988.

47. Collins, 1986, chapter 10, p. 93.

48. Quoted in Collins, 1986, p. 80.

49. *Pensamineto Propio*, Managua, May–June 1986.

50. Ohland & Schneider, 1983, p. 28–36. (M)

51. Mohawk, John & Davis, Shelton H., 'Revolutionary Contradictions: Miskitos and Sandinistas in Nicaragua' in Wright & Ismaelillo 1982.

52. Ibid.

53. Ibid.

54. Nietschmann, Bernard 'Nicaragua and the Indian Revolution' Geography Department, University of California, Berkeley, 1986; Miskito Indian refugees in interview with author, UNHCR-administered refugee camp near Limon, Costa Rica, April 1985.

55. Coburn & McKean Moore, 1987. (A)

56. Blum, 1986, chapter 21.

57. Coburn & McKean Moore, 1987. (A)

58. Blum, 1986, chapter 21.

59. *Tico Times*, 12 January 1990.

60. Rivera, Brooklyn, 1987. (A)

61. Dunbar-Ortiz, Roxanne, 1986. (A)

62. Linguists for Nicaragua, 1989.

63. Lamb, Sidni and Dunbar-Ortiz, Roxanne, 'Nicaragua: Return Flight from Exile' *Refugees*, United Nations High Commission for Refugees, August 1987.

64. *This Week*, 14 February 1986.

65. Cesar Samillan of Nicaraguan Institute of Economic and Social Investigation (INIES), quoted in *Mesoamerica* (San Jose, Costa Rica) May 1988.

66. Collins, 1986, pp. 184, 185.

67. Devereux, Don, 'Nicaragua Canal Plan Claimed' *Scottsdale Progress* (Az,) 25 November 1987.

68. *World Rainforest Report*, Earth Island Institute, San Francisco, March–May 1988b.

69. Collins, 1986, p. 114.

70. *Tico Times*, 17 July 1987.

71. *This Week*, 12 January 1987.

72. Rice, 1987. (A)

73. Ibid.

74. Sean Sweezey in telephone interview with author, August 1988.

75. Lorenzo Cardenal in interview with WBAI radio journalist Paul DeRienzo, New York City, June 1988 (portions included in Program 120, New Voices, Public Interest Video Network, Washington DC, 4 July 1988).

76. Cardenal, Ernesto, 'New Ecology' in *From Nicaragua With Love*, City Light Books, San Francisco, 1986.

77. Bill Hall in telephone interview with author, August 1988.

78. *New York Times*, 6 March 1990, Uhlig, Mark A., 'Sandinistas Warn They Want Control of Military'.

79. *Mesoamerica* (San Jose, Costa Rica) March 1987; *New York Times*, 12 September 1986, Kinzer, Stephen, 'Conscripts Come Home Well-Drilled Sandinistas'; and author's interviews with youth in Nicaragua, 1985 and 1987.

80. *New York Times*, 4 August 1989, Uhlig, Mark A., 'Sandinistas Suspend Army Draft Until After Election'.

81. *Mesoamerica*, March 1987.

82. *Amnesty International Report 1988*; *1987*; *1986*, Amnesty International, London.

83. *New York Times*, 22 October 1989, Uhlig, Mark A., 'Managua Puts Cloaks and Daggers on Display'.

84. *Amnesty International Report 1988*; *1987*; *1986*, Amnesty International, London.

85. *New York Times*, 3 March 1990, Uhlig, Mark A., 'Chamorro to Return Seized Land and Sell Large State Enterprises'.

86. Ibid., 27 February, 1990, Uhlig, Mark A., 'Violeta Barrios de Chamorro: Aristocratic Democrat'; and Violeta Barrios de Chamorro in interview with author, February 1987.

87. Nolan, 1984.

88. *Insight* (Washington DC) 14 May 1990. (M)

89. Chamorro, 1987, pp. 49, 50. (M)

90. *New York Times*, 23 June 1988, Volsky, George, 'Contra Split Widens as a Director Vows to Seek Commander's Ouster'; and ibid., 21 July 1988, Volsky, George, 'Contras Quit Group Over Colonel's Election'.

91. *New York Times*, 2 March 1990, Uhlig, Mark A., 'Ex-Exile Emerges at Core of Chamorro Alliance'.

92. Ibid.

93. MISURASATA advisor Bernard Nietschmann in telephone interview with author, June 1990.

94. Coburn & McKean Moore, 1987. (A)

95. *El Diario–La Prensa*, New York, 9 April 1991.

96. Ibid., 27 September 1991, and *Nicaragua News Update*, Nicaragua Solidarity Network of Greater New York, 30 September 1991.

Chapter 12

1. Woodward, 1976, chapter 6.

2. Ibid.

3. Ameringer, Charles D. 1978.

4. Ibid.

5. Blum, 1986, chapter 11; Ameringer, 1978, pp. 124, 125.

6. Blum, 1986, chapter 38.

7. Gerassi, 1965, p. 208.

8. Ameringer, 1978.

9. Weeks, 1985.

10. *Tico Times* (San Jose, Costa Rica) 24 September 1986.

11. *Costa Rican Information Services in Solidarity (CRISIS) Bulletin*, San Jose, Costa Rica, No. 1, June 1985.

12. *Tico Times*, 22 July 1988.

13. Ibid., 26 February 1988; 13 February 1987.
14. Ibid., 11 September 1987.
15. 1983 study by Costa Rican sociologist Beatriz Villareal, cited in *Tico Times*, 20 November 1987.
16. Hopfensperger, 1986. (A)
17. *Tico Times*, 10 June, 1988.
18. Ibid., 1 July 1988.
19. Marshall, et al, 1987, pp. 140–43.
20. *Tico Times*, 19 August 1988.
21. Ibid., 20 November 1987.
22. Cockburn, 1987, chapter 9.
23. *Tico Times*, 31 July 1987.
24. Hall, Bill and Karliner, Joshua, 1987. (A)
25. *Tico Times*, 20 February 1987.
26. Charles S. Siegel, attorney representing the banana workers, in telephone interview with author, August 1988.
27. *Tico Times*, 14 August 1987.
28. Ibid., 10 June 1988.
29. Ibid., 17 June 1988.
30. Ibid.
31. *Latinamerica Press* (Lima) 31 January 1985, 'United Brands Pressures Costa Rica'.
32. Norsworthy, Kent, 'Top Banana Peels Out of Costa Rica' *Multinational Monitor*, Washington DC, September 1983.
33. *Tico Times*, 13 March 1987.
34. Ibid., 12 January 1990.
35. Alexander Bonilla in interview with author, San Jose, Costa Rica, March 1988.
36. to 41. Karen Mogensen in series of interviews with author, Moctezuma, Costa Rica, March 1987 and San Jose, Costa Rica, March 1988.
42. *Tico Times*, 12 January 1990.
43. Ibid., 25 November 1983.
44. Ibid., 2 December 1983.
45. Ibid., 23 October 1987.
46. Ibid., 28 August 1987.
47. Niman, 1988. (A)
48. *Mesoamerica* (San Jose, Costa Rica) March 1989.
49. Ibid., May 1985.
50. *Declaracion de Organizaciones Campesinas de la Region Atlantica de Costa Rica Ante la 17a Asamblea General de la Union Internacional Para la Conservacion de la Naturaleza y los Recursos Naturales (UICN), Guacimo, Limon, 23 de Enero, 1988.*
51. to 56. Alexander Bonilla in interviews with author, San Jose, Costa Rica, March 1987 and March 1988.
57. 'A Third World Debt-for-Nature Swap' *Christian Science Monitor*, 18 January 1989; Umana, Alvaro (Costa Rican Minister of Natural Resources) 'Costa Rica Swaps Debt for Forests' *Wall Street Journal*, 6 March 1988.
58. Bonilla, Alexander, '*Bosque y Dueda Externa: Una Formula de Pago*' *La Republica*, San Jose, Costa Rica, 26 July 1987.
59. Bonilla in interview with author, San Jose, Costa Rica, March 1988.
60. *Tico Times*, 6 March 1987.
61. Ibid.

62. Bonilla in interview with author, San Jose, Costa Rica, March 1988.

63. *Tico Times*, 3 April 1987.

64. Ibid., 10 July 1987.

65. Bonilla in interview with author, San Jose, Costa Rica, March 1988.

66. *Tico Times*, 4 March 1988.

67. Ibid., 5 June 1987.

68. Ibid., 25 September 1987.

69. Ibid., 30 October 1987.

70. *New York Times*, 23 May 1989, Perlez, Jane, 'Only Radical Steps Can Save Wildlife in Kenya, Leaky says'.

71. Ruben, David, 1989. (A)

72. *Mesoamerica*, September 1984.

73. *Newsday*, 27 July 1987.

74. *Washington Post*, 4 February 1984.

75. *Mexico City News*, 25 February 1985.

76. Anderson & Anderson, 1986, p. 247.

77. *Mesoamerica* (San Jose, Costa Rica), July 1985.

78. Woodward, 1976, chapter 5.

79. *Mesoamerica*, July 1985.

80. Marshall, et al, 1987, p. 142.

81. *Costa Rican Information Services in Solidarity (CRISIS) Bulletin* San Jose, Costa Rica, No. 1, June 1985.

82. *Mesoamerica*, March 1986.

83. *Miami Herald*, 10 May 1987, Chardy, Alfonso, 'U.S. Used Threats on Latin Allies'.

84. Tripoli, Steve, 'Costa Rica Saves a High Dry Forest' *Christian Science Monitor*, 9 January 1989.

85. Cockburn, 1987, p. 131; US President's Special Review Board, p. 473; *Tico Times*, 27 February 1987.

86. *Tico Times*, 16 January 1987.

87. Karliner, 1987. (A)

88. *Tico Times*, 27 November 1987.

89. Ibid., 16 January 1987.

90. Ibid., 24 June 1988.

91. Ibid., 23 January 1987.

92. Cockburn, 1987, chapter 10.

93. Karliner, 1987. (A)

94. *Tico Times*, 31 July 1987.

95. Ibid., 17 July 1987.

96. Ibid., 18 December 1987.

97. Ibid., 28 July, 1989.

98. McGhie, Juliet, 1988. (A)

99. Lewis, Thomas A., 1989. (A)

100. Ibid., 17 July 1987.

101. Ibid.

102. *Tico Times*, 12 February 1988.

103. Ibid., 1989 Review.

104. *Mesoamerica*, October 1989.

105. Monteverde Conservation League, San Jose, Costa Rica; Monteverde Quakers in interviews with author, Monteverde, Costa Rica, April 1985.

106. Ibid.
107. Ibid.
108. *Tico Times*, 1989 Review.
109. *Friends Peace Center* newsletter, January/February 1987, San Jose, Costa Rica.
110. Leonard, 1985, p. 208.
111. Quoted in *Mesoamerica* July 1985.
112. *Tico Times*, 31 July 1987.
113. Ibid., 26 January 1990.
114. *Mesoamerica*, March 1986.
115. *Tico Times*, 22 July 1988.
116. Ibid., 26 January 1990.
117. Ibid.
118. Gannon, J. D., 'Tiny Costa Rica Gamely Tackles Drug Trafficking', *Christian Science Monitor*, 30 January 1989; *Tico Times*, 1989 Review, 12 August 1988.
119. Hopfensperger, 1986.

Chapter 13

1. Galeano, 1973, p. 121.
2. Gerassi, 1965, p. 172.
3. Galeano, 1973, p. 121.
4. to 10. Chace, 1988.
11. Conason, Joe & John Kelly, 1988. (A)
12. Marshall, et al, 1987. p. 99.
13. Marshall, Jonathan, 'Panama's Drug, Inc.' *Oakland Tribune* 22 January 1990; 5 January 1990.
14. *New York Times*, 10 January 1990, Pitt, David E., 'The Invasion's Civilian Death Toll: Still No Official Count'.
15. 'Panama: A Political Model Under Pressure' *Central America Report*, Inforpress Centroamericana, Washington DC, 8 May 1987.
16. Ibid.
17. Arkin & Fieldhouse, 1965, pp. 69, 228.
18. *Tico Times*, 8 January 1988.
19. Voelker, 1988a. (A)
20. Ibid.
21. Ibid.
22. Quoted in Nations & Leonard 1986.
23. *This Week* (Guatemala City) 17 March 1986.
24. Chace, 1988.
25. *Tico Times* 8 January 1988.
26. Ibid.
27. Navarro, Juan Carlos & Raul Fletcher 1988.
28. Ibid.
29. Ibid.
30. Bradt & Rachowiecki 1982, pp. 229, 240.
31. Myers, 1987. (A)
32. Howe, 1986. (A)
33. Myers, 1987. (A)
34. Voelker, 1988a. (A)

35. Myers, 1987. (A)
36. Wali, Alaka, 1989. (A)
37. *New York Times*, 28 April 1988, Pitt, David E., 'A Restive Island Tribe Adds to Noriega's Woes'.
38. Howe, 1986. (A)
39. Bradt & Rachowiecki, 1982, pp. 229–31.
40. Gjording, 1981. (M)
41. 'New Canal Planned', *Earth Island Journal*, San Francisco, Winter 1987.
42. Lewis, 1972, pp. 176–98.
43. Ibid.
44. Voelker, 1988a (A)
45. Ibid.
46. Ibid.
47. Chace, 1988. (A)
48. Marshall, Jonathan, 'Panama's Drug, Inc.' *Oakland Tribune*, 22 January 1990; 5 January 1990.
49. Myers, 1987. (A)

Chapter 14

1. Huxley, 1934, p. 21.
2. *New York Times*, 27 October 1985, Pitt, David, 'Belize Warily Considers Marijuana Herbicide'.
3. Woodward, 1976.
4. Wilk, Richard & Mac Chapin, 1989. (A)
5. 'Belize' *Book of the Year 1990*; *Encyclopedia Britannica*, 1990.
6. Grumbine, 1987. (A)
7. *Financial Times* (London) 16 October 1985, quoted in Grumbine.
8. Grumbine, 1987. (A)
9. Ibid.
10. 'Coke Pauses, Ecologists Refreshed', *Earth Island Journal*, San Francisco, Spring 1988; *Tico Times*, 27 November 1987.
11. Handy, 1984, pp. 177, 208; *Solidarity With Guatemalan Workers*, 1986 flyer, Industrial Workers of the World (IWW), Chicago.
12. 'Belize' *Book of the Year 1984*; *Encyclopedia Britannica*, 1984.
13. 'Belize' *Book of the Year 1985*; *Encyclopedia Britannica*, 1985.
14. 'Belize' *Book of the Year 1986*; *Encyclopedia Britannica*, 1986.
15. *This Week* (Guatemala City) 18 December 1985.
16. Gutman, Roy, 'U.S. Considers Military Aid for Peru, Belize Drug Raids', *New York Newsday*, 17 July 1986.
17. 'Belize' *Book of the Year 1990*; *Encyclopedia Britannica*, 1990.
18. *The Nature Conservancy*, Arlington, Va., September/October 1988.

Part 3

Chapter 15

1. Hall, Bill, 1987. (A)
2. Ibid.
3. Ibid.
4. *Tico Times*, 26 June 1987.
5. Ibid.

6. Karliner, Joshua, 'Peace Park or Clearcut?' *Earth Island Journal*, Spring 1987.

7. Karliner, Joshua, 'Costa Rica, Nicaragua Near Agreement on Peace Park' *Earth Island Journal*, Winter 1988.

8. Karliner, Joshua, 1988. (A)

9. Ibid.

10. Report on WBAI Radio news, New York City, 11 June 1990, 6:00 pm.

11. Geographer Bernard Nietschmann in telephone interview with author, June 1990.

12. Latin America Bureau, 1985, p. 89.

13. *Nuevo Diario* (Managua) 25 May 1987; 14 August 1986; *La Nacion* (San Jose, Costa Rica) 1 September 1986; 14 August 1986.

14. Alexander Bonilla in interview with author, San Jose, Costa Rica, March 1988.

15. Lorenzo Cardenal in interview with WBAI radio journalist Paul DeRienzo, New York City, June 1988 (portions included in Program 120, New Voices, Public Interest Video Network, Washington DC, July 4, 1988).

16. *EPOCA* publicity literature, Earth Island Institute, San Francisco.

17. *Bikes Not Bombs* publicity literature, Institute for Transportation & Development Policy, Washington DC.

Chapter 16
1. Galeano, 1979, pp. 14–17.

2. Cited in Pope, Carl, 'Family Planning Is Inherently Genocidal: True or False?' *Environmental Action*, Washington DC, 15 May 1971.

3. Brown, 1987, p. 29.

4. Brown, 1988, pp. 166–7.

5. Benjamin, et al, 1984.

6. Blum, 1986, pp. 211, 212.

7. Nations & Leonard, 1986.

8. Brown, 1987, p. 29.

9. *Statement on the Real Crisis Behind the 'Food Crisis'* Environmental Fund, Washington DC, 1976; cited in Durham.

10. Ehrlich, Paul R., Loy Bilderbach, and Anne H. Ehrlich, 1979, p. viii; cited in Hartmann, 1987, p. 15.

11. Hartmann, p. 15.

12. Rensberger, Boyce, 'Scientists See Signs of Mass Extinction' *Washington Post*, 29 September 1986.

13. Nations & Komer, 1987. (A)

14. AID, *Congressional Presentation*, FY 1985, p. 45; cited in Hartmann, 1987, p. 236.

15. Ibid.

16. *Observer* (London) 1 April 1984, O'Shaugnessy, Hugh, 'El Salvador Poor Given No Choice Over Sterilization'; cited in Hartmann, 1987, p. 237.

17. Hedges, Chris, 'Sterilization of El Salvadoreans Promoted by U.S. Agency' *National Catholic Reporter*, 11 November 1983; cited in Hartmann, 1987, p. 236.

18. *Tico Times*, 25 March 1988.

19. Ibid.

20. Ibid., 29 March 1988.

21. *New York Times*, 7 August 1987, 'Indian Health Service Dispenses Banned Contraceptive Drug'.

22. Hartmann, 1987, p. 189.

23. *Tico Times*, 27 November 1987.

24. *Overthrow*, Bleecker Publishing, New York, Spring 1986, reprinted from *Central America Newsletter*, New Orleans.

Chapter 17

1. Bahro, 1982.

2. Ibid.

3. Randy Hayes of the Rainforest Actions Network (Earth Island Institute, San Francisco) in address to Tropical Rainforest Conference, Hunter College, New York, 18 October 1987; quoted in Weinberg 1987.

4. Vananda Shiva in address to Tropical Rainforest Conference, Hunter College, New York, 18 October 1987; quoted in Weinberg 1987.

5. US Congressman John Porter in address to Tropical Rainforest Conference, 18 October 1987; quoted in Weinberg 1987.

6. Michael Oppenheimer, atmospheric physicist, Environmental Defense Fund, New York, in interview with author, *Downtown*, Soho Arts Weekly, New York, 19 October 1988.

7. Quoted in Nations & Leonard, 1986.

8. El-Ashry & Gibbons, 1986.

9. Tokar, Brian, 'Environmentalism Revisited' *Z Magazine* (Boston) February 1990.

10. Thropy, Ann, 1987 (A); Foreman, Dave, 1987. (A)

11. *Bloomsbury Review* (Denver) April/May 1986.

12. Ibid.

13. *Utne Reader* (Minneapolis) March/April 1988.

14. Menchu, 1984, Introduction.

15. Weinberg, Bill, 'Genocide in the Amazon: An Interview with Brazilian Workers' Party Organizer Zeze Weiss', *Downtown*, New York, 22 August 1990.

16. Otten, Mariel, *Transmigrasi: Indonesian Resettlement Policy, 1965–1985*, International Work Group for Indigenous Affairs, Copenhagen, 1986.

17. Weinberg, Bill, 'For One of the Biggest Environmental Disasters Ever, Try James Bay II!', *Downtown*, New York, 21 November 1990.

18. Barlow, 1990, pp. 151–2.

19. Ritchie, Mark, 'Trading Away Our Environment: GATT and Global Harmonization', *Journal of Pesticide Reform*, Washington DC, Vol. 10, No. 3.

20. Clark, Ron (moderator) 'Secession: 'The Case For and Against' Vermont Public Radio, 28 February 1990, 6:30 pm.

21. Tokar, 1988.

22. Bradford, George, 'Stopping the Industrial Hydra: Revolution Against the Megamachine' *Fifth Estate* (Detroit) Winter 1990.

23. *New York Times*, 10 May 1989, Oppenheimer, Michael, 'The Greening of Ms. Thatcher'.

Bibliography

Articles

Billes, Steve (1982) 'Indigenous People "Developed" Out of their Lands' *Multinational Monitor* (Washington DC) September.

Brooklyn, Rivera (1987) 'The Indian Struggle in Nicaragua' *Akwesasne Notes* (St Regis, NY) Spring.

Chace, James (1988) 'Getting to Sack the General' *New York Review of Books*, 28 April.

Chapin, Marc (1989) 'The 50,000 Invisible Indians of El Salvador' *Cultural Survival Quarterly* (Cambridge, Mass.) Vol. 13.

Coburn, Judith & Susanna McKean Moore (1987) 'US-Backed Forces Harass Indian Refugees'; 'Contragate Links to Central American Indians: Leaders Claim Miskitos used as Pawns' *Akwesasne Notes* Spring.

Colhoun, Jack (1989) 'El Salvador: US firms engineered electoral campaigns' *The Guardian* (New York) 12 April.

Conason, Joe & John Kelly (1988) 'Bush and the Secret Noreiga Report' *Village Voice*, 11 October.

Dunbar-Ortiz, Roxanne (1986) 'Towards Reconciliation: Atlantic Coast Autonomy' *Nicaraguan Perspectives* (Berkeley) Summer/Fall.

Foreman, Dave (1987) 'Whither Earth First!?'; '"Dangerous Tendencies" in Earth First!?' *Earth First! Journal* (Tucson) 1 November.

Gardener, Florence (1987) 'US Environmental Leaders Tour Central America' *Earth Island Journal*, Summer.

Grumbine, Ed (1987) 'On the Brink in Belize' *Earth First! Journal*, 1 May.

Hall, Bill (1987) 'Central Americans Confront Environmental Crisis' *Earth Island Journal* (San Francisco) Summer.

Hall, Bill & Joshua Karliner (1987) 'A Forgotten War: The Assault on Central America's Environment' *Greenpeace* (Washington DC.) Vol. 12, No. 4.

Hall, Bill, Joshua Karliner & Penelope Whitney (1987) 'Garbage Imperialism' *Earth Island Journal*. Fall.

Hopfensperger, Jean (1986) 'Costa Rica: Seeds of Terror' *The Progressive* (Madison) September.

Howe, James (1986) 'Native Rebellion & US Intervention in Central America: The Implications of the Kuna Case for the Miskito' *Cultural Survival Quarterly*, Vol. 10, No. 1.

Huss, Doug (1986) 'Reagan Rattles Saber, Wants Contra Funding' *The Guardian* (New York) 12 March; and *This Week* (Guatemala City) 18 March 1986.

Iwobi, Bosah (1988) 'From US with Malice . . .' *African Concord* (Lagos/London) 24 May.

Karliner, Joshua (1987) 'Contragate: The Environmental Connection' *EPOCA Update* Environmental Project on Central America, Earth Island Institute (San Francisco) Summer.

——— (1988) 'Costa Rica, Nicaragua Sign Agreement for Peace Park: Forging a New Development Model' *EPOCA Update*, Summer.

Kolankiewicz, Leon (1989) 'The Pesch of Honduras Face Uncertain Prospects' *Cultural Survival Quarterly* Vol. 13, No. 3.

Lambdin, Suzanne (1988) 'Third World Dumping Creates Concern *Water Pollution Control Federation Journal* (Alexandria, Va.) September.

Lewis, Thomas A. (1989) 'Daniel Janzen's Dry Idea' *International Wildlife*, National Wildlife Federation (Vienna, Va.) January/February.

Linguists for Nicaragua (1989) 'Language Rights on the Nicaraguan Atlantic Coast' *Cultural Survival Quarterly*, Vol. 13, No. 3.

McDonald, Marci (1987) 'The Comforts of 10 Lemp Alley' *MacLean's*, Toronto 23 February.

McGhie, Juliet (1988) 'Reclaiming a Natural Legacy' *The Ecologist*, Vol. 17, No. 4/5, January/February.

Maxwell, Clare (1984) 'Guatemala Counterinsurgency Plan Eradicating Native Way of Life' *Latinamerica Press* (Lima) 25 October.

Mohawk, John (1987) 'We the Original People . . .' *Daybreak* (Highland, MD) Autumn.

Moore, Jay (1985–86) 'The True Story of Sandino' *Kick It Over* (Toronto) Winter.

Myers, Norman (1985) 'How the Songbirds of America Choked on Fast Food' *The Guardian Weekly* (London) 6 January.

——— (1987) 'Kuna Indians: Building a Bright Future' *International Wildlife*, National Wildlife Federation July/August.

Nations, James D. & Daniel I. Komer (1987) 'Rainforests and the Hamburger Society' *The Ecologist*, Vol. 17, No. 4/5.

Navarro, Juan Carlos & Raul Fletcher (1988) 'Preserving Panama's Parks' *The Nature Conservancy Magazine* (Arlington, Va.) January/February.

Niman, Michael, I. (1988) 'Death of a Small Country: It's the US Presence that's Killing Costa Rica' *The Progressive* (Madison) August.

Padilla, Alejandra (1988) 'The Effects of the Contra War on the Honduran Environment' *Earth Island Journal*, Winter.

Pilger, John (1978) 'Vietnam: Do Not Weep for Those Just Born' *New Statesman* (UK) September.

Postel, Sandra (1988) 'A Green Fix to the Global Warm-up' *World-Watch* (Washington DC) September/October.

Reed, John (1988) 'Mass Movement Reappears in the Streets of Guatemala' *Overthrow* (New York City) Spring.

Rice, Paul (1987) 'Growing with Experience: Eight Years of Agrarian Reform' *Nicaraguan Perspectives* (Berkeley) Fall.

Rossdeutscher, Daniele (1987) 'Bizarre Spraying Campaign Haunts Guatemala' *Earth Island Journal*, Fall.

——— (1988) 'An Appeal from the Guatemalan Human Rights Commission' *Earth Island Journal*, Summer.

Ruben, David (1989) 'Can Lizard Meat Save the Rainforest?' *New Age Journal* (Brighton, MA) July/August.

Smyth, Frank (1987) 'Secret Warriors: US Advisors have taken up arms in El Salvador' *Village Voice*, 11 August.

Steif, William (1987) 'US Stalls Caribbean Ecology Program' *Earth Island Journal*, Fall.

Sweezey, Sean L., Douglas L. Murray & Rainer G. Daxi (1986) 'Nicaragua's Revolution in Pesticide Policy' *Environment* (Washington DC) January/February.

Terdre, Nick (1988) 'Bananas: A Ripening Bunch' *South* (London) March.

Thropy, Ann (1987) 'Population and AIDS' *Earth First! Journal*, 1 May.

Voelker, Denise (1988) 'Panama Canal: Falling Victim to Deforestation and Politics' *World Rainforest Report*, March–May.

Wali, Alaka (1989) 'In Eastern Panama, Land is the Key to Survival' *Cultural Survival Quarterly*, Vol. 13, No. 3.

Weinberg, Bill (1987) 'Debt, Deforestation, Disaster: A Report from the Tropical Rainforest Conference at Hunter College' *Downtown* (Soho Arts Weekly, New York) 25 November.

Wilk, Richard & Mac Chapin (1989) 'Belize: Land Tenure and Ethnicity' *Cultural Survival Quarterly*, Vol. 13, No. 3.

World Rainforest Report 1988, March–May.

Wurster, Charles F. (1988) 'Why We've Had Another Songless Spring' (Letter to Editor) *New York Times*, 20 June.

Books

Alvarado, Elivia (Benjamin, Medea, ed.) (1988) *Don't Be Afraid, Gringo: A Honduran Woman Speaks From the Heart* Institute for Food & Development Policy, San Francisco.

Ameringer, Charles D. (1978) *Don Pepe: A Political Biography of José Figueres of Costa Rica*, University of New Mexico.

Anderson, Scott & Anderson, Jon Lee (1986) *Inside The League: The Shocking Expose of How Terrorists, Nazis, and Latin American Death Squads have Infiltrated the World Anti-Communist League* Dodd, Mead & Co., New York.

Arkin, William & Fieldhouse, Richard W. (1985) *Nuclear Battlefields: Global Links in the Arms Race* Harper & Row, Cambridge, MA/Institute for Policy Studies, Washington DC.

Armstrong, Robert & Shenk, Janet (1982) *El Salvador. The Face of Revolution* South End Press, Boston/North American Congress on Latin America, New York.

Bahro, Rudolph (1982) *Socialism & Survival* Heretic Books, London.

Barlow, Maude (1990), *Parcel of Rogues: How Free Trade is Failing Canada*, Key Porter Books, Toronto.

Barry, Tom (1987) *Roots of Rebellion: Land and Hunger in Central America* South End Press, Boston/The Resource Center, Albuquerque, NM.

Benjamin, Medea, Joseph Collins & Michael Scott (1984) *No Free Lunch: Food and Revolution in Cuba Today* Institute for Food & Development Policy, San Francisco.

Blum, William (1986) *The CIA: A Forgotten History* Zed Books, London.

Bradt, Hilary & Rob Rachowiecki (1982) *Backpacking in Mexico & Central America* Bradt Enterprises, Cambridge, MA.

Brown, Lester R. (ed.) (1988) *State of the World 1988* W. W. Norton, New York/Worldwatch Institute, Washington DC.

Brown, Lester R. (ed.) (1987) *State of the World 1987* W. W. Norton, New York/Worldwatch Institute, Washington DC.

Browning, David (1971) *El Salvador: Landscape & Society*, Oxford University Press.

Cockburn, Leslie (1987) *Out of Control: The Story of the Reagan Administration's Secret War in Nicaragua, the Illegal Arms Pipeline, and the Contra Drug Connection* Atlantic Monthly Press, New York.

Collins, Joseph (1986) *Nicaragua: What Difference Could A Revolution Make? Food & Farming in the New Nicaragua* Grove Press, New York/Institute for Food & Development Policy, San Francisco.

Dixon, Marlene & Jonas, Susanne, (eds) (1984) *Nicaragua Under Siege* Synthesis Publications, San Francisco.

Doyle, Jack (1985) *Altered Harvest: Agriculture, Genetics, and the Fate of the World's Food Supply* Penguin, New York.

Durham, William (1979) *Scarcity and Survival in Central America: The Ecological Origins of the Soccer War* Stanford University Press.

Ehrlich, Paul R., Loy Bilderbach and Anne H. Ehrlich (1979) *The Golden Door: International Migration, Mexico and the United States*, Ballantine, New York.

Galeano, Eduardo (trans. Cedric Belfrage) (1973) *Open Veins of Latin America: Five Centuries of the Pillage of A Continent* Monthly Review Press, New York.

Gerassi, John (1965) *The Great Fear In Latin America* Collier, New York/London.

Handy, Jim (1984) *Gift of the Devil: A History of Guatemala* South End Press, Boston.

Hartmann, Betsy (1987) *Reproductive Rights & Wrongs: The Global Politics of Population Control & Contraceptive Choice* Harper & Row, New York.

Hodges, Donald C. (1986) *Intellectual Foundations of the Nicaraguan Revolution* University of Texas Press.

Huxley, Aldous (1934) *Beyond the Mexique Bay* Chatto & Windus, London.

LaFeber, Walter (1984) *Inevitable Revolutions: The United States in Central America* W. W. Norton, New York.

Lappe, Frances Moore & Joseph Collins, with Cary Fowler (1978) *Food First: Beyond the Myth of Scarcity* Ballantine Books, New York/Institute for Food & Development Policy, San Francisco.

Leonard, H. Jeffrey (1985) *Divesting Nature's Capital: The Political Economy of Environmental Abuse in the Third World* Holmes & Meier, New York.

Lewis, Richard S. (1972) *The Nuclear Power Rebellion: Citizens Vs. The Atomic Industrial Establishment* Viking Press, New York.

Marshall, Jonathan, Peter Dale Scott, & Jane Hunter (1987) *The Iran–Contra Connection: Secret Teams and Covert Operations in the Reagan Era* South End Press, Boston.

Menchu, Rigoberta (Elisabeth Burgos Debray (ed.) & introduction) (1984) *I, Rigoberta Menchu: An Indian Woman in Guatemala* Verso, London.

McNeill, William H. (1982) *Plagues & Peoples* Doubleday, New York.

Nations, James D. & H. Jeffrey Leonard (1986) 'Grounds of Conflict in Central America' in Andrew Maguire and Janet Welsh Brown (eds) *Bordering on Trouble: Resources and Politics in Latin America* Adler/World Resources Institute, Washington DC.

Nolan, David (1984) *The Ideology of the Sandinistas and the Nicaraguan Revolution* University of Florida Press.

Schlesinger, Stephen & Kinzer, Stephen (1982), *Bitter Fruit: The Untold Story of the American Coup in Guatemala* Doubleday, New York.

Seeley, Robert (1986) *The Handbook of Non-Violence* Lawrence Hill & Co. Westport, CT.

Tokar, Brian (1988) *The Green Alternative* R&E Miles, San Pedro, CA.

United States President's Special Review Board (1987) *The Tower Commission Report* Bantam/Times, New York.

Weeks, John (1985) *The Economies of Central America* Holmes & Meier, New York.

Weir, David & Schapiro, Mark (1981) *Circle of Poison: Pesticides & People in a Hungry World* Institute for Food & Development Policy, San Francisco.

Williams, Robert G. (1987) *Export Agriculture and the Crisis in Central America* Chapel Hill University, NC.

Wolf, Eric (1959) *Sons of the Shaking Earth: The People of Mexico & Guatemala* University of Chicago Press.

Woodward, Ralph Lee, Jr. (1976) *Central America: A Nation Divided* Oxford University Press.

Wright, Robin & Ismaelillo (1982) *Native Peoples In Struggle: Cases From the Fourth Russell Tribunal & Other International Forums, Akwesasne Notes*, St. Regis, NY/Anthropology Resource Center, Boston.

Monographs

Biotechnology Working Group (1990) *Biotechnology's Bitter Harvest*, New York.

Chamorro, Edgar (1987) *Packaging the Contras: A Case of CIA Disinformation* Institute for Media Analysis, New York.

El-Ashry, Mohamed & Diana C. Gibbons (1986) *Troubled Waters: New Policies for Managing Water In the American Southwest* World Resources Institute, Washington DC.

Gjording, Chris N. (1981) *The Cerro Colorado Copper Project and the Guaymi Indians of Panama* Cultural Survival, Inc., Cambridge, MA.

Hunter, Jane (1987) *No Simple Proxy: Israel In Central America* Washington Middle East Associates, Washington DC.

Karliner, Joshua & Daniel Faber, with Robert Rice (1986a) *EPOCA Green Paper No. 1: Nicaragua: An Environmental Perspective* Environmental Project On Central America (EPOCA), Earth Island Institute, San Francisco.

Karliner, Joshua & Daniel Faber, with Robert Rice (1986b) *EPOCA Green Paper No. 2: Central America: Roots of Environmental Destruction* Environmental Project On Central America (EPOCA), Earth Island Institute, San Francisco.

Karliner, Joshua & Daniel Faber, with Robert Rice (1986c) *EPOCA Green Paper No. 3: Militarization: The Environmental Impact* Environmental Project On Central America (EPOCA), Earth Island Institute, San Francisco.

Latin America Bureau (1985) *Honduras: State For Sale* Latin America Bureau, London.

Nesmith, Jeff, (1986) 'Mexico, Central America: Robbing the Future', *Natural Disasters: The Human Connection*, Cox Newspapers, Atlanta.

Ohland, Klaudine & Robin Schneider (eds) (1983) *National Revolution and Indigenous Identity: The Conflict Between Sandinistas and Miskito Indians on Nicaragua's Atlantic Coast* International Work Group for Indigenous Affairs, Copenhagen.

Stephen, David & Phillip Wearne (1984), *Central America's Indians* Minority Rights Group, London.

Wasserstrom, Robert (1975) *Revolution In Guatemala: Peasants & Politics Under the Arbenz Government* Comparative Studies in Society & History, Cambridge University Press, MA.

Index

2,4,5-T herbicide, 53, 106

A.H.Robins company, 155
Abbey, Edward, 163, 164
Abraham Lincoln Brigade, 147
aerial spraying: of chemicals, as violation of Geneva Convention, 53; of pesticides, 17; of defoliants, 58; of paraquat, 136
Agee, Philip, 60
Agent Orange, spraying of, 52, 58
agrarian reform, 43, 44, 45, 54, 59, 60, 86, 90, 99, 102, 113, 124; in Nicaragua, 79-81
agribusiness, 137-8; capital-intensive, 150
agro-industry, 11, 61, 90, 114, 130
aid: US, 4, 62, 95, 98; US military, 4, 53, 103, 156 (to Israel, 55)
AIDS, seen as salvation of earth, 162
Ailes, Roger, 123
airstrip discovered in Costa Rica, 119-20
Alaska wilderness, 167
Alcoa company, 34
Alliance for Progress, 60
Alliance for the Progress of the Miskito and Sumo (ALPROMISO) (Nicaragua), 88
Alvarado, Elvia, 73
Amazonian Alliance of the Peoples of the Forest, 166
American Institute for Free Labor Development (AIFLD), 60
Amnesty International, 27, 73
Amoco company, 51, 52, 162
anarchism, 13, 170
Angola, 52
animals, extinction of, 10
anti-communism, 43, 101
anti-nuclear movement, in US, viii (decline of, viii)
Applied Recovery Technologies company, 38

Arana, Carlos, 27-8
Arbenz, Jacobo, 43-4, 138
Arbenz regime (Guatemala), 10, 46, 54
archaeological relics, Mayan, sale of, 50
ARCO company, 162, 167
Arenal hydro-dam, 33
Arenal national park, 122
Arevalo, Juan José, 43
Arias, Arnulfo, 127
Arias, Fr Elias, 105
Arias, Oscar, 3, 104, 118, 119, 120, 123, 143
asparagus, growing of, 48, 54
assassinations, in El Salvador, 63
Association of Rural Workers (ATC) (Nicaragua), 80, 99
Atlacatl Battalion (El Salvador), 62
Atomic Energy Commission (AEC) (US), 133
Augelli, John P., 29
austerity, 103, 112
Aztec empire, 7

Bahro, Rudolph, 157, 163
banana companies, 67, 68
banana plantations, 10, 17, 105, 131
banana republics, 53
'Bananagate' scandal, 28
bananas, 11, 19, 26, 30, 54, 107, 139; chemical treatment of, 161; consumption of, 161; nationalization of, 10; trade in, 77, 130
Banco Exterior de España (BEE), 34
Bank of America, 31
banks, 128, 160; international, and land pillage, 33
Barnaby, Malcolm, 139
Barra de Colorado reserve, 145
beans, growing of, 12, 13, 19, 22, 28, 90, 93, 102, 109; breeding of, 85; shortage of, 62
beef industry, x, 6, 11, 25, 43, 45, 86, 107,

84842

Zed Books Ltd

is a publisher whose international and Third World lists span:

- **Women's Studies**
- **Development**
- **Environment**
- **Current Affairs**
- **International Relations**
- **Children's Studies**
- **Labour Studies**
- **Cultural Studies**
- **Human Rights**
- **Indigenous Peoples**
- **Health**

We also specialize in Area Studies where we have extensive lists in African Studies, Asian Studies, Caribbean and Latin American Studies, Middle East Studies, and Pacific Studies.

For further information about books available from Zed Books, please write to: Catalogue Enquiries, Zed Books Ltd, 57 Caledonian Road, London N1 9BU. Our books are available from distributors in many countries (for full details, see our catalogues), including:

In the USA
Humanities Press International, Inc., 165 First Avenue,
Atlantic Highlands, New Jersey 07716.
Tel: (201) 872 1441;
Fax: (201) 872 0717.

In Canada
DEC, 229 College Street, Toronto, Ontario M5T 1R4.
Tel: (416) 971 7051.

In Australia
Wild and Woolley Ltd, 16 Darghan Street, Glebe, NSW 2037.

In India
Bibliomania, C-236 Defence Colony, New Delhi 110 024.

In Southern Africa
David Philip Publisher (Pty) Ltd, PO Box 408, Claremont 7735,
South Africa.